THE
LATTER-DAY
SAINT
IMAGE
IN THE
BRITISH
MIND

Malcolm Adcock
and Fred E. Woods

THE LATTER-DAY SAINT IMAGE IN THE BRITISH MIND

Greg Kofford Books
Salt Lake City, 2022

ISBN 978-1-58958-558-4 (paperback)
Also available in ebook.

Greg Kofford Books
P. O. Box 1362
Draper, UT 84020
www.gregkofford.com
facebook.com/gkbooks
twitter.com/gkbooks

Library of Congress Control Number: 2022942122

To our beloved parents:

Denis and Joyce Adcock, pioneers in the faith,
& Fred and Shirley Woods

who supported their children in all their undertakings.

They inspired their families
and their influence
will touch the lives
of generations to come.

Contents

Foreword

The *Latter-day Saint Image in the British Mind* is a welcome, careful, and accessible account of the transformation and growth of The Church of Jesus Christ of Latter-day Saints, and the changing attitudes of British culture towards this community.

In this volume, Malcolm Adcock and Fred E. Woods track these changing attitudes that began with suspicion and hostility, directed at the perceived weird beliefs and threat of bogeymen from Utah coming to abduct local women to America. Adcock and Woods show how the curiosity of Latter-day Saint presence in a nation—where "everything stops for tea" and where local pubs serving ale had a central social function—provoked a sense of Latter-day Saints as somewhat puritanical alien Americana through the nineteenth and early twentieth centuries.

But Adcock and Woods show that this is far from the whole picture. Citing Charles Dickens, Latter-day Saint service in wartime Britain, missions through popular music and sport, the building of temples, and networking in public and political life, they illustrate how Latter-day Saints patiently faced ridicule and won respect through consistent integrity.

Dickens came to judge not by the hearing of the ear, but by what he saw as the fruits of "Mormon" endeavour. Examples of uprightness and sustained service led judgments—such as those of the Architect of the London Temple, Sir Thomas Bennett—to be transformed. He came to value Latter-day Saints as "the finest people for whom I work."

This volume also shows how a more nuanced series of theological engagements and interfaith dialogue is fruitful and equips further understanding and appreciation.

The profile of Latter-day Saints in the United Kingdom continues to change and deepen. Missionaries may be ridiculed in the West End's production of *The Book of Mormon*, but the refusal to react aggressively has positively surprised many.

In addition to these diverse images, Latter-day Saints are also increasingly celebrated for profound humanitarian work in the United Kingdom and beyond, with missionaries showing that Latter-day Saints are indeed "friends of all nations" through their self-forgetfulness and outward focus. This service was noted in their charitable assistance during the floods of 2019 in Wales and Yorkshire, and through the coronavirus pandemic of 2020. In this, The Church of Jesus Christ of Latter-day Saints in Britain shows consistency with the classic Anglican desire to serve the whole nation, yet it does so with an intensity and dynamism that seems to have dissipated in more traditional, established faith traditions.

From the earliest Latter-day Saint missions in England, the community has endured persecution but has persevered, proving resilient, innovative, and committed to sharing faith and life with non–Latter-day Saint neighbours. The transformation of culture, for example, by the Osmonds in popular mission is appreciated. In contemporary estimation, the accessibility of Latter-day Saint family history work is also an increasingly valued contribution in showing the connectedness of the whole human family.

This well-written, carefully evidenced book provides a broad and hopeful foundation for the future mission of Latter-day Saints in Britain; it invites us to continue to commit to witness and service together, and to grow in authentic love and appreciation of one another. I commend it wholeheartedly.

Reverend Dr. Andrew Teal
Chaplain, Fellow, & Lecturer in Theology
Pembroke College, Oxford, 2020

Preface

Since the coming forth of the Book of Mormon in 1830, The Church of Jesus Christ of Latter-day Saints has added millions of people to its global membership. Crucial to its initial growth were converts from Great Britain who emigrated to join with other Latter-day Saints in the United States. Many, however, stayed in the United Kingdom in order to establish a presence of the Church there. The faith's reputation among the British is the focus of this work. Although both authors have British roots running back several centuries, Malcolm was brought up in the Latter-day Saint faith and lives in the United Kingdom, while Fred has no Latter-day Saint ancestry and lives in America.

Malcolm Adcock's parents became Latter-day Saints in 1959, during an era of significant expansion. Malcolm vividly recalls many childhood experiences reflecting the Latter-day Saint cultural realities of the time, including working at meetinghouse building sites with his family ("Put down that sledgehammer!" he was once told by a worried adult) and clearing away cigarette butts and beer bottles (discarded by Saturday night revelers) in rented halls to prepare the area for Sabbath day meetings.

Malcolm graduated from the University of Kent Law School and served a Latter-day Saint mission in Ontario, Canada. Soon after returning home, he was able to follow his passion for journalism and writing (specifically investigative coverage) by working with the BBC as a consumer issues journalist and producer. During his time as Mayor of Daventry, Northamptonshire, he had two chaplains: an Anglican and a Latter-day Saint. Now heading the UK-based Communication office (previously Public Affairs[1]) for The Church of Jesus Christ of Latter-day Saints, he is in regular contact with opinion leaders who share a mutual desire to focus on common touchpoints, including the vital need for freedom of religion and belief in the United Kingdom and globally. Malcolm has participated in many of the high-profile events described within the book.

---

1. "Public Affairs" is used in this book to refer to public outreach activity by staff or volunteer Church representatives. Over the years, various designations have been used, including Public Communications, Public Affairs, and now Communication (incorporating public affairs).

Fred E. Woods was raised near Los Angeles, California. His immediate family members, each of a different Christian denomination, reflected the multi-faith cultural influence of his local neighborhood and city. Although he grew up in a metropolitan region, Fred was naïve when it came to understanding the Latter-day Saint tradition. He had been told that The Church of Jesus Christ of Latter-day Saints was a cult and was unaware that it is a Christian faith. Fred envisioned the Latter-day Saints as a bizarre sect whose people were garbed in black. Aside from these misconceptions, he had learned of early Latter-day Saint pioneer leader Brigham Young via a student report in his sixth grade class and later heard the buzzword "polygamy." This was the extent of his exposure to the faith.

Just shy of his twentieth birthday, Fred became a member of The Church of Jesus Christ of Latter-day Saints. He later obtained a PhD in Hebrew Bible and encountered the Talmudic idea "We do not see the world as it is. We see the world as we are."[2] Certainly this idea was indicative of Fred's revised perspectives through the lens of his newfound faith. He discovered that the Jews and the Latter-day Saints have a similar number of adherents[3] but wondered why so many people knew more about Judaism than about the doctrines and practices of those belonging to the Church.

The purpose of this book, *The Latter-day Saint Image in the British Mind*, is to explore the multifaceted perspectives of British people outside the Latter-day Saint faith tradition and how these perceptions of The Church of Jesus Christ of Latter-day Saints and its members generally have improved over time. In the context of the book, the term *image* refers to an "impression of something" or a "mental conception held in common by members of a group that's symbolic of a basic attitude and orientation."[4] Our intent is that this study will provide a better understanding and serve as a reminder that how people view things has everything to do with correct information blended with their personal biases and experiences. Along those lines, although the Church and its leaders, beginning with Joseph Smith, have largely embraced the nicknames

---

2. William Berry, "The Truth Will Not Set You Free."

3. As of this printing, there are over fifteen million Jews and over sixteen million Latter-day Saints among the world's population. See "Vital Statistics: Jewish Population of the World (1882–Present)," AICE; and "Facts and Statistics," The Church of Jesus Christ of Latter-day Saints.

4. *Merriam-Webster*, s.v. "image."

"Mormon" and "Mormonism,"[5] in October 2018 the President of the Church, Russell M. Nelson, requested that Church members and the media no longer use those terms: to instead use the full name of the Church whenever possible and to refer to its members as "Latter-day Saints."[6] We have thus strived to follow this request, except in quotations in which members or others use those terms as they would have naturally adopted them at the time.

In this book, we present historical accounts via literature, film, and media reviews of Latter-day Saints and their faith. In addition, we have conducted over a hundred face-to-face interviews and surveyed a thousand Brits to determine how UK citizens perceive The Church of Jesus Christ of Latter-day Saints in the twenty-first century and why they hold those views.

We have also produced a documentary as a companion to our book. This 2021 award-winning film, directed by Martin Andersen, captures the expressions and voices of many of those we interviewed. It can be accessed via this link:

https://truth-and-reason.com/LDS_Image_BritishMind.htm

We hope that our exploration and analysis of these evolving public views—with reference to how Church members see themselves—coupled with the combined lens of our blended perspectives will enable us to identify and demystify naïve conceptions about Latter-day Saints and make what may once have seemed strange appear quite sound. We also hope readers will be left with a keen sense of the contribution Latter-day Saints have made to British society and of their concerted efforts to join hands with neighbors in their local communities in rendering multidimensional service for the benefit of all.

---

5. For example, in a March 20, 1839, letter to Latter-day Saints that was later published in the Church's *Times and Seasons*, Joseph Smith wrote: "No, they [critics] may rage, with all the powers of hell and pour forth their wrath, indignation and cruelty like the burning lava of mount Vesuvius, yet, shall Mormonism stand. Truth is Mormonism, and God is its author." See Joseph Smith, et al, "Copy of a Letter, Written by J. Smith Jr. and Others, while in Prison," 103.

6. Russell M. Nelson, "The Correct Name of the Church." In that address Nelson stated: "If we allow nicknames to be used or adopt or even sponsor those nicknames ourselves, [God] is offended."

Acknowledgments

We are so grateful to the very many individuals and organizations who have made it possible for us to produce this work, whether named or unnamed below. We especially acknowledge the time and insight provided by those whom we have interviewed. We deeply value our association with everyone who has advised on the book in a wide range of capacities.

Fred's time as Summer Oxford research fellow to Harris Manchester College, Oxford, for the Trinity trimesters for 2017 and 2018 was an inspirational and foundational experience for the book. Malcolm and Fred are especially appreciative of the invaluable contribution to the project by Revd. Dr. Andrew Teal, Chaplain, Fellow & Lecturer in Theology, Pembroke College Oxford, whose public dialogue on Latter-day Saint theology continues to be deeply enlightening. Professor Eileen Barker OBE, Professor Emeritus of Sociology with Special Reference to the Study of Religion at the London School of Economics, provided very important perspectives on how religious groups have been perceived over the years. Dr. Terryl L. Givens, Neal L. Maxwell Senior Fellow at Brigham Young University, conveyed the context within which the Latter-day Saint faith has often been significantly mischaracterized in popular culture. Dr. James Holt, Associate Professor of Religious Education, University of Chester, suggested that The Church of Jesus Christ of Latter-day Saints would be categorized as a "restorationist" Christian faith, thus going beyond the three main traditional groupings of churches as Catholic, Orthodox, or Protestant.

We thank Michael Otterson, former managing director of the Public Affairs Department of The Church of Jesus Christ of Latter-day Saints, for his time in carefully reading the pre-publication manuscript. Likewise, we are appreciative of the support of Richard E. Turley Jr., previously Assistant Church Historian and latterly managing director of the Church's Communication Department. Previous employees of the Church's Public Affairs Department providing valuable insight include Lynn Driscoll, RoseMarie Loft, Marion McLaverty, Kym Reichart, and Lesley Smith. Malcolm has warm memories of association with the late Bryan Grant and David Fewster, previous UK-based Area Public Affairs Directors, who provided professional mentorship over the decades (and who are referenced in the book).

We appreciate Greg Kofford Books' publication of this volume and thank Loyd Isao Ericson for his support in the production process. The tireless work of those who provided the interview transcripts and other administrative support must not go unnoticed, especially Beverly Yellowhorse.

We thank Dr. Brian Cannon and Dr. David Kirkham, both from BYU, for their insightful interviews. We are also grateful to Joel Campbell, associate teaching professor in journalism at BYU's School of Communications, for his additional material.

We acknowledge the help of the BYU College of Religious Education, BYU Religious Education Faculty Support, and the Church History Library of The Church of Jesus Christ of Latter-day Saints.

It has been a pleasure to work with filmmaker Martin Andersen, who accompanied us on many interviews across the length and breadth of Great Britain and Ireland. His humor and professionalism helped buoy our spirits during very long days. We thank Chris Wills, former UK-based video producer at The Church of Jesus Christ of Latter-day Saints, who also assisted—with his wife Jeannie Wills—in locating archive sources and in other ways. Utah-based radio host and book reviewer Terry Hutchinson provided insightful editorial steers. In the United Kingdom, we also thank Dr. David Cook and Professor Simon J. Gibson, CBE DL, Frank Blease, and many others for background material on the mid-twentieth-century Church building program. We are most grateful to Rosalie West for her detailed research on British newspaper archives.

It was fun to spend time with members of the Osmond family, who did—and do—so much to help bring the Church out of obscurity in the United Kingdom. Thank you to Donny and Marie Osmond, and brothers Alan, Jay, and Merrill, and the rest of the family.

We are very conscious of the tireless work of so many Public Affairs volunteers and leaders from the Church, as well as interfaith representatives in many churches and faith groups who do so much to connect with community and promote goodwill across the faith spectrum. Every individual with whom we interacted on this "book journey" has had an impact on our own lives, and if we have failed to acknowledge anyone by name, then we offer our sincere apologies. The following people deserve special mention for their time providing further understanding of their individual experiences and for their support in other ways: Chris Abbas, Bill Baldock, William Bodine, Eric Bowyer, Eileen Connolly, Martin

Cook, Brian Dawson, Michael Dockrill, Aled Edwards, Anne Edwards, Cath Finlay, Dr. Ian Finlay, Jen Forward, Steve Forward, Wayne Gardner, Charlie Gee, Rachel Gee, Geoff Green, Arlene Jones, Gabe Jones, Julian Jones, Craig Marshall, Robert Mawle, Sheila Maxwell, Ruth Nevison, Bernard O'Farrell, Nor'dzin Pamo, Malcolm Ross, Jason Spragg, Julie Wagner, Cathy Walton, Keith Walton, Ian Walton, Margaret Watson, and Pippa Wright.

Above all, we thank our respective wives, Sharon Adcock and JoAnna Woods, for their love, patience, constructive input, and support.

The writers take full responsibility for the book's content. Views expressed do not necessarily reflect the position of The Church of Jesus Christ of Latter-day Saints or of Brigham Young University.

The Latter-day Saint Image

It was nevertheless a fact that I had beheld a vision . . . but still there were but few who believed.
— Joseph Smith History 1:24

On central London's congested public transportation system (with capital-wide annual passenger numbers of 1.35 billion), next to crowded escalators and on the sides of iconic red buses, "I love Mormon" posters shout for attention.[1] The London promoters of *The Book of Mormon* musical reportedly spent one million dollars for the launch marketing of one of the world's top entertainment hits, and the sizeable British ad spending for *The Book of Mormon* musical continues.[2]

The portrayal of Latter-day Saints in melodramatic fashion—with hackneyed recycling of stereotypes—has pulled crowds to the box office over the decades and has captured readers' attention even before the turn of the twentieth century. What *The Book of Mormon* musical (with its raw, excessive adult humor) is to the twenty-first century, *A Study in Scarlet* (with its sensationalized reports of Latter-day Saints) was to the Victorian era. Early depictions of "Mormons" in this novel helped launch Sir Arthur Conan Doyle's literary career. *A Study in Scarlet*, Doyle's first novel, was published in Britain during 1887 when Latter-day Saint persecution for polygamy—seen then as the religion's chief feature—was at a peak. (Following a visit to Utah, Conan Doyle softened his view of the Latter-day Saints.[3])

On both sides of the Atlantic, television shows such as *Big Love* and *Sister Wives* continue to promote the myth of polygamous "Mormons." Thankfully, many reality-based programs are now increasingly making it clear that the multiple-wived men featured in these shows are not members of The Church of Jesus Christ of Latter-day Saints, but some confusion continues.

---

1. TfL Community Team, "Tube Trivia and Facts."

2. Paul Scott, "The Book of Mormon Review: The Most Over-Hyped Show on God's Earth."

3. Sebastian Lecourt, "The Mormons, the Victorians, and the Idea of Greater Britain," 85.

Latter-day Saints well known to Brits include the Osmonds, Brandon Flowers, Gladys Knight, and Mitt Romney. Romney's political run as Republican 2012 US presidential candidate raised the Church's profile to a huge extent in the United Kingdom—during a time dubbed "the Mormon Moment." A spiritual legacy of inspiring musical tours from the Mormon Tabernacle Choir—now named The Tabernacle Choir at Temple Square—has also enthralled British audiences.

So, what do people really think about Latter-day Saints? We found that in modern Britain, the perception of Church members is perhaps more like the view through a kaleidoscope than through a telescope; there are multiple views, informed by personal experiences and interactions with Latter-day Saints individually and with the Church as an organization. There is no overriding "groupthink" norm, no overall prejudgment; yet, generally speaking, the British perception of the Latter-day Saint image has improved in the modern era. After all, there are over 189,000 Latter-day Saints living in the United Kingdom, including members of the judiciary, members of parliament (MPs), and West End talent (London's Broadway), as well as people in more traditional jobs.[4] Latter-day Saints then are members of a sizeable minority faith. (By comparison, there are just over 263,000 Jews in England and Wales.[5])

In our survey of one thousand UK residents, we discovered that nearly a quarter expressed the individual view that "I would not mind learning more about Latter-day Saints if I could learn it from a friend without feeling any pressure to join."[6] This is perhaps a surprising response at a time when church attendance in Britain is at an all-time low. Other questionnaire answers were revealing too.

Members of the Church are active in community building, as is the Church institutionally. For example, The Church of Jesus Christ of Latter-day Saints supports religious and secular rights of conscience through the All Party Parliamentary Group for International Freedom of Religion or Belief. In its early days, the Church was not strong enough in the United Kingdom to lend support to religious freedom since its own rights for religious freedom were unassured. Over a century ago, it was Winston Churchill as Home Secretary who, during House of Commons exchang-

---

4. See "Facts and Statistics," The Church of Jesus Christ of Latter-day Saints.

5. See "Jews in Numbers," Board of Deputies of British Jews.

6. This professional survey conducted with one thousand British citizens is in possession of authors.

es, advocated religious tolerance towards Latter-day Saint missionaries.[7] Now, members of the Church are reaping the benefits of that tolerance supported by Churchill.

Latter-day Saints in the United Kingdom are not a homogeneous social group and instead display significant racial and political diversity. For example, the first Latter-day Saint elected to Parliament was Terry Rooney MP, who represented the Labour party in Bradford North.[8] All the major political parties have had parliamentary candidates, campaigners, and elected MPs who are Latter-day Saints. Latter-day Saint singer and entertainer Alex Boyé was born in the United Kingdom and is of Nigerian heritage.

The Britain of today is a far cry from late nineteenth- and early twentieth-century Britain when the Church's worship services in varied locations were disrupted by angry locals,[9] or from the 1950s when many people saw families converting to what was seen as a strange new American sect. The public perception of the Church began to change more quickly in the 1960s, however; it was a time of major growth for the Church in Britain, as Latter-day Saints constructed large chapels and rapidly baptized tens of thousands across the land.

The spiritual yearnings of Latter-day Saint British converts were satiated as they embraced a new faith route for their Christianity that they felt was borne of a sure spiritual witness; the concept of "Zion in Britain" was in their hearts. They would have strongly related to the words of William Blake's "Jerusalem," which builds off the folk story of a young Jesus visiting the British Isles:

> And did those feet in ancient time
> Walk upon England's mountains green?
> And was the holy Lamb of God
> On England's pleasant pastures seen?

---

7. See "Mormon Missionaries: Volume 25: Debated on Monday 8 May 1911."

8. See "Church Member Elected to British Parliament."

9. See, for examples, "A Mormon Riot," *Mormon Chronicle* [London], 7; "Mormon Riot at Sheffield," *Shields Daily Gazette and Shipping Telegraph*, 4; "The Anti-Mormon Riots at Brightside," *Sheffield Daily Telegraph*, 2; "Anti-Mormon Riot in London," *Western Daily Press*, 7; "A Welsh Anti-Mormon Meeting," *Huddersfield Daily Chronicle*, 4; "Anti-Mormon Riot," *Derby Daily Telegraph*, 7; "Anti-Mormon Riot," *Manchester Courier*, 10.

And did the Countenance Divine
Shine forth upon our clouded hills?
And was Jerusalem builded here
Among these dark Satanic mills?

Bring me my bow of burning gold:
Bring me my arrows of desire:
Bring me my spear: O clouds unfold!
Bring me my chariot of fire.

I will not cease from mental fight,
Nor shall my sword sleep in my hand
Till we have built Jerusalem
In England's green and pleasant land.[10]

The spiritual and emotional resonance new members felt was linked to the social backgrounds of many earlier converts to The Church of Jesus Christ of Latter-day Saints. New followers in the nineteenth century may have literally worked in Blake's "dark Satanic mills"—the industrial factories—of northern England. Those joining in the middle of the nineteenth century were often from the working class, and they formed large groups and gathered to Zion in America, ready to build up a "New Jerusalem." Their more modern counterparts were urged to build up a Zion in the British Isles—this was a place of gathering too.

Building the Kingdom of God

It was the physical building of the kingdom that British Latter-day Saints took literally in the late 1950s. That time was designated by David O. McKay, then President of the Church, as a "new era" in Great Britain, and Church meetinghouses sprang up all over the land.[11] Currently, 320 congregations are established in the United Kingdom.[12]

Permanence and stability for the Church has been demonstrated via the chapel building programs and the construction of the Latter-day Saints' two British temples—impressive structures in Chorley, Lancashire, and in the Surrey countryside. As it was with the ancient Jews, the temple is regarded by Latter-day Saints as the most sacred place on earth—a place where heaven and earth meet. One of the most fascinating episodes in the history of construction of Latter-day Saint chapels in the United Kingdom

---

10. William Blake, "Jerusalem."
11. Derek A. Cuthbert, "Breakthrough in Britain."
12. "Facts and Statistics," The Church of Jesus Christ of Latter-day Saints.

is the relationship between renowned architect Sir Thomas Bennett and the British Latter-day Saints. Bennett was the architect for the Latter-day Saint London Temple in Surrey (dedicated 1958) and the London Hyde Park Chapel (dedicated 1961), and he could justifiably be seen as Blake's knight who helped "build Zion in England's green and pleasant land." This greater physical prominence was accompanied in the 1970s by the musical superstardom of the Osmonds, who indelibly made their mark on the United Kingdom. Tens of thousands of people began to see the Latter-day Saint faith in a new light as this popular musical family exemplified good, wholesome living.

Fifty years ago, most of the Church's full-time missionaries in Britain were from the United States. As designated Church representatives to the community, they were clean-cut and clad in white shirts and ties; it was thus easy to get the impression that this was indeed an American religion. While it was true then that most Church members worldwide were US-based (less than half are now), the heritage of The Church of Jesus Christ of Latter-day Saints is just as much British as it is American. The Church's oldest extant meetinghouse in the world is located near the village of Pendock, Worcestershire—the Gadfield Elm Chapel.[13] And the Church's longest continuous congregation globally, founded in 1837, is in Preston, Lancashire.[14]

During the Victorian era, nearly 90,000 European converts, prior to sailing on over four hundred chartered voyages, made their way (often by rail) to Liverpool, then the most important point of embarkation from Europe.[15] Most of these fledgling converts were from the British Isles, many of whom immigrated to the United States even before the pioneer prophet Brigham Young led the epic trek to the western US settlement of Salt Lake City. This all came about because Joseph Smith, the founder and first President of The Church of Jesus Christ of Latter-day Saints, commissioned the Church's Quorum of the Twelve Apostles to travel to Britain. This was a mission to rescue the Church from major challenges. It led to significant results and probably saved the Church numerically, energizing the American-based religion. During the second half of the nineteenth

---

13. "Gadfield Elm Chapel," The Church of Jesus Christ of Latter-day Saints.

14. "History of the Church in the British Isles," The Church of Jesus Christ of Latter-day Saints.

15. Fred E. Woods, "The Tide of Mormon Migration Flowing Through the Port of Liverpool, England," 60–86.

Statue of Latter-day Saint emigrants at Liverpool Docks. Courtesy Craig Ostler.

century, Latter-day Saints from Britain formed the backbone of the new church.

In more recent times, the Church has been no stranger to challenges—some of these resulting in extensive publicity and increased name recognition for Latter-day Saints among fellow Brits, despite regrettable contexts. One of the most remarkable challenges is the series of bizarre episodes surrounding Joyce McKinney and her accomplice Keith May who kidnapped Church missionary Elder Kirk Anderson in 1977. After Anderson escaped, McKinney and May were arrested, but they eventually jumped bail, using unusual disguises, and fled to the United States. Media coverage at the time was extensive—covering front pages for days. Understandably, many members of the Latter-day Saint faith were concerned. The very unfortunate incident, however, gave the Church an opportunity to tell its own story.

This book dives deep into the British people's perceptions of Latter-day Saints through interviews with Church members and those of other faiths. In the process of researching this volume, we spoke to Latter-day Saints who were involved in or lived through many different moments of the Church's history in Britain, such as those who worked to build the first modern Latter-day Saint meetinghouses in the 1960s, converts who discovered the Church during the earlier era of "baseball baptisms," and Michael Otterson, who was the UK public communications director in the late 1970s and later headed the Church's global Public Affairs department.

Not limiting our examination to the past, we bring readers up to date with the Latter-day Saint image in the British mind. The Church of Jesus Christ of Latter-day Saints is no longer an obscure sect meeting in cold, damp rented halls with just a few congregants—though many long-term British members fondly recall that heritage. It has grown and faced new challenges while striving to appeal to those seeking a practical, Christ-centered lifestyle and worship system. Far outnumbering the handful of apostles sent on missions to the British Isles by Joseph Smith, today there are typically around one thousand Latter-day Saint missionaries serving in the United Kingdom—many of whom are either women or not from the United States. [16]

In addition, we look at the lives of modern British Latter-day Saints and examine how they reconcile their apparently strict moral code—including no alcohol or extramarital sex—with modern existence in the United Kingdom and a desire to be part of and serve their local communities and the larger society. Although Latter-day Saints are distinct, they are also inclusive; anyone who wants to maintain positive values within local communities, educational institutions, and society as a whole through public service will typically find common ground with Church members.

Following the first publication of his work *The Uncommercial Traveller*, Charles Dickens endorsed the view that "The Mormon ship is a Family."[17] While no family is perfect, the avowed aim of Latter-day Saints is to share their message of hope aimed at strengthening people as they sail on their grand voyages of life.

---

16. During the COVID-19 national lockdown of early 2021, UK in-field missionary numbers were fewer, at around 600.

17. See Charles Dickens, *The Uncommercial Traveller and Reprinted Pieces etc.*, 220–32, annotation included in reprinted edition; referencing conversation with Lord Houghton, and (article by) Lord Houghton, *The Edinburgh Review*, January 1862, citing the Select Committee of the House of Commons on emigrant ships in 1854. Dickens had referred to his June 4, 1863, experience observing Latter-day Saints aboard the ship *Amazon*.

CHAPTER 1

Church Beginnings
and Foundational Teachings

*And we talk of Christ, we rejoice in Christ, we preach of Christ,
we prophesy of Christ, and we write according to our prophecies, that our children may know to what source they may look
for a remission of their sins.*

— 2 Nephi 25:26

It was a clear, beautiful day in early spring 1820. Within a secluded
forest area in upstate New York, a young teenage boy was determined
to seek a solution to his inner turmoil and entered the woods with
ironclad resolution. He had experienced spiritual confusion, even darkness, and was severely conflicted by the religious bitterness spewing from
the mouths of local ministers. Joseph Smith, an obscure fourteen-year-old
farm boy, had finally made the decision to pray out loud for the first time
in his life. The theophany that followed was to change Smith's life irrevers-
ibly; it would ultimately impact millions of people and eventually lead to
his own murder.

This was the genesis of The Church of Jesus Christ of Latter-day
Saints. Smith had been searching for which of the many competing denominations he should join. After fervent prayer, Smith reported that he
had seen a vision of God the Father and His Son Jesus Christ and was
instructed by them not to join any of the existing churches. Three years
later, after another fervent prayer, Smith described how he was visited by
an angel who told him about an ancient book that testified of Jesus Christ
and His visit to the ancient Americas shortly after His resurrection.

By early spring of 1830, Smith had translated this record and established what he proclaimed to be the Restoration of the primitive Church
of Jesus Christ. Although it had small beginnings (six members) in
Fayette, New York, The Church of Jesus Christ of Latter-day Saints now
has more than sixteen million members in tens of thousands of congregations dispersed over an excess of 160 countries. Around sixty percent of
the Church membership is located outside the United States.[1]

---

1. See "Facts and Statistics," The Church of Jesus Christ of Latter-day Saints.

Headquartered in Salt Lake City, general Church leaders supervise a missionary force of over 67,000 men and women (easily recognizable by their nametags and conservative, professional dress). Although the missionary message is focused on the tenets that Christ atoned for the sins of humankind, rose from the dead, and lives still, because of the faith's additional scripture and doctrines that differ from traditional Christian theology, some Christian denominations do not recognize The Church of Jesus Christ of Latter-day Saints as a Christian sect.

Mainstream Christian Objections

Various doctrines held by The Church of Jesus Christ of Latter-day Saints today do not follow traditional Christian beliefs. One example of this diversity is the nature of the Godhead that had been agreed upon by Christian authorities in AD 325 in the Nicaean Creed. (In practice, these doctrinal differences are more likely to arise in scholarly theological debate than in interreligious dialogue.) Whereas traditional Christianity embraces the belief of a literal oneness of the Trinity, Latter-day Saint doctrine holds that God the Father, His Son Jesus Christ, and the Holy Ghost are separate and distinct beings who are one in purpose.

Connected to this departure from traditional Christian theism is the Latter-day Saints' belief that following the death of Christ's original Apostles in the first century AD, there was a general apostasy in the early Christian Church, which Latter-day Saints believe to be a fulfillment of Paul's teaching that before Christ would return to the earth a second time, there would be "a falling away first" (2 Thess. 2:3). Consequences of this falling away include that there was no longer divine authority to perform saving ordinances or sacraments such as baptism and that without prophetic authority some truths, such as the nature of the Godhead, had become lost. However, central to their belief in a full restoration of the original Church of Jesus Christ is their claim that Christ sent the resurrected John the Baptist and His Apostles Peter, James, and John to restore that authority in 1829 and 1830, and that "a man must be called of God, by prophecy, and by the laying on of hands by those who are in authority, to preach the Gospel and administer in the ordinances thereof" (A of F 1:5).

Thus, another example of differences in foundational tenets that some other Christians take exception to is the Church's claim that the authority of God still resides in prophets and apostles and that Christ directs the affairs of His living Church through these ordained men today, beginning with Joseph Smith. And this "restoration" includes new scripture and revelations that both restore and newly reveal important truths about God, Jesus, and salvation. For example, Latter-day Saints accept the Book of Mormon, alongside the Bible, as divine scripture, and they believe that both works testify of the divinity of Jesus Christ. Because of their belief in the Book of Mormon, members of The Church of Jesus Christ of Latter-day Saints are often called "Mormons," and the Church is sometimes referred to as the "Mormon Church"—though these nicknames are no longer embraced by the Church as they had been in the past.[2]

Despite these differences, The Church of Jesus Christ of Latter-day Saints holds central to its beliefs the Christian doctrine of relying on faith in the name of Jesus Christ for salvation (grace)—though unlike their evangelical Christian counterparts, they also maintain the importance of living in faith daily (works). Christian apologist C. S. Lewis reasoned the issue with this analogy and perspective:

> Christians have often disputed as to whether what leads the Christian home is good actions, or Faith in Christ. I have no right really to speak on such a difficult question, but it does seem to me like asking which blade in a pair of scissors is most necessary. . . . The Bible really seems to clinch the matter when it puts the two things together into one amazing sentence. The first half is, "Work out your own salvation with fear and trembling"—which looks as if everything depended on us and our good actions: but the second half goes on, "For it is God who worketh in you"—which looks as if God did everything and we nothing.[3]

Latter-day Saints frame it in a similar vein. Citing the Book of Mormon, they maintain, "It is by grace that we are saved, after all we can do" (2 Ne. 25:23). Further noting, "And we talk of Christ, we rejoice in Christ, we preach of Christ, we prophesy of Christ, and we write according to our prophecies, that our children may know to what source they may look for a remission of their sins" (2 Ne. 25: 26).

Respecting Religious Freedom

Although Latter-day Saints believe The Church of Jesus Christ of Latter-day Saints to be "the only true and living church upon the face of the whole earth" with the authority to perform all saving ordinances (D&C 1:30), they also acknowledge that there are many good people of

---

2. Russell M. Nelson, "The Correct Name of the Church."

3. C. S. Lewis, *Mere Christianity*, 148.

other faiths who will be saved. Church members desire to be inclusive and to build upon the truths others have embraced. Thus, religious freedom is a fundamental foundation of the Church: "We claim the privilege of worshiping Almighty God according to the dictates of our own conscience, and allow all men the same privilege, let them worship how, where, or what they may" (A of F 1:11).

In a letter to former New York publisher and educator, Joseph Smith explained:

> All men ought to be free . . . to think, and act, and say as they please, while they maintain due respect to the rights and privileges of all other creatures, infringing upon none. This doctrine I do most heartily subscribe to and practice.[4]

He also explained the appropriate course one should pursue when encountering differing beliefs:

> If I esteem mankind to be in error, shall I bear them down? No. I will lift them up, and in their own way too, if I cannot persuade them my way is better; and I will not seek to compel any man to believe as I do, only by the force of reasoning, for truth will cut its own way.[5]

Several years prior to Smith's death, the Nauvoo Charter was established in the city of Nauvoo, Illinois, in late 1840. In his history of the Church, Elder B. H. Roberts, of the First Council of the Seventy, writes,

> When this document was crafted, Joseph was serving on the Nauvoo City Council, and would soon serve as the city's second mayor. Section one of the charter reads: Be it ordained by the city council of the city of Nauvoo that the Catholics, Presbyterians, Methodists, Baptists, Latter-day Saints, Quakers, Episcopalians, Universalists, Unitarians, Mohammedans [Muslims], and all other religious sects and denominations, whatever, shall have free toleration and equal privileges in this city.[6]

Smith's expanded benevolence is also apparent in his statement regarding the salvation of those who have been unable to receive the message of Christ:

> While one portion of the human race are judging and condemning the other without mercy, the great parent of the universe looks upon the whole of the human family with a fatherly care, and paternal regard; he views them as his offspring, and without any of those contracted feelings that influence the chil-

---

4. "Letter to James Arlington Bennet, September 8, 1842," 1–2.

5. "History, 1838–1856, Volume E-1 [1 July 1843–30 April 1844]," 1666.

6. B. H. Roberts, *A Comprehensive History of the Church of Jesus Christ of Latter-day Saints*, 2:55–56.

dren of men, causes "*his sun* to rise on the evil and on the good; and sends *his rain* on the just and the unjust." He holds the reins of judgment in his hands; he is a wise lawgiver, and will judge all men, [not according to the narrow, contracted notions of men, but] "according to the deeds done in the body whether they be good or evil;" or whether these deeds were done in England, America, Spain, Turkey, India.[7]

Unfortunately, the tolerance advocated for was not always reciprocated. Smith's unorthodox teachings, new scripture, and revelations, coupled with his claims of authority and the "gathering" of Latter-day Saints together into centralized populations, resulted in conflicts and persecution. Such violence followed the Saints from place to place as they gathered in New York, Ohio, Missouri, and Illinois. Eventually this culminated in the murders of Joseph Smith and his brother Hyrum in 1844. Unable to find peace within the United States, the Saints were forced to flee Nauvoo, Illinois, during the winter of 1846. The following summer, the President of the Quorum of the Twelve, Brigham Young, led a vanguard company into the Salt Lake Valley, establishing the Latter-day Saint capital for decades to follow. Salt Lake City flourished as headquarters for the Church, and it continues to flourish there today.

From its fledgling origins in 1830, the Church focused on energetic proselytizing despite extreme harassment. With Bible and Book of Mormon in hand, members of this newly restored religion witnessed significant expansion. But opposition to the Latter-day Saints came from the pen as well as the sword.

---

7. Joseph Smith, "Baptisms for the Dead," 759; emphases and brackets in original.

CHAPTER 2

Nineteenth-Century Perceptions
of Latter-day Saints

What the Mormons do seems to be excellent; what they say, is mostly nonsense.

— Charles Dickens

Since its genesis, The Church of Jesus Christ of Latter-day Saints has been attacked in the press. During the spring of 1831, just one year after the Church's establishment, Joseph Smith described how "many false reports, lies, and fo[o]lish stories, were published in the newspapers, and circulated in every direction to prevent people from investigating the work or embracing the faith."[1] The following summer he noted, "So embittered was the public mind against the truth, that the press universally had been arrayed against us."[2]

News about this new movement traveled quickly across the Atlantic, and the print media was fast to exploit the situation. As early as 1831, a caricature of "the Mormons" had been drawn in the British press, six years before the first missionaries arrived in Liverpool. With the headline "Fanaticism," the *Morning Advertiser* reported, "We noticed . . . the progress of a new religious order in the western part of Ohio. It would seem that good materials are found in that district for such a work." The newspaper then quoted from an Ohio paper, referenced as the *Painsville Gazette*, "The believers in the sacred authenticity of this miserable production, are known by the name of 'Mormonites,' and their book is commonly called 'the Book of Mormon.'"[3] The British publication continued the syndication, including claims of unusual occurrences:

> It is alleged that some of them have received white stones promised in the [second] chapter of the Revelations. Such of them as have "the spirit" will declare that they see a white stone moving about the upper part of the room, and will jump and spring for it, until one more fortunate than the others

---

1. "History, 1838–1856, Volume A-1 [23 December 1805–30 August 1834]," 104.
2. "History, 1838–1856, Volume A-1 [23 December 1805–30 August 1834]," 216.
3. "Fanaticism," 4. We are very grateful to Rosalie West, Bridlington, East Yorkshire, for her research into British newspaper archives relating to the Church (1830–1950).

catches it, but alone can see it. Others however profess to hear it roll across the floor. These . . . stories, and others of a similar character, are told by them with solemn asseverations of their truth.

Later that year, the same paper incorporated an article on its front page from an Illinois newspaper, the *Jacksonville (Illinois) Patriot*, that described "Mormonites" as "unfortunate lunatics." The report asserted that the sect is "a deluded set of men, whose doctrines are not only dangerous—but, notwithstanding all their professions, they are calling down the curse of God on their own heads."[4]

Why Such Persecution?

Why did this obscure and seemingly peculiar church attract so much persecution? In his official history written the year after the missionaries came to Britain, and later canonized as Latter-day Saint scripture, Joseph Smith recounted that in answer to his prayers regarding which church he should join, he had a vision from God the Father and his Son Jesus Christ. The instruction given to him was simple and direct: "join none of them, for they were all wrong" (JS—H 1:19). When this teenaged boy told others of his spiritual experience, he described that he "felt much like Paul, when he made his defense before King Agrippa . . . , he was ridiculed and reviled" (v. 24). Smith explained that one Methodist preacher who responded to his reported theophany said, "It was all of the devil, that there were no such things as visions or revelations in these days; that all such things had ceased with the apostles" (v. 21).

Writing nearly two decades after his vision, Smith recalled his surprise at the vehement reactions to his story: "[It] was the cause of great persecution, which continued to increase;" especially since he was "an obscure boy . . . of no consequence in the world," there was "bitter persecution . . . common among all the sects——all united to persecute me" (v. 22).

How did Smith react to this maltreatment? Instead of raising his fists, he pulled out his pen. In the very first verse of his official history, written in 1838, came the response:

> Owing to the many reports which have been put in circulation by evil-disposed and designing persons, in relation to the rise and progress of The Church of Jesus Christ of Latter-day Saints, all of which have been designed by the authors thereof to militate against its character as a Church and its progress in the world—I have been induced to write this history, to disabuse

---

4. "The Mormonites," 1.

the public mind, and put all inquirers after truth in possession of the facts, as they have transpired, in relation both to myself and the Church, so far as I have such facts in my possession. (JS—H 1:1)

It was difficult to offset the abundant ridicule and misrepresentation that was penned both nationally and internationally from the press as well as through biased literary works that targeted the Saints. By 1850, just twenty years after the Church was established, and a half dozen years after the martyrdom of Joseph Smith, there were two hundred exposés and articles written; in addition, by century's end, over fifty anti-Mormon novels were published.[5] Venomous writings spiked when the Church publicly announced the practice of plural marriage from Salt Lake City in 1852. In response to the ubiquitous criticisms and the press's unwillingness to accept rebuttals, the Church established various periodicals at home and abroad to defend their doctrines and practices.

Church Periodicals Launched

During the 1850s, several newspapers and pamphlets were launched in various regions by competent Church leaders. These included *The Seer* (1853) by Orson Pratt in Washington, DC; *The St. Louis Luminary* (1854) by Lorenzo Snow in eastern Missouri; *The Mormon* (1855) by John Taylor in New York; and *The Western Standard* (1856) by George Q. Cannon in San Francisco. Internationally, the Saints released the *Zion's Watchman* (1853) in distant Sydney, Australia. However, the earliest Church periodical outside of Latter-day Saint centers was *The Latter-day Saints' Millennial Star*, inaugurated in the spring of 1840 by Apostle Parley P. Pratt in Manchester, England.[6] Pratt's prospectus stated that the *Millennial Star* was "a periodical devoted entirely to the great work of the spread of truth. . . . [D]evoted to . . . the restoration of the ancient principles of Christianity . . . the gathering of Israel."[7]

The *Millennial Star* was not conceived to combat opposition to polygamy because that practice was not publicly proclaimed until a dozen

---

5. Terryl L. Givens, *The Viper on the Hearth: Mormons, Myths, and the Construction of Heresy*, 134–35.

6. *The Latter-day Saints' Millennial Star* ran continuously from 1840 to 1970, the longest-running Latter-day Saint periodical. For more information on the establishment and purpose of the *Millennial Star*, see Alan K. Parrish, "Beginnings of the *Millennial Star*: Journal of the Mission to Great Britain," 133–49.

7. Parley P. Pratt, "Prospectus," 1.

years later. Rather, the publication's intent was to proclaim the message of the restoration of primitive Christianity and the "gathering of Israel"—preaching Smith's message and bringing together converts from around the globe to one of the "stakes" or communities of Latter-day Saints in America.[8] In the *Millennial Star*, British converts were given useful information to assist them with the emigration process via Liverpool and across the Atlantic as well as with their journey traversing America to Salt Lake City. The paper apprised departing emigrants of travel dangers and encouraged the use of guidance from Church immigration agents. In April of 1841, the following apostolic counsel via the "Epistle of the Twelve" was published with this advice:

> We have found that there are so many "pick pockets," and so many that will take every possible advantage of strangers, in Liverpool, that we have appointed Elder Amos Fielding, as the agent of the church, to superintend the fitting out of the Saints from Liverpool to America. . . . It is also a great saving to go in companies, instead of going individually. First, a company can charter a vessel, so as to make the passage much cheaper than otherwise. Secondly, provisions can be purchased at wholesale for a company much cheaper than otherwise. Thirdly, this will avoid bad company on the passage. Fourthly, when a company arrives in New Orleans they can charter a steamboat so as to reduce the passage near one-half. This measure will save some hundreds of pounds on each ship load. Fifthly, a man of experience can go as leader of each company, who will know how to avoid rogues and knaves.[9]

The *Millennial Star* was founded in the same year that Latter-day Saint immigration to America commenced in Great Britain. British converts by the hundreds and thousands gathered to Liverpool (the main port of embarkation) to journey to what they considered the American Zion: first to Nauvoo, Illinois (1840–1845), and later to Salt Lake City, Utah Territory, commencing in 1848. Even with all the immigration to the United States, there were actually more Saints in Great Britain in the mid-nineteenth century than in all North America combined.[10]

---

8. A stake is an ecclesiastical area similar in size to a diocese.

9. Brigham Young et al., "An Epistle of the Twelve," 311. Church leaders also assisted over 30,000 foreign converts through a revolving fund known as the Perpetual Emigrating Fund between 1849 and 1887. It was maintained through Church donations and private contributions. Immigrants who received funds to gather were expected to repay what they borrowed as soon as they were able. See David F. Boone, "Perpetual Emigrating Fund," 3:1075.

10. Richard O. Cowan, "Church growth in England, 1841–1914," 202.

British Perceptions of Latter-day Saint Emigrants

Perceptions of the Saints came not only through newspapers and magazines but other channels as well: novels, films, travel literature, and caricatures. Though the channel varied, the message was often the same: the Latter-day Saints were outsiders who were odd, unfit for society, and the subject of unrelenting ridicule.

British journalists catching sight of the unseemly converts bound for the "promised land" of America summarized them as mindless dupes foolishly leaving the British Empire.[11] Those working within the maritime emigration business observed the fruits of the Saints' modus operandi throughout the nineteenth century and held vastly different views. Emigrating and immigrating Latter-day Saint converts and agents received high marks in ports on both sides of the Atlantic. For example, a Liverpool shipping agent interviewed in 1852 made this comment about the Latter-day Saints:

> With regards to Mormon Emigration and the class of persons of which it is composed, they are principally farmers and mechanics, with some few clerks, surgeons, &c. They are generally well-behaved, and many of them highly respectable.[12]

Two years later in 1854, a London newspaper correspondent reported how a Latter-day Saint emigration agent, Samuel W. Richards, had been interviewed by the House of Commons concerning the agents' success in bringing Latter-day Saint converts across the Atlantic:

> I heard a rather remarkable examination before a committee of the House of Commons. The witness was no [none] other than the supreme authority in England of the Mormonites, and the subject upon which he was giving information was the mode in which the emigration to Utah, Great Salt Lake, is conducted. . . . At the close of the examination, he received the thanks of the committee in rather a marked manner. According to his statements,

---

11. The *Liverpool Mercury* published several negative reports about the departing Latter-day Saint emigrants during the early 1840s (e.g., October 12, November 4, 1842; and February 23, March 22, 1844). However, one impartial article appearing in the *Liverpool Albion*, September 1842, stated, "The emigration of the Mormons . . . is daily increasing. . . . The class of persons thus emigrating are in appearance and worldly circumstances above the ordinary men of steerage passengers." This article is cited in W. H. G. Armytage, "Liverpool, Gateway to Zion," 39.

12. Charles Mackay, *The Mormons or Latter-day Saints*, 244–45.

Samuel W. Richards, British Mission president, who supervised the 1854 Mormon emigration from Europe. From a portrait by Frederick Piercy, 1854.

about twenty-six hundred Mormonite emigrants leave Liverpool during the first three months of every year, and are under the care of a president. On arriving at New Orleans they are received by another president, who returns to Mr. Richards an account of the state in which he found the ship, etc. . . . At any rate there is one thing which, in the emigration committee of the House of Commons, they can do—viz., teach Christian ship owners how to send poor people decently, cheaply, and healthfully across the Atlantic.[13]

A year later, the *New York Tribune* reported the excellent condition of the ship *S. Curling* when its cargo of European Latter-day Saint immigrants disembarked at the New York port: "The vessel was the cleanest emigrant ship we have ever seen; notwithstanding the large number of passengers, order, cleanliness and comfort prevailed on all hands, the between decks were as sweet and well-ventilated as the cabin." The journalist further stated, "It would be well if the packet ships that ply between this port and Liverpool were to imitate the system of management that prevailed on this ship."[14]

In the same year that Richard Burton published his interest-piquing book, *City of the Saints*,[15] *The Edinburgh Review* reported on the superior Latter-day Saint travel system:

---

13. London correspondent of the *Cambridge Independent Press*, May 24, 1854, concerning Mormon emigration agent Samuel W. Richards. See "Missionary Experience," 158–59, which also contains a firsthand account of this unusual evidence by Richards himself. For additional information on the exceptional Latter-day Saint emigration process from Liverpool, see Fred E. Woods, "The Tide of Mormon Migration Flowing through Liverpool," 60–86.

14. P. A. M. Taylor, "Mormons and Gentiles on the Atlantic," 204.

15. Richard Burton wrote about the Saints after living among them for a time. However, like other works of the day, both histories and in the form of novels, these writings were not aimed at framing the Church in a positive light but rather in a

The ordinary emigrant is exposed to all the chances and misadventures of a heterogeneous, childish, mannerless crowd during the voyage, and to the merciless cupidity of land-sharks the moment he has touched the opposite shore. But the Mormon ship is a Family under strong and accepted discipline with every provision for comfort, decorum, and internal peace. On his arrival in the New World the wanderer is received into a confraternity which speeds him onwards with as little hardship and anxiety as the circumstances permit and he is passed on from friend to friend, till he reaches the promised home.[16]

A year later, Charles Dickens observed Latter-day Saint converts in London bound for America on an immigrant ocean vessel, the *Amazon*. He admitted that he went on board

to bear testimony against them if they deserved it, as I fully believed they would . . . to my great astonishment they did not deserve it; and my predispositions and tendencies must not affect me as an honest witness. I went over the *Amazon's* side feeling it impossible to deny that, so far, some remarkable influence had produced a remarkable result, which better known influences have often missed.

Of the Latter-day Saint British converts themselves, he noted they were "in their degree, the pick and flower of England."[17] Dickens's issue against the Saints was particular to their beliefs but never their practices. He summarized, "What the Mormons do seems to be excellent; what they say, is mostly nonsense."[18]

On the heels of Dickens's confessions, American humorist Artemus Ward's 1865 *His Travels*, under a section titled "Among the Mormons," reflected the begrudging acknowledgement of the exemplary industrious model that Dickens had observed in the Saints.[19] Additional positive ob-

---

sensational manner, apparently for book sales and attention. See Richard F. Burton, "The City of the Saints, and across the Rocky Mountains to California," 99.

16. Burton, 101.

17. Charles Dickens, "The Uncommercial Traveller," *All the Year Round*, 444, 446.

18. Quoted in Givens, *Viper on the Hearth*, 63.

19. Artemus Ward, *Artemus Ward; His Travels*, 1865. But the humorously mocking influence of Artemus Ward's satirical performances cannot be underestimated. Charles Farrar Browne (Ward's real name) was one of America's most well-known nineteenth-century humorists; his work was beloved by President Abraham Lincoln. Ward's funny "lectures" were a big hit in London too. His stretching of facts about the Mormons for comedic impact would have hugely swayed public perceptions on both sides of the Atlantic. That influence even reached into the twentieth century. "This famous 'genial showman' had much to do with setting the

servations surfaced through the writings of William Hepworth Dixon in his 1867 *New America*. In this work he compared the English, whom he maintained wasted energy in doctrinal debates, with the Latter-day Saint community, which, in his opinion, had become quite successful in implementing their religious faith into everyday living. Dixon cited a sermon that Brigham Young, who felt it his duty to teach the Saints practical salvation, gave to recent inbound foreign Saints:

> Don't bother yourselves much about your religious duties. . . . Your first duty is to learn how to grow a cabbage, and along with this cabbage an onion, a tomato, a sweet potato; then how to feed a pig, to build a house, to plant a garden, to rear cattle and to bake bread. . . . These things you must do first; the rest will be added to you in proper season.[20]

George Ramsden and the Guion Line

By the end of the decade, the Saints found a shipping company to safely transfer immigrant Saints across the Atlantic. The esteemed Guion shipping line could readily be identified because the majority of its vessels bore the names of American states, though the ships were British by law.[21] George N. Ramsden was employed by the Guion line as a shipping agent. With a reputation of having great principles and utmost integrity, Ramsden could no doubt observe the favorable qualities of the Latter-day Saints coupled with an opportunity for economic profit. Under his direction, forty thousand European Latter-day Saint converts crossed the Atlantic Ocean to gather in Utah via a dozen steam vessels owned and operated by this British maritime company.[22]

---

stage for American and British views of Mormonism. Numerous articles have been made available from British papers in the British Library through the digitization of several collections. The newspapers from 1850 through 1900 chronicle the popularity of Ward's Mormon lecture in England and the long-term effect of Ward on the Mormon image into the twentieth century. In that time period, there are more than 15,000 references to the combined search terms 'Artemus Ward' and 'Mormons.'" (See Joel J. Campbell and Kristoffer D. Boyle, "Artemus Ward: The Forgotten Influence of the Genial Showman's Mormon Lecture on Public Opinion of Mormons in the United States and Great Britain," 1107–26).

20. Sebastian Lecourt, "The Mormons, The Victorians, and the Idea of Greater Britain," 93.

21. George Chandler, *Liverpool Shipping: A Short History*, 122–23.

22. Conway B. Sonne, *Saints on the Seas: A Maritime History of Mormon Migration 1830–1890*, 117, 173.

The beginning of Ramsden's warm relationship with the Saints began on May 13, 1869, when he met with Latter-day Saint British Mission President Albert Carrington in Liverpool. There, an arrangement was made for the transatlantic conveyance of a company of Latter-day Saint converts aboard the *Minnesota*.[23] According to their plan, the Saints boarded the vessel in Liverpool on June 1, 1869. The "British Mission Manuscript History" records, "On their arrival on board they were provided with tea, and everything was done by the manager, Mr. G. Ramsden, for the comfort of the Saints. They had the best part of the steamer entirely for themselves and could use the aft part of the ship in common with the cabin passengers."[24]

Five years later, Joseph F. Smith, president of the European Mission, found he could secure a better financial deal with a different shipping firm than what the Guion Line was offering. Therefore, Ramsden, whom Smith defined as "a very shrewd, keen man, with both eyes open to business,"[25] quickly made a counteroffer to keep the Latter-day Saints' business. This proposal affected the entire shipping conference cartel, which decided to permit the Guion Line to lower the rates of Latter-day Saint passengers only.[26]

The extraordinary relationship between Ramsden and the Saints was kept alive and lasted for a quarter of a century. In praise of the trust he enjoyed with the Saints, Anthon H. Lund, the British Mission president from 1893 to 1896, pointed out that Ramsden worked for decades with the Church in absence of a written contract.[27] Furthermore, by 1880, the entire maritime industry held the Guion Line in great esteem inasmuch as it had "never lost a life" during its shipping years.[28] Not only did the sea-going Saints receive exceptional service, but they could travel in peace, confident of the Guion's impeccable safety record. In addition, the successful transition from sail to steam on the journey westward significantly reduced travel time to America.[29] Ramsden's trusted leadership, paired

---

23. "British Mission Manuscript History," 24 (1869–1871), May 13, 1869.

24. "British Mission Manuscript History," 24 (1869–1871), June 1, 1869.

25. Joseph F. Smith letter to Franklin D. Richards, September 9, 1874.

26. Richard L. Jensen, "Steaming Through: Arrangements for Mormon Emigration from Europe, 1869–1887," 7.

27. Jensen, 6–7.

28. Edward Cloward, *The Steam-Ship Lines of the Mersey and Export Trade Register*, May 1880, 17.

29. The Guion Line shortened the length of the Atlantic crossing from 32–36 days to 10–16 days.

with the timely and safe voyage the Guion Line offered to the Saints, melded into a prosperous synergistic partnership and business.

Ramsden also came to the defense of the Saints when others wished them harm. For example, in 1879, US Secretary of State William M. Evarts tried to campaign against the Latter-day Saint practice of polygamy by sending a circular letter to a number of European countries, ultimately hoping to halt the immigration of Latter-day Saints to America. In an article for the *Millennial Star*, Lund reported:

> Several of Mr. Ramsden's friends engaged in the shipping business warned him of the risk he ran of having our people sent back should he attempt to land them in America; but this did not deter him from booking them. He saw how unjust this measure was and knew that it had its origin in prejudice and religious intolerance.[30]

According to Lund, just as a consul put up posters announcing Latter-day Saints could not land in American ports, Ramsden came aboard a Guion ship and took charge:

> In a towering rage [Ramsden] commanded the Consul to pull down the notice. The latter said he was acting [on] order from the government. Ramsden replied that the government had nothing to do with his ships, and that he did not ask a passenger what his religion was. His strong stand saved our emigration from being stopped.[31]

Ramsden was successful in Liverpool, but posters and persecution against the Saints ran rampant on both sides of the Atlantic during the decade of the 1880s, mainly resulting from the American laws of the Edmunds Act (1882) and later the Edmunds Tucker–Act (1887), which aimed at ceasing the practice of plural marriage and criminalized even unlawful cohabitation.

In the same year as the Edmunds–Tucker Act, Sir Arthur Conan Doyle launched his legendary character Sherlock Holmes in his novel *A Study in Scarlet*, wherein the Saints are depicted as a murderous group whose actions led to the deaths that Holmes is investigating. Three and a half decades later, when he was in Salt Lake City as a visiting lecturer, Doyle admitted that this fictitious work was "sensational and overcolored"

---

30. Anthon H. Lund, "A Good Friend Gone," 360–62.

31. Anthon H. Lund, letter to Heber J. Grant, March 22, 1905, as cited in Jensen, "Steaming Through," 7. For more information on the relationship between Ramsden, the Guion Line, and the Saints, see Fred E. Woods, "George Ramsden, the Guion Line, and the Mormon Immigration Connection," 83–97.

but refused to apologize because it represented the best information he could gather at the end of the nineteenth century.[32]

In his study on early literary accounts of the Latter-day Saints, Terryl L. Givens explains how the Saints were marginalized during the Victorian era: "Nineteenth century writers of fiction were . . . sensationalistic [and] exploitive."[33] As a result, many people misperceived The Church of Jesus Christ of Latter-day Saints, and some thought its adherents were members of a cult and far from Protestant mainstream Christianity.

---

32. Lecourt, "Mormons," 85.

33. Givens, *Viper on the Hearth*, 130.

CHAPTER 3

The First Half of the Twentieth Century: Opinions Regarding the Saints

Their missionary work is chiefly directed to making converts of young and comely girls with a view to induce them ultimately to go out to Utah . . . and there become the plural wives of Elders.
— London *Times*

Perceptions about Latter-day Saints in the twentieth century were greatly influenced by an event that occurred a decade preceding it. In 1890, Church President Wilford Woodruff issued the Manifesto announcing an end to the practice of polygamy in response to both persecution and prosecution by the US Government against the Saints. Woodruff said he was shown in a vision what would occur if Church members did not desist from the observance of plural marriage: temples would be closed, and the Latter-day Saints' proxy ordinance work (sacred ceremonies for deceased persons) would cease.[1] This document was very influential in the decision to have Utah admitted into the Union in 1896. Despite the Manifesto, repercussions stemming from polygamy continued at home and abroad and influenced how the Church would be viewed in the twentieth century.

Although the official statement by Woodruff prompted some welcomed softening towards the Church generally, one prominent Church leader was carefully scrutinized and harassed because of the stigma associated with plural marriage. Senator Reed Smoot served on the US Senate and as a Church apostle concurrently for three decades from 1903 to 1933. Rumors and accusations that polygamous practices continued into the twentieth century led to the "Smoot hearings," which ran a lengthy four years beginning in 1903 and prompted a second manifesto completely prohibiting polygamy among the Latter-day Saints, this time issued by

---

1. Woodruff stated, "The Lord showed me by vision and revelation exactly what would take place if we did not stop this practice. If we had not stopped it, you would have had no use for . . . this temple in Logan; for all ordinances would be stopped throughout the land of Zion." See "Excerpts from Three Addresses by President Wilford Woodruff Regarding the Manifesto," The Church of Jesus Christ of Latter-day Saints.

President Joseph F. Smith in 1904. In the end, Smoot kept his Senate seat; however, the Church continued to have a difficult time eliminating its reputation of polygamy from the public consciousness.

Continued Persecution via Slanderous Media

Coverage of the Smoot hearings rekindled a wave of anti-Mormon sentiment in film and literature throughout the early decades of the twentieth century, with polygamy continuing to be fodder for this slander. The United States was passing through the Progressive Era, and a reform-minded society remained committed to publishing articles condemning what the public perceived to be the Latter-day Saints' persistent practice of polygamy.

Across the Atlantic, things were no better. According to one Church historian,

> In England, the anti-Mormon crusade reached its height in 1911, when people like the Rev. Daniel H. C. Bartlett, an Anglican vicar, led an anti-Mormon rally in Liverpool; and Hans Peter Freece, . . . a former member of the Church, described how well-dressed Mormon elders flattered thousands of English girls into joining the harems in Utah.[2]

In this same year, the London *Times* baselessly stoked these fears:

> The great charge brought against them is that their missionary work is chiefly directed to making converts of young and comely girls with a view to induce them ultimately to go out to Utah . . . and there become the plural wives of Elders, for, it is said, though . . . declared illegal, [polygamy] is still secretly practised in Utah.[3]

These messages had the intended effect on the British population. For example, Abraham Wright recalled first hearing of the "Mormons" as a seven-year-old in Sunderland during 1911:

> When I was a kiddie, . . . my auntie . . . said, "Now come on home or I'll let the Mormons catch you." . . . That was the first time I ever heard the word Mormon referring to anybody. . . . In those days there used to be stories . . . that Mormons used to trap girls into going to America. . . . The newspapers . . . used to think anything scandalous was fine.[4]

This stirring up of fear led to some governmental leaders investigating the matter themselves. One Church periodical reported that due

---

2. Richard Cowan, "Church Growth in England, 1841–1914," 226–27.

3. "Mormonism In England," 8.

4. Abraham Wright, interviewed by Ron Walker, 5–7.

to the negative reports against the Saints, the "British Home Secretary, Winston Churchill, directed that a nationwide survey of the activities of the 'Mormon' missionaries be made. However, when pressed as to what action the British government intended to take . . . he replied: I have not so far discovered any grounds for legislation in the matter."[5]

Not all periodicals were swept up in the anti-Mormon fervor. For example, the *Daily Express* kept a cool head during this tumultuous period, noting,

> The whole so-called crusade is an outbreak of sectarian savagery worked up by journalists, who in their zest for sensation appear to be quite indifferent to the fact that the only permanent result of their exploit will be to advertise and to spread the 'Mormon faith' among the masses, who love fair play, and who hate religious persecution.[6]

Anti-Mormon sentiments, however, continued in the media. In 1922, *Cosmopolitan* magazine used the phrase "viper on the hearth" to heighten awareness of the Latter-day Saints' polygamous threat to society via the destruction of "the domestic sphere."[7] The following year, Zane Grey's 1912 *Riders of the Purple Sage* became another best-selling popular novel that focused on the Saints' perceived practice of luring women into plural marriage.[8]

These years preceding World War I in Great Britain were viewed as the most hostile assault against the Church since the Latter-day Saint missionaries first arrived at Liverpool in 1837. This prejudice and the anti-Mormon films and literature that flung such epithets as the "Mormon Peril" or the "Mormon Menace" were widely distributed through the British press and often resulted in violence.[9]

Among these, perhaps the most damning influence during this era stemmed from British novelist Winifred Graham, who penned several sensational novels with a similar theme: Latter-day Saint missionaries deceiving gullible young women into plural marriage. During these peak years of anti-Mormon assaults in Great Britain, she published *The Love Story of a Mormon* (1911), *The Sin of Utah* (1912), and *A Popular History* (1913). As one historian noted, Graham was "a popular Edwardian novelist . . . [who] portrayed the Mormons as the personification of evil," though

---

5. Richard L. Evans, *A Century of "Mormonism" in Great Britain*, 211.

6. Evans, *Century of "Mormonism,"* 211.

7. Terryl Givens, *The Viper on the Hearth*, 4.

8. Givens, *Viper on the Hearth*, 145, 151.

9. See, for example, "Anti-Mormons Riot," 7; "Anti-Mormon Riot," 10.

Cecil B. DeMille (left) and David O. McKay (right), ca. 1956. Photo courtesy L. Tom Perry Special Collections, BYU.

her writings suggest she knew few facts regarding The Church of Jesus Christ of Latter-day Saints.[10]

Several years later, *A Mormon Maid* (1917), an anti-Mormon silent film that also carried this damaging theme, was shown in movie theaters throughout the United States and later in Britain. The film producer was none other than the famous Cecil B. DeMille, who would later produce and direct the epic *The Ten Commandments* starring Charlton Heston. Although DeMille was not directly responsible for the content of the film, he was responsible for the decision to release it. The film has been described as "arguably the most potent and important anti-Mormon film in the history of cinema" and "the most-advertised picture in the history of American cinema up to that time."[11]

Decades later, DeMille was introduced to Church President David O. McKay and over time they became dear friends. DeMille not only changed his view of the Latter-day Saints; he actually became an advocate for McKay and the Church. As the ultimate goodwill gesture, DeMille chose to preview *The Ten Commandments* in Salt Lake City, and there he publicly praised what he saw as the fine character and goodness of The Church of Jesus Christ of Latter-day Saints.[12]

This happy ending was not the case with other films produced to mar the image of the Church during this period. Although World War I brought a bit of a reprieve, a harmful motion picture that was released in 1922, titled *Trapped by the Mormons*, again sent the message that English girls must be warned of the mesmerizing Latter-day Saint missionaries sent to lure them back to Salt Lake City to join a harem. Based on Graham's

10. Malcolm R. Thorp, "'The Mormon Peril': The Crusade against the Saints in Britain, 1910–1914," 69, 75–76; see also Thorp, "Winifred Graham and the Mormon Image in England," 107–21.

11. "A Mormon Maid," Mormon Literature and Creative Arts.

12. Fred E. Woods, "Cecil B. DeMille and David O. McKay—an Unexpected Friendship," 78–104.

Three Latter-day Saint missionaries posing with a London advertisement for *Trapped by the Mormons*, 1922. Courtesty Church History Library.

venomous novel *The Love Story of a Mormon* (1911), this film was also heavily influenced by Bram Stoker's 1897 novel, *Dracula*.

Trapped by the Mormons proved to be another stumbling block for the missionary work in the British Isles. In fact, the film was so detrimental that McKay, at that time a member of the Church's Quorum of the Twelve Apostles and serving as the president of the European Mission, wrote to then Church President Heber J. Grant stating, "The activity of the Saints in Britain in tracting [proselytizing] is arousing the devil, who is manifesting his evil designs through his co-partner Winifred and her ilk."[13]

Desiring Protection from Physical Abuse

During this tumultuous period of the early 1920s, missionaries such as future Church President Ezra Taft Benson and his companions had to rely on the police for protection.[14] Abraham Wright, a teenaged Saint from Sunderland, recalled that Benson and another elder "were stoned outside our railway station by a mob. His companion [William Harris]

---

13. James V. D'Arc, "The Mormons as Vampire: A Comparative Study of Winifred Graham's *The Love Story of a Mormon*, the Film *Trapped by the Mormons*, and Bram Stoker's *Dracula*," 168–69.

14. Sheri L. Dew, *Ezra Taft Benson, A Biography*, 62.

got his face or his cheek cut and had to go to the local infirmary and have some stitches put in."

When Wright went tracting with Benson himself, Wright noted that Elder Benson told him, "When we go tracting like this there's one thing we must always remember. If we come to a close [dead end street], don't start at one side and go around the close delivering tracts. Go to the middle and work outwards so that if by any chance you met with any antagonism, at least your way wouldn't be blocked to get out of the street." Wright also explained, "The general feeling of the people at that time was antagonistic. . . . Some areas were very, very, very bad. When you got into some of these villages or some of these smaller places, the antagonism was greater."[15]

Another Saint from Sunderland, Frederick W. Oates, captured the intense persecution during this era:

> I can remember coming out of the chapel with my father, and just seeing what looked to me at that time as hordes of people. They were throwing flour bags and grass sods at the Saints as they were coming out of church to make their way home. They then would break up into groups and follow the Saints to their homes, break into their homes, and look under the beds and in the wardrobes and see if they had any missionaries there. So it was very bitter. . . . The police weren't too helpful. The Saints would ask them for protection, but I guess they were afraid and we very seldom got any real help.[16]

Wisely Dealing with Attacks

The 1922 releases of *Trapped by the Mormons* and its sequel *Married to a Mormon* were quickly met with a plucky, preemptive response as reported to the *Deseret News* by G. Osmond Hyde, president of the Hull Conference:

> We secured permission from the police and the manager of the hall to tract the people as they left the show. . . . We distributed a large number of pamphlets and tracts. Of course some of the people would not accept them, others tore them up in our faces, but others were anxious to get them and would not leave until they had secured one. That was the best stroke of advertising that we have put forth since coming over here. In three evenings we let more people know that we are here than we could have done in three months at ordinary tracting from door to door. It was a rare experience but one in which, I am sure, we did a great amount of good.[17]

---

15. Abraham Wright, interviewed by Ron Walker, 5–7.

16. Frederick W. and Gladys Q. Oates, interviewed by Richard L. Jensen, 11–12.

17. G. Osmond Hyde, "Movie Campaign against 'Mormons' Leads Many to Investigate Message," 40.

Two years later Graham launched yet another work, *Eve and the Elders.* This, however, did not flourish like the previous films largely due to the public image of the Church at this time quickly transforming into just another of the many sects coming out of America.[18] It was also a time of some needed respite for the Church because of the rippling impact of the end of World War I and the changes brought by the Roaring Twenties, which flooded America and also managed to pour over onto Britain's shores. Notwithstanding, Elder James E. Talmage, a Church apostle seasoned in dealing with anti-Mormon attacks in the press, was sent to preside over the British Mission from 1924 to 1927 and to fortify the Church and be ready for any additional onslaughts.[19]

Upon his arrival to replace David O. McKay as mission president, Talmage explained the current media problem: "Mission authorities had been unable to reach the men at the decision-making level of the offending journals. . . . Always the man at the top . . . was unavailable—for a variety of reasons, or, rather, of conventional fictions."[20]

During his presidency, Talmage confronted these media leaders head-on, and the tide ebbed. For example, one Church periodical noted the change evident in Cardiff, South Wales:

> Credit for bringing this about must be given to President Talmage. With an influence born of his scholarly achievements, and his recognition by, and his membership in, various Royal Societies, together with his sincerity of purpose . . . President Talmage exerted a powerful influence upon the editors.[21]

Summarizing the extent of his influence on the media during his leadership in Great Britain, Talmage's son wrote, "The change in the attitude of the press was not reflected only in the disappearance of scurrilous anti-Mormon attacks but also in positive ways, including objective reporting of Latter-day Saints activities and even occasional articles directly praising the Mormons and their work."[22]

Talmage was replaced by Apostle John A. Widtsoe, who followed the counsel of his friend and mentor. Widtsoe served three consecutive two-

---

18. Thorp, "Mormon Image in England," 113.

19. Alan K. Parrish, "Turning the Media Image of the Church in Great Britain, 1922–1923," 179.

20. John R. Talmage, *The Talmage Story: Life of James E. Talmage—Educator, Scientist, Apostle,* 206.

21. Lewis F. Hansen, "The Work in Wales," 469–70.

22. Talmage, *Talmage Story,* 211.

year terms as mission president from 1927 to 1933 due largely to his success with the media. One technique he employed that proved effective was to invite the press to mingle with Church members so that they could feel of their goodness.[23] After only one year in office, Widtsoe reported to the *Sheffield Daily Telegraph*: "The old bogey of young men coming to this country from Salt Lake City to take young women back to America is dead and buried, and what is more, it had a respectable funeral."[24]

Using Sport to Create a More Favorable Image

The decade of the 1930s provided a more favorable image of the Church as British citizens became more accepting, understanding, and—to some degree—even admiring of the Saints. Transitioning the Church's British Mission headquarters in 1932 and the European Mission headquarters in 1933 from Liverpool, where they had been located for nearly a century, to London significantly and positively affected the Church's public image.

One particular impact on the Church's image in the 1930s was the successful participation of Latter-day Saint missionaries in both baseball and basketball associations. In 1935, the first year of organized league baseball in Britain, two teams of Latter-day Saint missionaries gained national reputations. One of the teams, the Rochdale Greys, made it to the British championships that year; as did the other team, the Catford Saints, the following year. The Rochdale Greys soon won the national championship in 1938.[25]

In 1936 and 1937, the Rochdale Greys won first place in the baseball northern division.[26] In 1936, the Catford Saints were placed second in the southern baseball division, being defeated in the final championship by the White City team. Shortly thereafter, the secretary of the White City

---

23. Parrish, "Media Image of the Church," 182–83.

24. "The Mormon Mission: One of the Twelve Apostles," 7.

25. Louis B. Cardon, "The First World War and the Great Depression, 1914–1939," 357–58. See also Josh Chetwynd et al, "National Champions of British Baseball."

26. The Rochdale Greys caught the attention of the media, who knew they were Latter-day Saint missionaries. For example, in announcing the north division championship baseball game in 1937, one journalist wrote, "They are in England as missionaries of the Church of Latter-day Saints." See "Rochdale Greys to Visit Craven Park," 9.

team sent a tribute to Elder Wendell J. Ashton, manager of and player for the Catford Saints. This tribute was later published in the *Millennial Star*:

> We always hoped and needed to play our best game against our L.D.S. friends. Most important of all, however, was the sporting spirit in which every game was played, and I regard those games in which I was privileged to participate against you last year as ample reward for the work which has devolved upon me in connection with baseball. Although you came to this country as missionaries of your Church, your success as ambassadors of goodwill has earned a special debt of gratitude from the general public both here and in the States.[27]

The elders continued to participate successfully in athletic contests, with the team names of the Catford Saints and the Rochdale Greys also being used for missionary basketball teams.[28] Because of their success, the Catford Saints were allowed to compete in the international basketball competition—and won. After returning to Britain, their manager, E. W. Browning, made this report to the national committee of the praiseworthy Latter-day Saint missionary team:

> It was a pleasure to accompany such an exemplary group of young men on this trip as manager. Their conduct at all times was above reproach. On the basketball floor their clean play and sportsmanship made them very popular with the large crowds who saw them play. . . . [T]hey were a distinct credit to the highest traditions of British sportsmanship.[29]

Building Bridges with Music

During the same decade, music was also used by missionaries to build bridges in the British Isles. Under the direction of Joseph J. Cannon, who served as British Mission president from 1934 to 1937, the Millennial Chorus was formed, and they sang for thousands of people throughout Britain. Made up of a total of sixteen missionaries out of ninety possi-

---

27. Parry D. Sorensen, "A New Kind of Pioneering," 668; also cited in Cardon, "First World War," 358.

28. Cardon, "First World War," 357–59. Again, the media was aware that the Rochdale Greys were Latter-day Saints. For example, one reporter wrote, "Take a look at the Rochdale Greys, a team of sturdy, non-smoking, teetotal American missionaries." See "Basketball Makes New Speed Thrill," 11.

29. Parry D. Sorensen, "Mormon Missionaries Under the Union Jack," 476, 502–3; "Catford Saints Win European Tournament," 292; also cited in Cardon, "First World War," 359.

ble candidates, these missionaries continued to tract, but they also held musical street meetings and sang at district conferences. In addition, the Millennial Chorus performed for various church and school functions and entertained at cinemas and on the radio.[30] By 1938, these talented missionaries had become an outstanding choir, wielding a tremendous positive impact on how the Church was viewed.[31] This is evident in supportive articles from the British media. For example, a reporter from the *Gloucestershire Echo* observed,

> The Millennial Chorus . . . are missionaries of the Church of Jesus Christ of Latter-day Saints, and are on a goodwill tour of England. . . . Their work is entirely voluntary, and extends over a period of two years. . . . There are 180 such missionaries in Great Britain, and 3,000 in the world. . . . This particular chorus is well known in this country for its singing.[32]

The fame and influence of the Millennial Chorus soon spread as far as Northern Ireland, where the media similarly offered up praise. For example, the *Northern Whig and Belfast Post* announced,

> Fifteen young missionaries of the Church of Jesus Christ of Latter-day Saints are at present staying in Northern Ireland. They are known as the Millennial Chorus, and . . . they are to broadcast some songs in the B.B.C. Northern Ireland programme. The Chorus . . . possesses some very fine voices.[33]

Among the Saints, the *Millennial Star* reported on the choir's impact:

> With two or three performances each day . . . before audiences of up to two and three thousand each session it is not over estimating to say that in one week more than 25,000 people are coming in contact with these singing ambassadors . . . [who] cannot help but admire the views and conduct of this outstanding group of young men. . . . There is not a more effective means of making friends for the Church in Britain than through the efforts of the members of the Millennial Chorus.[34]

---

30. For an overview of how the Church was using the radio for missionary work in the decade of the 30s, see Jessie L. Embry, "'New Ways of Proselyting': Radio and Missionary Work in the 1930s," 117–50.

31. Cardon, "First World War," 359.

32. "Goodwill Tour of Britain," 4. See also, "Mormon Singers in Hull," 9; "Male Voice Choir," 6.

33. "American Chorus in Belfast," *Northern Whig*, 10, cited in Evans, *Century of "Mormonism,"* 213.

34. Robert S. Stevens, "Broadcasting with the Millennial Chorus," 92–95; Marvin J. Ashton, "Singing Ambassadors," 520–21.

A Season of Positive Press

Perhaps an even better barometer of the change in public perceptions of the Church can be seen in reports by those not of the Latter-day Saint faith in local newspapers during the 1930s. For example, in 1932, London's *East Ham Echo* noted,

> Probably no section of the human race is more unfairly criticized, more libelled and slandered or more misunderstood by the ignorant, than members of the Church of Jesus Christ of Latter-day Saints. . . . Sensational fiction and crude films have created among the uninformed in England, many queer impressions.[35]

The following year, a journalist from the *Birmingham Weekly Post* likewise reported on the disparity between rumor and reality: "Everywhere in Salt Lake City . . . you begin to appreciate the sterling qualities of this once despised sect."[36]

Similar reports that decade also came from the *Liverpool Evening Express*:

> Let us hope that readers will no longer look upon the Mormons as decadent ministers luring women to a shameful life in Salt Lake City. They are a clean-living band of young men, anxious to convert Gentiles. . . . And they do it without reward of any sort.[37]

The London-based *Daily Express*:

> The faith of the Mormons, which began in ridicule, now stands in dignity and respect. They have created a worthy and useful institution whose members do good by teaching and by the example of their upright lives.

And the British magazine *Cavalcade*:

> Since [the Latter-day Saints] arrived in this country one hundred years ago they have had to fight against blind prejudice brought about by untrue stories. . . . In the years that have passed they have succeeded in living down this calumny.[38]

Some old stereotypes persisted but, at times, supposed "Mormon" polygamy was referenced in lighthearted ways. This included the 1933 newspaper advertisement for a British breakfast cereal, with the strapline

---

35. Charles Eade, "Salt Lake City and Utah," 342.
36. Evans, *Century of "Mormonism,"* 212.
37. Eargle M. Charmsen, "Making Friends with Fleet Street," 443.
38. Both these articles were cited in Cardon, "First World War," 360.

"All the wives a Mormon ever had couldn't prepare a better breakfast than you get in Scott's Porage Oats."[39]

Centennial Commemoration of the Church in Great Britain

In the year leading up to the celebration of the centennial commemoration of the Church in Britain, the Saints would reflect on what it took to get them to this point. Apostle Richard L. Evans was commissioned to write the centennial history, which would culminate in a variety of celebratory activities. Although the statistics for the year 1937 placed Church membership in Britain at only a bit more than six thousand, by the end of the first century of the Church in Britain, over 125,000 had been baptized and nearly six thousand missionaries had labored there.[40] In addition, it is thought that at least 52,000 British converts immigrated to America between 1837 and 1937.[41]

Attending the commemorative activities were Church President Heber J. Grant and his counselor J. Reuben Clark. The *Millennial Star* noted, "Never in the history of the [British] Mission have two members of the First Presidency been here at the same time."[42] A week later, Elder Parry D. Sorenson, a missionary serving in England, observed, "Never in the eventful history of the British Mission have so many Church leaders been in Britain at one time as there are at present to attend the Centennial Conference."[43] Ironically, however, as noted by Derek A. Cuthbert fifty years later, due to the mass nineteenth-century British emigration from the British Isles to Zion, "[s]adly, few were left in Britain to join in these [centennial] celebrations."[44]

Throughout this period, President Grant also dedicated seven chapels, which no doubt thrilled the local Saints who generally met in rented facilities for Church meetings. In addition, the media took notice of the

---

39. February 2, 1933, *Hull Daily Mail* advertisement, referenced in Rosalie West, "HULL Newspapers 1830–1950."

40. Alexander L. Baugh, "The Church in Twentieth-Century Great Britain: A Historical Overview," 242–43.

41. Cardon, "First World War," 355.

42. "Greetings to President and Sister Clark," 452.

43. Parry D. Sorenson, "Our Centennial Visitors," 485.

44. Derek A. Cuthbert, *The Second Century: Latter-day Saints in Great Britain*, 1:1.

centennial event, and on several occasions during the festivities, the BBC invited missionaries to participate in their programs.[45]

The War Years

The threat of Nazi Germany sweeping over Europe dulled the happy echoes of Latter-day Saint commemorations, missionary athletic cheering, and even the inspirational singing of the Millennium Chorus. On August 24, 1939, the First Presidency of the Church ordered an evacuation of the missionaries throughout Europe, including in the British Mission. Soon, these missionaries would return to their homes in the United States. This was the first time in over a century of British Latter-day Saint history that Great Britain would be left without American missionaries. [46]

Anticipating the impending withdrawal, Mission President Hugh B. Brown (a Canadian who had fought in World War I and knew something of the impact of global warfare) reserved one hundred tickets to ship home his missionaries in advance of the First Presidency's evacuation order. After sending the missionaries safely home, Brown stayed in England several more months to make sure that leadership of the mission was taken care of. He then transferred authority for the mission into the hands of Andre K. Anastasiou, a native Russian who had come to England as a nineteen-year-old during World War I. Though it was challenging, Anastasiou and his counselors continued to publish the *Millennial Star* to keep the scattered European Saints informed of what was going on in the Church during the war years.[47]

In order to maintain some stability for the Church and its members, Anastasiou successfully petitioned the British government to allow presidents of local branches and districts to have exemption from wartime service. Still, in some areas, there was only one priesthood leader to carry out the work of conducting church meetings and performing ordinances and rituals. Due to these trying circumstances, Anastasiou called upon

---

45. Cuthbert, 1–2.

46. Bruce Van Orden, *Building Zion: The Latter-day Saints in Europe*, 138.

47. Van Orden, 141; Cardon, "War and Recovery," 365, explains that Anastasiou's first counselor directed the publication of the *Millennial Star*. Further, after only a few months of service in the presidency, Hill was replaced as counselor by George H. Bailey, but Hill continued to direct the editing of the *Millennial Star* throughout the war years. The second counselor in the mission presidency was James R. Cunningham.

local men who had disability deferments or health challenges, as well as some women, to serve full-time missions. In addition, hundreds more were called as part-time home missionaries in their local regions. One Latter-day Saint historian commented on the successful home missionary program launched by Anastasiou during World War II:

> Church members who were called to this program agreed to contribute four to eighteen hours of Church service each week, visiting members, . . . proselytizing door to door, and doing the duties the full-time elders had performed. Over five hundred British Saints labored as home missionaries during the war years.[48]

In the spring of 1944, a year before the war in Europe would end, Brown returned to inspect the British Mission and congratulated Anastasiou and his associates for what they had achieved since the outbreak of war. During his four-and-a-half-year tenure as mission president, the branches in England had actually increased in number, and Anastasiou had collected over eighty thousand dollars in tithes and offerings.[49] Having passed through a season of limited availability of priesthood leaders wherein the scars of war-torn Europe took their toll, the British Saints arose from the ashes and stood stronger in their spiritual independence—not in spite of but because of the agonizing, adverse conditions of the war years.

By spring of 1945, the shout of victory heralded across Europe as the war came to its bitter end and Brown was able to fully reestablish the British Mission, with Selvoy J. Boyer presiding over the mission from 1946 to 1950. Adding to the strength of the region, Apostle Ezra Taft Benson was called in 1946 to preside over the neighboring European Mission and help restore stability in the area. Soon, there was a rapid increase of missionaries, and by 1950, Boyer was replaced as British mission president by Stayner Richards. As the mid-twentieth century concluded, missionaries were back in the throes of building bridges through sports programs. They also started a poster campaign to promote Church awareness.[50]

---

48. Baugh, "Historical Overview," 244.
49. Van Orden, *Building Zion*, 141–42.
50. Cuthbert, *Second Century*, 4.

CHAPTER 4

The 1950s: The Opening of a New Era

It took a little bit of time to grasp that we were going to have a temple in the British Isles. . . . They wanted the temple built, and built quickly.

— Frederick W. Oates

The dark days of World War II were now in the past. Britain still faced tough times, with food rationing continuing until 1954, but postwar governments went ahead with ambitious rebuilding programs. For The Church of Jesus Christ of Latter-day Saints too, brighter days lay ahead, though not without some challenges. It had been a century since plural marriage was publicly acknowledged from the Salt Lake Tabernacle and over half a century since the official Manifesto ending the practice was issued. Yet, the first thing that popped into the mind of average British citizens when they heard the words "Mormon" or "Latter-day Saint" was still polygamy. Despite this continued association, in several ways, the 1950s became a progressively positive decade for the Church in the United Kingdom.

Conversions, a Temple, and the Choir

Looking back on this decade, Derek Cuthbert, a British convert who later was to serve as a Church general authority, observed:

> 1951 was a turning point. That year almost one thousand converts entered the Church—the highest number in forty-three years. We were happy to see them listed in the *Millennial Star,* which we eagerly read each month to learn what was taking place throughout the country.

According to Cuthbert, three things came together to increase British convert baptisms:

> [T]he first set of [standardized] missionary discussions . . . ; an increased use of the Book of Mormon in tracting; and the largest missionary force yet seen in the British Isles—250 strong. Then the great challenge of newly sustained President David O. McKay, "Every member a missionary," was taken up in our district conferences, and many responded.[1]

---

1. Derek A. Cuthbert, "Breakthrough in Britain."

London Temple and grounds, present day. Courtesy Martin Andersen.

Another evidence of progress within the Church was the escalation of genealogical research throughout the British Isles. Of the seventy-five branches in the United Kingdom, sixty-nine of them had a genealogical organization for such research.[2] This proved most timely, considering the forthcoming announcement of a temple in Britain, which would occur in August of 1953 by David O. McKay as President of the Church. That same month, McKay dedicated the temple site in Newchapel, Surrey, with much jubilation for the British Saints. Frederick Oates, who served in multiple local church leadership roles, recalled,

> It took a little bit of time to grasp that we were going to have a temple in the British Isles. . . . They were so surprised, and yet so overjoyed, that it was just wonderful. It seemed to be the main topic of conversation . . . the temple in the British Isles and what we're going to do, and so forth. . . . They wanted the temple built, and built quickly.[3]

The groundbreaking in 1955 brought over a thousand joyous Saints together as well as several notable leaders in the project, including Edward O. Anderson, temple designer, and Sir Thomas Bennett, the British super-

2. Cuthbert, *The Second Century: Latter-day Saints in Great Britain*, 1:23.
3. Frederick W. and Gladys Q. Oates, interview by Richard L. Jensen, 65.

vising architect.[4] Apostle Spencer W. Kimball was also present and encouraged the British Saints to build Zion in their own homeland now rather than immigrate to the United States. This new direction would be greatly emphasized throughout this era. The groundbreaking also included a rare visit from the well-known Mormon Tabernacle Choir from Salt Lake City.

Taking advantage of this occasion, the Tabernacle Choir also performed in various venues in Britain and throughout Europe. The tour was planned to coincide with both the 1955 groundbreaking of the London Temple and the dedication of the Swiss Temple that same year. Being welcomed by dignitaries throughout its tour increased the legitimacy of the Church, and media coverage of their concerts helped increase awareness of the Church throughout Britain and abroad.[5]

One performance of the choir was held in London's iconic Royal Albert Hall on Sunday, August 28, 1955. The *Times* gave a thoughtful description of this unique performance:

> Nearly 400 strong, this long-established body is comprised . . . [of singers] from all walks of life. . . . Their singing was admirable. The tone quality was outstandingly beautiful . . . when the sopranos . . . could float their voices with an ethereal purity of effect. . . . [T]he spoken commentary . . . came as a reminder that the singers were here as much in the role of evangelists as musicians.[6]

The *Daily Mail* reported that the program was a mixture of classical pieces, sacred music, and even American rallying cries like "Mine Eyes Have Seen the Glory" sung to the tune of "John Brown's Body." The newspaper's critic offered the following review: "Some of their arrangements were too dramatic and some of their harmonies too syrupy for English taste, but they sang from memory with a bright, resonant tone, precise attack and immense fervour."[7]

For the Saints, it would have been nothing but pure delight. Three years later, in September 1958, the London Temple was dedicated and became a tremendous blessing to the UK Saints, then numbering about 11,000. Church members David and Mary Porch, both from Glasgow, Scotland, were present on that sacred occasion. David recalled,

4. "First Mormon Temple in Britain," 4.

5. Craig L. Foster, "Sacred Structure and Public Print: Mormon Public Relations and the British Response during the Building and Dedication of the London Temple," 4–5.

6. "Albert Hall," 10.

7. E. M. M., "Syrupy but So Fervent," 3.

We were in the Celestial Room when the temple was dedicated. . . . And we had the Hosannah Shout.[8] That was . . . a really uplifting experience. . . . We'd never been in a temple before. Of course, we'd seen pictures of it and we'd read books about it, the purpose of the temple and so on. [Yet] I went there with a wee bit of lack of knowledge.[9]

Information about the construction and upcoming dedication of the London Temple was spread through the press. Clifton G. M. Kerr, president of the British Mission from 1955 to 1958, enthused, "The best advertising the Church received was free," referencing the many articles that were published surrounding the dedication.[10] Kerr estimated that there were more than five hundred articles published about the Church in either newspapers or magazines between the groundbreaking in August 1955 and just prior to the dedication three years later. In the actual month of the dedication (September 1958), over 140 articles appeared.[11]

These articles no doubt helped advertise the open house that preceded the dedication, but there was no official Church Public Affairs office yet in place in the United Kingdom. According to historian Craig Foster, "the emphasis of public relations efforts by the Church itself occurred at the time of the open house and dedication ceremonies of the Temple. Clifton Kerr said that although this was, up to the time, the greatest public relations effort of the Church in Britain, the technicalities of such an undertaking were left up to his missionaries and himself."[12]

One journalist who took up the humble offer to be escorted by a missionary through the temple wrote detailed descriptions of the various rooms and her experience. She took note that Latter-day Saints attended the temple to participate in sacred ordinances, which included eternal marriage and the sealing (uniting) of eternal families, as well as proxy work on behalf of ancestors.[13] Tens of thousands of others would likewise take advantage of the tour invitation.

---

8. *Hosanna* is a Hebrew word ("please save us") and can be used as part of Latter-day Saint worship, including during temple dedications.

9. David M. and Mary B. Porch, interviewed by Ronald K. Esplin, 33.

10. Clifton G. M. Kerr, interviewed by Gordon Irving, 35–36, cited in Foster, "Sacred Structure," 2.

11. Kerr interview by Irving, 13, cited in Foster, "Sacred Structure," 2–3.

12. Foster, "Sacred Structure and Public Print," 5.

13. Rhona Churchill, "The Strangest Church I've Ever Visited," 6.

One British newspaper comically noted, "The Mormon Temple is the only Church in Britain with a quarter-mile queue waiting to get in."[14] Another announced, "Not since the days of Billy Graham have people turned out to a place of worship in such numbers."[15] The London *Times* reported:

> Day after day they came, sloshing through England's summer rain, jamming the road from London to the Surrey town of Lingfield. . . . The new temple was opened to the public for 17 days. . . . The crowds of visitors (76,324 by head count) were handled by 40 young American missionaries who first guided their charges into a green tent to watch a movie showing the spread of Mormonism through the world. Then the visitors, warned not to talk or smoke within the temple, were escorted in groups through the building. . . . They had plenty of questions. . . . Whispered one woman to her husband: "I'd like to come here for a holiday." . . . Said the temple's president, Selvoy J. Boyer: "Hundreds of people who have been through the temple have asked our missionaries to visit them in their homes to talk to them about our faith."[16]

Under the able direction of Kerr, advertisements, newspaper articles, and posters were put up all around London to announce the open house. Further, because of the distance from greater London to the temple, buses were rented and bus stops were coordinated to bring thousands of people to this special event. Kerr explained,

> To introduce visitors to the Temple . . . a coloured film . . . was shown in two tents. . . . In a third tent, . . . a missionary gave a short introductory talk before the tour began. And on the ground, from the loudspeakers conveniently located, came recorded Tabernacle Choir music. The crowds emerged from the tents divided into 30–50 people, with a guide for each group.[17]

When the successful seventeen-day temple open house concluded, the Saints gathered for the dedication taking place on September 7–9, 1958. The night before the first dedicatory session (September 6), there was a terrible storm that brought a deluge of rain, partially flooding the temple basement. Later Church President Gordon B. Hinckley, who had served a mission to England two-and-a-half decades earlier and was a newly called Assistant to the Quorum of the Twelve Apostles at the time of the dedication, explained,

---

14. Cuthbert, *Second Century*, 30.

15. Clifton G. M. Kerr, "Now it is History," 293–94.

16. See "London's Mormon Temple."

17. Kerr, "Now it is History," 294. For a life sketch of Kerr, see "Obituary: Clifton G. M. Kerr," *Deseret News*.

Brother Selvoy J. Boyer, who became temple president, and I stood in water up to our waists, bailing it out of the stairwell that at the time led to the downstairs area of the temple. The water flooded in there and we worked until we were exhausted to keep it from getting in the temple.

This incident was not made public and the dedicatory services went forward as planned.[18]

A New Era

During the dedication, President David O. McKay proclaimed, "This is a great day for the members of the Church in Great Britain. . . . The temple is the opening of a new era."[19] Over the six dedicatory sessions, more than twelve thousand Saints attended and left with a firm resolve to assist in bringing about this fresh epoch of change.[20] With the push of an energetic British Mission president, a plan for implementing the "new era" began to take shape.

Derek Cuthbert noted that the stirring words "new era" really resonated with the local members of the Church. He explained what he saw as a timely change in leadership:

We had experienced steady growth and training, . . . but now came dynamic growth under [new British Mission President] T. Bowring Woodbury. . . . [I]n January 1959, the "Prospectus for the New Era" was presented to us. This was a three-pronged thrust: to reduce and eliminate emigration, to develop local leadership, and to launch a concerted meetinghouse construction program.[21]

Efforts to "eliminate emigration" were a challenge because the call to leave "Babylon" (Europe) and gather to Utah to build an American Zion had resounded for over a century. In the twentieth century, the Church's senior global leadership had begun to scale back on the old paradigm. Frederick Oates recalled a time, decades before the London Temple was erected, when McKay (as president of the European Mission) visited with him in Sunderland.

---

18. Foster, "Sacred Structure," 10.

19. Cuthbert, "Breakthrough in Britain."

20. Ben Bloxham, James R. Moss, and Larry C. Porter, eds., *Truth will Prevail: The Rise of the Church of Jesus Christ of Latter-day Saints in the British Isles 1837–1987*, 402.

21. Cuthbert, "Breakthrough in Britain." See also Cuthbert, *The Second Century*, 39.

Frederick W. and Gladys Q. Oates. Courtesy BYU Special Collections.

"Well, young Brother Oates, I understand from your mother you are going to Zion." I said, "Yes, President." He said, "Is that so?" Then he said, "Now, what if I was to tell you that if you go to America, it will not be Zion to you? But if you will stay in this country, you will receive callings and you'll have responsibilities. You'll be a leader. So what you [sic] going to do?" I said, swallowing my heart, I think, "Well, I guess, I had better stay, President McKay." He patted me on the shoulder, and he said, "Good boy! Good boy!" . . . So I stayed here, and it is remarkable how that blessing has come to pass, as you can see from callings I have received.[22]

Such callings (or church assignments) included serving as counselor to five British mission presidents.[23] Indeed, Oates was blessed as he heeded the call to remain in his homeland—including the blessings that came from the British temple—but many others did not follow this counsel even after the London Temple was erected. Cuthbert wrote,

Despite the very strong counsel of the mission president to the contrary, some emigration continued. In the first year following the Temple dedication

22. Frederick W. Oates interview by Richard L. Jensen, 17.

23. For a biographical sketch of Frederick W. Oates, including a summary of his Church callings, see Pamela Johnson, "This Month We Honour Fred W. Oates," 395–96.

Dedicatory

Programme

THE SONG 'THE MORNING BREAKS'
BY THE CONGREGATION

INVOCATION

THE SONG 'HOLINESS BECOMES
THE HOUSE OF THE LORD' BY THE CHOIR

REMARKS

SOLO 'BLESS THIS HOUSE'

REMARKS

REMARKS AND DEDICATORY PRAYER
BY PRESIDENT DAVID O McKAY

'HOSANNA SHOUT'
LED BY PRESIDENT DAVID O McKAY

'HOSANNA ANTHEM'
BY THE CHOIR AND CONGREGATION

BENEDICTION

London Temple Dedication Program, September 1958. Courtesy Church
History Dept, UK archive.

Dedicatory

Sessions

Sunday 7 September

10 a m British Mission members and official guests
2.30 p m British Mission members, invited guests
and Netherlands members and missionaries

Monday 8 September

10 a m Scandinavian Missions' members and missionaries
in Scandinavian language
2.30 p m German Mission members and missionaries
and invited guests

Tuesday 9 September

10 a m French members and missionaries and invited guests
2.30 p m British Mission members and others

Choirs

Combined Manchester and Sheffield Districts choir
South London Branch choir and others

Soloists

Ardyth Twitchell, Jean Taverner and others

Accompanists

Vonda Sedgwick, Wilma Pulsipher and others

Ushers

British missionaries

London Temple Dedication Program, September 1958. Courtesy Church History Dept, UK archive.

[emigration] was reduced to less than one percent of the membership. Thereafter it continued to decline, as the members realised there were more blessings to be gained by staying than by leaving.[24]

The thrust now was clearly to build Zion in Britain. With the London Temple in full operation, the land transformed from a Babylon to another Zion. It could also be said that Old Albion was restored to a sacred Zionic state. For as William Blake's poem "Jerusalem" so beautifully asked (and implicitly envisioned),

> And did those feet in ancient time
> Walk upon England's mountains green?
> And was the holy Lamb of God
> On England's pleasant pastures seen?

More than a century before the London Temple was dedicated, Joseph Smith enlightened Latter-day Saint Apostle Heber C. Kimball regarding the great lands of the British Isles. Kimball told Smith about the rich outpouring of the Holy Spirit he had experienced as a missionary outside Clitheroe, near Pendle Hill, where earlier both George Fox and John Wesley had held special communion with heaven. Smith then asked Kimball, "Did you not understand it? That is a place where some of the old prophets travelled and dedicated the land, and their blessing fell upon you."[25]

It appears that a similar blessing fell upon the Saints and again on the ancient land of Albion after McKay offered his stirring dedicatory prayer at the London Temple. In this prayer, he recalled important events that had taken place in the British Isles: "It is fitting that we express appreciation of the signing of the Magna Carta in the county of Surrey, the same county in which we meet today wherein the promise is given that no freeman shall be taken or imprisoned or seized or outlawed or exiled without proper trial by his peers or by the law of the land."[26]

McKay also called to memory God's dealing with this sacred place:

When in the Middle Ages the church departed from Christ's teachings Thou didst inspire honest, upright men here in Great Britain to raise their voices against corrupt practices. Mingling with the denunciatory messages of Luther and Melanchthon in Germany, and Swingli in Switzerland, were the voices of George Wishart and later John Knox of Scotland. We thank Thee

---

24. Cuthbert, *The Second Century*, 39.

25. Heber C. Kimball, April 6, 1857, Journal of Discourses 5:22, cited in Bloxham et al., eds., *Truth Will Prevail*, 4.

26. See the full dedicatory prayer in Appendix A.

that before the scorching flames silenced his tongue and reduced his body to ashes Thou didst permit George Wishart to glimpse that "This realm shall be illuminated with the light of Christ's evangel, as clearly as ever was any realm since the days of the apostles. The house of God shall be builded in it; yea, it shall not lack the very copestone."

In addition, in his prayer, McKay spoke of how "authorized messengers were sent to Great Britain to announce to the people of the British Isles that God had again spoken from the heavens and reestablished in its purity and fullness the gospel of Jesus Christ."[27] The ancient royal Britain would again become a "nursing" mother to provide suck.[28] Subsequently, the building of many chapels in the land strengthened these claims.

Constructing Chapels while Building Saints

During the nineteenth century the early Saints gathered in homes or rented halls to have their meetings. Historian Matthew L. Rasmussen observed in his study of the Church in Britain:

> The rented accommodations used by the saints fluctuated in size and description, proportionate to the ebb and flow of membership numbers. Because the cost of renting meeting halls was met by the members, there was an obvious relationship between the number of saints in any one location and the quality of the accommodation.[29]

The low quality of rented and converted meeting places continued into the twentieth century. One Welsh Latter-day Saint, Arnold Jones, remembered when the Merthyr Tydfil congregation met in a mere hut during the depression years. He noted, "By 1936 the Saints had built a wooden hut . . . which we always called it our chapel, but it was nothing more than a little wooden hut."[30] Thomas Entwistle also remembered having a priesthood meeting in a wooden hut in Cardiff and recalled meeting in an "old house converted into a place where we could worship."[31] Rowland Elvidge mentioned memories of "when we used to meet in halls where we had to

---

27. "Dedicatory Prayer London England Temple, September 7, 1958," The Church of Jesus Christ of Latter-day Saints.

28. This allusion is derived from the thought based on Isaiah 49:23, that Great Britain has been used by God to fulfill his divine purposes.

29. Matthew Lyman Rasmussen, *Mormonism and the Making of a British Zion*, 165.

30. Arnold Jones, interviewed by Fred E. Woods.

31. Thomas Entwistle, interviewed by Fred E. Woods.

clean it all up Sunday morning."[32] Similarly, Gordon Sherlock recalled that when the Saints met in a men's club for their Sunday meetings, "we use[d] to have to sweep the cigarette ends up and the beer bottles . . . and open the windows, where we could get a bit of fresh air."[33]

The poor conditions of rented or converted spaces hampered the Saints' efforts to bring their friends and "investigators" (people looking into the faith) to church services.[34] Horace Hayes from the Wigan Branch drew a comparison with other Christian places of worship in the area and where the Latter-day Saints met. Whereas the local Saints met in a simple hall on the fourth story of a building, the Methodist, Baptist, and Catholic church members gathered in their own lovely places of worship.

Hayes recalled, "Sometimes I'd feel a little uncomfortable inviting my friends there and then having them comment, 'Is this where you go to church? What a place this is. I wouldn't go to church there.' You know comments like that. So I think this played a big part in not being able to have converts."[35] In addition, due to the doctrine of gathering to the American Zion, there had often been more plucking than planting in British congregations—numbers, as well as conditions, were low.

Much of this changed, however, when the mid-twentieth century ushered in an unprecedented building wave throughout the British Isles. Members of the Church now felt pride in their places of worship instead of embarrassment. As the physical structures brightened, so did the image of the Church in the minds of its members, those of different faiths, and others.

With the Saints' own dedicated buildings, there would no longer be a need to rent halls. During the period of the fifties, one historian summarized the process for meetinghouse improvements from smoky rented halls or small huts to larger places for congregations to assemble:

> [T]he Saints purchased large homes and converted them into chapels where missionaries or older LDS couples lived. The larger rooms were utilized for Church services and other activities. As the Church members met in these converted homes, construction was begun on the rear portion of the property for a new chapel. When the chapel was completed, the homes in the

---

32. Rowland Elvidge, interviewed by Fred E. Woods.

33. Gordon William Sherlock, interviewed by Stephen C. Young, 14–15.

34. Rasmussen, *British Zion*, 166.

35. Horace Hayes, interviewed by Chad M. Orton, 19. The account continues, "Yet others kept coming as they felt the kindness of the Saints, in spite of their poor meeting accommodations." See, for example, Lucy Ripley Bradbury, interview by Richard L. Jensen, 1–3, 59–61.

front were removed to make way for parking lots or landscaping. This two-phase approach to chapel building was followed in many lands in Europe, providing adequate and attractive physical facilities for the first time.[36]

One catalytic change for the management of the Church in Britain was the decision made by British Mission President Woodbury to call five percent of the total British Church membership to serve as local district missionaries. When Apostle Marion G. Romney toured the British Isles in the summer of 1959, he was quite impressed with the British Mission, where over six hundred district missionaries were serving. Romney commented, "I think the district missionary work is the greatest thing I have seen in Great Britain."[37]

With greater numbers of missionaries came the expectation of additional converts.[38] More new chapels were needed, so an improved building program that perpetuated the thrust of the "new era" was launched near the conclusion of the 50s. Shortly after the dedication of the temple in Surrey, a grand chapel in London was begun in August 1959. Cuthbert explained,

> Meetinghouse construction got off to a flying start with the Hyde Park Chapel . . . when Elder [Romney] broke ground. The following month, the building program was launched in earnest; over the next six months, fourteen projects were started and sixty-three sites purchased. The British Saints were delighted with the announcement that fifty new chapels would be constructed in the next five years.[39]

This robust building plan would be in full operation during the following decade.

---

36. James R. Moss, "Building the Kingdom in Europe," 91.

37. Cuthbert, "Breakthrough in Britain."

38. Many of those converts received immediate responsibilities within their newfound congregations. Mary Boswell, baptized as a 24-year-old in Ashton-under-Lyne (Manchester area), even played the piano at her own baptismal service. She attended the branch for the first time on the day after her baptism and found herself sitting quite near the piano. She related, "It was about 10 minutes before it [Sunday School] was due to begin. And I turned around to the person behind me who was a complete stranger and I said, 'Is there not going to be someone to play music?' She said, 'Oh yes, *you* are!' I just went to the piano and played." Mary Boswell, interviewed by Malcolm Adcock.

39. Cuthbert, "Breakthrough in Britain."

CHAPTER 5

The 1960s: A Period of Growth and Change

When we were in the hut we were just odd. . . . But when the
building came, of course everything changed.

— Freda Entwistle

The decade of the 1960s, a period of wholesale societal change, also brought enormous changes in the look and feel of The Church of Jesus Christ of Latter-day Saints within the United Kingdom. Facing new worldwide challenges, the Church's global leadership responded with initiatives that impacted the stability and growth of the Church in Britain. Under President David O. McKay's supervision, general Church administrators were asked to review the curriculum and programs of the Church. Home teaching,[1] part of the Church from early days, was re-emphasized, and the Family Home Evening program was highlighted.[2] Although the family remained a constant Church focus, a concerted effort to spread the good news of the gospel took center stage. Latter-day Saints were also introduced to a courageous new program spearheaded by McKay: the "Every Member a Missionary" program that strongly encouraged local members to assist the missionaries' evangelizing efforts. Shortly thereafter, the Church introduced a more systematized approach for supervising missions. Senior leadership at Church headquarters were assigned mission areas to directly supervise, thus increasing global coordination.[3] Such bold initiatives from Salt Lake City sent waves sure to reshape the bonny shores of Great Britain.

First Stake in Great Britain

In the spring of 1960, the very first stake in Great Britain was organized not far from where the first Latter-day Saint missionaries began their labors, reflecting the British Saints' spiritual status and diligent efforts.

---

1. In-home pastoral visits by lay priesthood holders.
2. One night per week devoted exclusively to family time, with flexibility to include spiritual and social pursuits.
3. The Church of Jesus Christ of Latter-day Saints, *Church History in the Fulness of Times Student Manual*, 592.

T. Bowring Woodbury, president of the British Mission, recorded details of this historic event and noted its significance:

> March 27, 1960—This day marks an event that will long be remembered in Great Britain and in the history and in the annals of the history of the church. As Harold B. Lee said, this is the greatest event to happen in the history of the British Mission since its organization. I feel to concur in this expression and it was felt by all who crowded into the Manchester Hippodrome Theatre for the organization of the Manchester Stake. On the stand were in excess of 200 singing mothers, beautifully dressed in their white blouses. There was a perfusion of flowers on the stand. . . . [T]here were many newspaper people in the audience. . . . I felt a rich outpouring of the [S]pirit.[4]

Sue Kureczko, then seventeen years old, was excited about the new organization. Looking back on this event, she recounted, "I can remember going to the meeting where we were made a stake. We were all thrilled to bits about it. . . . [I]n those days, none of us had cars. . . . We were willing to travel all over the place, so there was a different feeling then than there is now."[5]

In his history of the British Saints, Derek Cuthbert summarized this transitional decade and the obstacles British Church leadership faced head-on:

> The three main challenges that were thrust upon us were, firstly, the need to integrate new members, whose influx became almost a deluge, considering the small base from which the Church was starting. Secondly, the need to accommodate these new Saints, [for] our facilities were inadequate and catered for 100 small congregations in a population of almost sixty million people. Thirdly, there developed a desperate need for supplies and curriculum materials.[6]

Singing Mothers

The Singing Mothers choir, began during the Great Depression and made up of Latter-day Saint women, performed at the stake organization and continued to bring inspiration, assimilation, and appreciation to Church members and others throughout the United Kingdom.[7] Scores of women gathered and traveled in order to lift others through their music.

---

4. T. Bowring Woodbury Journal, March 27, 1960.

5. Sue Kureczko, interviewed by Fred E. Woods, in possession of authors.

6. Derek A. Cuthbert, *The Second Century: Latter-day Saints in Great Britain*, 1:51.

7. "In the middle of the Great Depression, under the direction of General Relief Society President, Louise Y. Robison, what would become the world-famous Relief Society 'Singing Mothers' was organized. . . . Singing Mother

Singing Mothers, ca. 1960. Courtesy Sally Brown.

They were a blessing to the Saints, and their beautiful, harmonious music helped to improve the look and feel of the Church in general. One historian noted,

> In February 1961 forty-eight LDS women gave a concert at the Royal Albert Hall in London, as well as concerts in Manchester, Nottingham, Cardiff, Newcastle, Glasgow and Belfast. As had been the case in the Tabernacle Choir tour of 1955, the Singing Mothers tour of 1961 brought both critical acclaim and renewed interest in the Church.[8]

Under the direction of Florence Jepperson Madsen, American and British Latter-day Saint women joined together to lift thousands. The press took notice and reports were favorable. The *Sunderland Echo* noted,

> The whole concept is remarkable—50 American singers who have come over specially for these events joined with 200 British singers, who have formed a choir whose performance was an absolute object lesson in choral singing. . . . [T]here was absolute unanimity in everything they did.[9]

---

groups formed in various Relief Societies all over the world." See Jan Tolman, "The Singing Mothers."

8. James R. Moss, "The Great Awakening," 410. See also Pamela Johnson, "Music is International: The Story of the Triumphant Singing Mothers Tour of Great Britain," 147.

9. Moss, "The Great Awakening," 411.

Both their music and dress echoed unity. Sally Brown, a Scottish Singing Mother, recalled, "We always had music resolves in three parts. First soprano, second soprano, and alto. And . . . we always had to wear white blouses and black skirts."[10]

Church Building Program

Another great boost to member morale and the positive perceptions of community members was the aggressive Church building program, with local Latter-day Saints working alongside specially called building missionaries. Sue Kureczko noted,

> They would go down, the men and the women, regularly and build. No health and safety. . . . And we used to have, of course, the building program, where there were missionaries who got ten shillings[11] a week at the time. They lived, in Manchester, on site. So we would feed them, the members would feed them, and they would build the chapels.[12]

Another sister involved with the building program was Freda Entwistle, from Merthyr Tydfil. She described her involvement and contrasted the reaction the town had after the Saints moved out of an old wooden hut into a beautiful new chapel:

> When we were in the hut we were just odd, I guess. But when the building came, of course everything changed. People were amazed at the kind of building that we were building. I enjoyed the building program. It was great. I learned to make concrete much better than I could make cake at the time. I had to move the cement around the building for the men to work. In the evenings we would go down and put down the bricks in different positions around the site so the brick layers could carry on the work in the morning. All sorts of things. I've been on the roof, I've put the knockings in the corridors, I fell off the scaffolding, I've done quite a few things. But it was great, it was great fun to be a part of the building program. And when people saw the building after and were able to come . . . inside to see it, they were just amazed.[13]

Leighton Jones, a Welsh building missionary during this same period in Merthyr Tydfil, remembers the creative way they brought people in from the community to see the finished building. The members organized

---

10. Sally Brown, interviewed by Fred E. Woods and Malcolm Adcock, in possession of authors.

11. A modest amount of pocket money.

12. Sue Kureczko, interviewed by Fred E. Woods.

13. Freda Entwistle, interviewed by Fred E. Woods.

Pouring concrete, Merthyr Tydfil Chapel c. 1963. Courtesy Frank Blease.

pantomimes, he recalled, "a cast, of about 50 people on the stage, the children, teenagers, and all age groups would perform. Mostly it was nursery rhyme stories, like Jack and the Beanstalk, that type of thing."[14]

But the real magic was the unity that formed among the Saints as they labored together building their sacred meetinghouses. Men and women, side by side, simultaneously united and strengthened their resolve to establish Zion in their native homeland. As historian Matthew L. Rasmussen correctly assessed, "the saints' involvement in chapel construction diverted their attention from the enticing Salt Lake Valley and fixed it firmly upon their own communities. Zion, through permanent places of worship, had become a reality for the Saints of Britain." To summarize, "The chief lesson learned from the building program was that Zion and Britain were not just compatible, but synonymous."[15]

As scores of Latter-day Saint chapels sprang up in the United Kingdom during the 60s, the press took notice and occasionally resuscitated remnants of old suspicions.[16] One historian observed that in the Oldham

14. Leighton Jones, interviewed by Fred E. Woods.

15. Matthew Lyman Rasmussen, *Mormonism and the Making of a British Zion*, 181.

16. For example, in 1966, the tabloid *Sunday People* ran a series of "investigations" into the activities of the "new religions," with Latter-day Saint missionaries and other "door-to-door persuaders" characterized as "the new 'doorstep salesmen'

chapel, "it was rumored that the large floor mat installed in the building's entrance was a carefully disguised trapdoor through which attractive young women would vanish." He also noted that while the Liverpool chapel was under construction during the early 1960s, "local youths believed the building was a portal to a transatlantic tunnel through which unsuspecting converts, and perhaps curious children were abducted. Local lore maintained that the tunnel terminated in Salt Lake City."[17]

Hyde Park Chapel

The most impressive and significant structure to draw attention to the Church in Britain during this decade was the Hyde Park Chapel, dedicated February 26, 1961. The day after the dedication, the headlines in the *Daily Express* were "The 'Press-button' Church" and "Beneath the Golden Spire it's All Mod[ern] Con[veniences]—Basketball Court and even Iced Water."[18] The newspaper referred to the chapel's architect, Sir Thomas Bennett, whose initial reticence was quoted by Woodbury during his talk at the dedication service, "I wonder whether I can afford to do business with the Mormons?"[19] But Bennett soon changed his tune and said, "The Mormons are the finest people for whom I work."[20] President David O. McKay addressed the over 1,600 Church members in attendance,[21] emphasizing the importance of chapels. Among other things, he said, "[W]e need these meetinghouses, these chapels. . . . In 1922, 1923, 1924, when Sister McKay and I were in the British Mission, and in the European Mission, they [the British Saints] had to meet in rented halls. People would ask, 'Where is your meeting place?' . . . We [would] say it is in hall

---

. . . peddling their creed from house to house." The report actually contained no shocking revelations and its sensational style did much to captivate readers. See Eric Tyson, "The Faith Merchants," 2.

17. Rasmussen, *British Zion*, 179.

18. John Redfern, "The 'Press-Button' Church," 11.

19. Redfern, 11.

20. Redfern, 11. It is worth noting that the newspaper's Canadian-British publisher Lord Beaverbrook admired "Mormons" and did not approve of subsequent attacks on Latter-day Saints within his newspapers. In a letter to the *Sunday Express* he opined, "I protest. Paragraphs and interviews denouncing Mormon missionaries should not be given publicity in the Sunday Express. . . . Their people . . . lead wholesome lives and indeed give an admirable example of devotion and sacrifice to lesser Christian communities in Britain." See "I Protest—by Lord Beaverbrook."

21. Cuthbert, *Second Century*, 40.

Hyde Park Chapel, London, 2021.

so-and-so, giving the impression to an investigator that the Church was not permanently established."[22]

Mel Alexander, a missionary who attended the dedication, recalled,

President David O. McKay came to dedicate the Hyde Park Chapel, which was the first chapel that had been built within this area of England. . . . The Spirit was extremely strong, and President McKay dedicated every part of the building [even] the drinking fountain. . . . In the chapel, itself, they had a classic organ, and they had several people—Brother [Roy M.] Darley came, Alexander Schreiner came,[23] and they would stay a period of time, and we would take people up to hear organ recitals. . . . [W]hen President McKay dedicated the Hyde Park chapel, he included the organ in his prayers for the missionary work.[24]

The exact wording in McKay's dedicatory prayer was this:

We dedicate the organ, built especially to render up music to thy name and holiness, built by able and capable men who devoted long hours to the establishment of this wonderful instrument. May it be held sacred in thy sight. Bless those who would play the organ that they will render such music that it will touch the heart and bring them to know thee and thy work.[25]

Schreiner, the Mormon Tabernacle Choir organist at the time, gave a series of weekly recitals a year after the Hyde Park Chapel dedication. The following month, the *Millennial Star* noted:

Representatives from practically every walk of life and profession attended the recitals, and the attendance figures went so high in several of the concerts that the audience completely filled the chapel and flowed out into the recreational hall.[26]

---

22. David O. McKay, "A Dream Fulfilled. Remarks of President David O. McKay at the Dedication of the Hyde Park Chapel, Morning Session, February 26, 1961," 176.

23. Both Roy M. Darley and Alexander Schreiner were organists for the Mormon Tabernacle Choir, now known as The Tabernacle Choir at Temple Square. Darley was a Choir organist for the years 1947–1984 and Schreiner from 1924–1977. See Molly Farmer, "Tabernacle Organist Leaves Resonating Legacy," 77–78. While Schreiner played for most of the month of May 1961, Darley played for an entire year at the Hyde Park Chapel.

24. Melvin C. Alexander, interviewed by Fred E. Woods and Martin L. Andersen, in possession of authors.

25. David O. McKay, "Text of the Dedicatory Prayer by President David O. McKay at the Hyde Park Chapel, February 26, 1961," 182.

26. Anthony Middleton, "Alexander Schreiner, Organist Supreme," 284.

In speaking of his performances, Schreiner said, "When I play these hymns I feel that I am playing of the restoration of the gospel, and that I am playing something which must touch the hearts of the people."[27]

At the end of the 60s, the Hyde Park Chapel was still used to attract attention. One missionary recalled,

[W]e would arrange guest speakers to come. People like Billy Casper and folks like that and organ recitals from accomplished musicians and so the Hyde Park Chapel became a place for missionaries to bring their contacts and we thought that was a very helpful thing so they could see a bigger view of the church.[28]

About the same time the building program was up to full speed, another plan was hatched to hopefully increase the number of Church members and fill the chapels being erected. Under the supervision of Woodbury, missionaries began introducing boys to baseball in the hopes of teaching them the gospel.

The Baseball Baptism Program

Mel Alexander observed how this "new era" tied in with the baseball (softball) program: "The 'new era' was . . . a push to increase the baptisms in England and where in the old era there were few missionaries and very few people that joined the Church. During my time, we were pressed with a goal to seek out and find people that were ready to hear the gospel." Alexander further explained,

We played softball, . . . and a mission meeting was held, and President Woodbury . . . had an individual come up to tell us about [how] he had these seven baptisms, and told of how he went and got a baseball bat and went out in the field and played baseball with the kids, and that's how he was successful.

My aspect, like my companion's, would be: we'd find a field, a park, and we'd start playing baseball. Kids would come and want to play, and so we taught them how to play baseball, and we wrote down their names and their addresses so that we could go and meet their parents and get permission for them to play, but also to get to know the parents. They became our referrals. And it was very positive, and what we did if the parents weren't interested, was "Okay," the kids still played. We would open a town, we'd get a place

---

27. Alexander Schreiner, "Music and Fervent Faith," 292.

28. Dennis A. Wright, interviewed by Fred E. Woods and Martin L. Andersen, in possession of authors.

to hold church, and in that place, one night a week, we'd have what you'd call "MIA."[29] Since the towns we were in generally didn't have members, the ones that came were those that played baseball. We would play games, and we'd teach them the Gospel, and we'd go back to their parents, and it was a successful way of finding families to teach, and this was our goal: to find families that were interested. . . .

There were a few that abused the program with the baseball and I can honestly say that many of my companions always used it as a missionary tool to meet families, teach families, invite them to church.[30]

Although there were mission rules requiring parental permission, often the elders—eager to achieve baptism goals—did not follow the details of the rules and parents were not fully aware that with the bat and ball often came a baptism. Haydn D. Morgan explained,

In 1960, 1961, 1962 there were a tremendous amount of baptisms under the baseball program which originated in Swansea. It was a wonderful program had it been carried out correctly.[31] Regretfully, in many cases, it was just sufficient if you want to join our baseball club you had to be baptized. That was rather sad because youngsters forced their parents into agreement. Later when we had to resolve the mass of youngsters who were inactive, we discovered that in many cases they didn't even know that they'd joined the Church. They had joined the baseball club.[32]

On the other hand, Leighton Jones recalls this aspect of their missionary labors more positively: "I thought Woodbury was fantastic, because he wanted people to join the church. There's a lot of things being said about baseball baptisms, but a lot of people . . . joined and stayed."[33]

---

29. Mutual Improvement Association, the Church's recreational organization for youth.

30. Alexander, interviewed by Fred E. Woods and Martin L. Andersen.

31. For example, Dr. Lee Burke, who served in the British Mission from June 1960 to June 1962, said he saw instances of families being baptized via the baseball program and referred to "one of our very strong families in Plymouth" who was introduced to the Church by it. Lee Burke, interviewed by Malcolm Adcock.

32. Haydn D. Morgan, interviewed by Ronald D. Dennis. For a critical treatment of this program, see D. Michael Quinn, "I-Thou vs. I-It Conversions: The Mormon 'Baseball Baptism' Era," 30–44; Richard Mavin, "The Woodbury Years: An Insider's Look at Baseball Baptisms in Britain," 56–60.

33. Leighton Jones, interviewed by Fred E. Woods. Additionally, Linda Tucker joined the Church in 1961 when she was nearly fourteen years old, after getting involved in Saturday morning baseball games with the missionaries and her

Myrtle Mawle, who served as a sister missionary in the north of London during the early 1960s, explained the purpose and operation of the baseball program from her point of view:

> Well, really it was to get more converts into the Church, and the way to attract the young people. . . . [W]e were tracting to peoples' houses, and if they had children, and that was it to attract the children. We would say to the children, "Oh, we have . . . a youth program, perhaps they'd like to come along." So we're going to start up a little baseball team, which attracted them because it was baseball, a bit different from football. And then we'd arrange perhaps a Saturday morning to meet on a nearby field and just have baseball practices and bits of competition, and get around to asking the parents if they would like to come and attend church. . . . I can't remember anyone that said they would like to, but if the children would like to come, we could take them to church.[34]

According to Mawle, the boys would be gathered and transported to the baseball games by bus, which proved challenging because it was not easy for the missionaries to control the rambunctious boys. The few sisters (female missionaries) serving at the time were a bit more mature at twenty-three than the elders (male missionaries) who, commencing in 1960, could begin serving missions at age nineteen.[35] There were not many years separating the youth playing baseball and the elders who supervised them. In addition, the sudden flood of thousands of young converts brought with it challenges to supply adequate Church leadership because most of these young men were being baptized without their parents also joining the faith.[36]

The legacy of baseball baptisms lived on into the 1970s. The Church's home teachers would attempt, largely unsuccessfully, to reengage the grown men who had joined the Church during the previous decade because of missionary outreach through sport.[37] On reflection, the program was generally seen as controversial by British church leaders and was abandoned by global Church leadership and missionary leaders a few years after it had begun.

---

friends. One day, she was invited to be baptized at the Handsworth Chapel, Birmingham. She had not received any formal teaching from the missionary elders by that time but fairly soon became involved in youth activities and gospel learning. Linda Tucker, interviewed by Malcolm Adcock.

34. Myrtle Mawle, interviewed by Malcolm Adcock and Fred E. Woods.

35. Mawle, interviewed by Malcolm Adcock and Fred E. Woods.

36. Cuthbert, *Second Century*, 52.

37. Personal experiences of Malcolm Adcock as a home teacher in the UK.

Elder Dennis Wright Interviewed on Television

Dennis Wright, a seasoned young missionary serving in the England East Mission between 1968 and 1970, had a keen intellect and could think well on his feet. Because of his talents, he was given the opportunity to be the first Church missionary interviewed on a television talk show in the United Kingdom.

Wright was interviewed on Thames Television as part of a series titled "On the Fringe." After the interview, Mavis Airey from the show sent a letter to Wright thanking him for the interview, noting that it proved to be "very lively and interesting" and mentioned, "We were all pleased."[38] The talk show host actually helped the Church by asking some sensitive questions that Wright responded to in an informed and candid manner. Wright vividly recalled the experience fifty years later:

> In April of 1969, we received a message from the mission home that we were to come to the mission office. . . . [W]e went in and saw the mission president who at that time was Reed Callister, a lawyer from California, who was an excellent mission president. He said, "Elder Wright, we have a wonderful opportunity. Thames Television is running a series on cults in England and they want us to be on TV." And I said, "President, you want us to be on TV as a cult?" He said, "They can call us whatever they want, because once they see us, they are going to know that we are something special."[39]

Wright also explained that he, his missionary companion, and President Callister met with the interviewer prior to Wright's interview. The interviewer told them that he had been to Salt Lake City and heard the Mormon Tabernacle Choir and commented, "You guys are great." He also said, "The people in England have no idea what you people are like. You are wonderful people." He added, "I love the Mormons. . . . Let's make this happen on TV. . . . I know some of your difficult points and

---

38. Mavis Airey to Elder Dennis A. Wright, April 21, 1969, in private collection of Dennis A. Wright. Thanks is expressed to Wright for granting the authors a copy of the letter, now in their possession. This letter was written to thank Wright for the taped program, which occurred on April 14, 1969, and noted that the actual showing of the program would take place during the week of May 5–11, 1969. (The show was telecast on May 11, 1969.)

39. Dennis A. Wright, interviewed by Fred E. Woods and Martin Andersen. Author Malcolm Adcock has a vivid early childhood memory of President Reed Callister's positive approach when he presented the young Adcock with a shiny sixpence, along with the declaration that the coin was a donation for his mission fund.

Elder Dennis Wright and his companion at the time of the interview, Elder Ronald Barrett, 1969. Courtesy Dennis Wright.

I am going to try and avoid those so that we can have a really positive experience." And Wright said, "Great," but noted, "I just had this feeling that it wasn't going to be as simple as he portrayed it."[40]

Wright's premonition proved to be correct. The talk show host concluded the television interview by asking the young missionary a couple of difficult questions about Latter-day Saint history in the nineteenth century. Wright remembered him stating, "Now, Elder Wright, before we conclude, there [are] just a couple things I would like to ask you about." The talk show host then asked Wright about the Mountain Meadows Massacre, one of the darkest moments in Church history.[41] It seemed the TV host was surprised that Wright knew something of this tragic history

40. Wright, interviewed by Fred E. Woods and Martin Andersen.

41. The Mountain Meadows massacre was an attack on a westbound emigrant wagon train that occurred in September 1857 led by a local Latter-day Saint Utah Territorial Militia and some Paiute Native Americans resulting in the slaughter of

and admired that this young missionary admitted it was wrong. The TV host then questioned the television audience, "Which one of our vicars would openly apologize for the mistakes they made?" He said, "These Mormons are straight up."[42]

Wright also recalled,

> Now he says, "I want to ask you about polygamy. Are you a polygamist?" And of course I said no. We just talked about it and he said, "Well, why do you practice polygamy?" [I responded], "Well, it is just very simple, a prophet of God, . . . commanded us to live polygamy for a short period of time in our history for specific purposes of membership growth. It was successful and when the purpose was complete, the revelation was withdrawn, and we are no longer polygamists." . . . So he said, "All right, hasn't this been wonderful?" He said, "The next time these guys come, let them in. They are great guys and maybe they will even play one of their Mormon [T]abernacle songs for you." And then we closed and they were singing the Battle Hymn of the Republic again. And . . . that was the end of the interview. It was a lot of fun, it was exciting, it was a moment when a missionary was given a little bit of extra help to glue this thing together and we had a friendly person who liked the church.[43]

After the show, the host invited Wright and his companion over for dinner. Wright remembered, "We had a most pleasant visit . . . and presented him with a copy of the Book of Mormon. For the time I spent on television, I received £10, which my Mission President said was for me and my companion to spend on a real restaurant."[44]

The pay that truly brought missionaries the greatest satisfaction was seeing hundreds and thousands of Brits join the Church. Individual conversions brought tremendous joy into the lives of missionaries and strengthened branches. Melvin Alexander felt he was generally treated well as he labored with his companions in various places in the British Isles, even though most individuals he taught did not embrace their message. Alexander recalled,

> The ones we came in contact with, primarily through tracting, were . . . positive, because we'd go, and people would say, "I belong to this church," or "I

about 120 people. For the complete story, see Richard E. Turley Jr., Ronald W. Walker, and Glen M. Leonard, *Massacre at Mountain Meadows*.

42. Wright, interviewed by Fred E. Woods and Martin Andersen.

43. Wright, interviewed by Fred E. Woods and Martin Andersen.

44. Dennis A. Wright, "Remembrances Regarding April 1969 Thames Television Appearance."

belong to that church," and we thanked them and [in] some places they'd let us in and . . . offer us tea or coffee. . . . And . . . we thanked them . . . [a]nd we'd have a conversation.

Alexander further noted, "Very few people that we met were antagonistic. . . . By and large, the British people were kind. . . . When we baptized—the ones that were against us were really the ministers. . . . [W]e were taking away their flock."[45]

The Latter-day Saint mission presidents and their international priesthood leaders were ambitious and focused. During the mid-1960s, the Church is reported to have expressed interest in buying a television station in Britain: "The American-based Mormon Church is to apply for an ITV contract to set up a commercial TV company in Britain," related the *Daily Mail*. President of the British Mission, O. Preston Robinson, "wanted to see uplifting material going into the home."[46]

The growth of the Church in this decade was truly unprecedented, pioneered by female and male leaders alike. Derek Cuthbert surmised, "Little did we realize that in the decade of the 1960's the Church would have a larger harvest than did those early missionaries. In fact, over 57,000 were baptized from 1960–1969."[47]

---

45. Alexander, interviewed by Fred E. Woods and Martin L. Andersen.
46. "Mormons Bid for Channel on ITV," 3.
47. Cuthbert, *Second Century*, 52.

CHAPTER 6

The 1970s: Coming of Age and Reaching Out

The Church is coming of age in Great Britain and is being built up and strengthened here among some of the best people on earth.

— President Joseph Fielding Smith

August 27, 1971, saw a historic gathering take place in the United Kingdom. Up to twelve thousand British Latter-day Saints waited in reverent expectation at Manchester's Belle Vue Exhibition Centre to be addressed by the ninety-five-year-old leader Joseph Fielding Smith, President of the Church and regarded by the Saints as "prophet, seer, and revelator" for the globe.[1]

Manchester was a suitable setting for the gathering—the city had been the base for the Church's British operations when Brigham Young and other early apostles served their missions, addressing "Mancunians"[2] in street meetings and larger gatherings at Carpenter's Hall between 1840 and 1841. In the next century, during March 1960, the United Kingdom's first stake had been formed in this city.[3]

First British Area General Conference

For the 1971 event, many from far-flung areas of the British Isles stayed in local hotels and guest houses, with some even setting up at nearby camping and caravan sites and battling the British weather. This was the Church's first ever area general conference. The faith's Salt Lake City–based world leaders came en masse to the people in the United Kingdom, with most members of the Latter-day Saints' international governing councils present in Britain for the event. The occasion was groundbreaking for the Church and very exciting for the British Saints.

"My dear brethren and sisters," began Smith as he spoke to a hushed congregation, "I am grateful beyond measure to greet the members of the Church

---

1. *Official Report of the First British Area General Conference of The Church of Jesus Christ of Latter-day Saints, Held in Manchester, England, August 27, 28, 29, 1971, with report of discourses*, 162.

2. Manchester-dwellers are known as Mancunians.

3. See also David Cook, "Manchester, England," 698–99.

Church President Joseph Fielding Smith, Area General Conference, Manchester, August 1971. Courtesy *Deseret News.*

in this goodly land of Great Britain, and I do so in love and in fellowship and in unity."[4] The prophet's heart would have been especially tender on this trip because his wife Jessie Evans Smith had died earlier that month;[5] however, he wanted to be in the country that had such meaning to him in his ministry.

Smith's conference address was electrifying. "We all went across the Pennines [Pennine Hills] from Sheffield to Manchester for those sessions and I remember Joseph Fielding Smith was the Prophet," recalled Julian Bell, whose parents had joined the Church in the 1950s.

> That was the first time I saw a prophet, and we sang "We Thank Thee, O God, for a Prophet," and I remember that kind of spine-tingling feeling that you got on those kind of occasions. I remember as a young deacon that I went to the Priesthood session . . . and a group of Priesthood brethren went over the Pennines in heavy fog and rain, and it was all a big adventure. . . . Very happy memories.[6]

---

4. *British Area General Conference*, 5.

5. Sheri Dew, *Insights from a Prophet's Life: Russell M. Nelson*, 102.

6. Cllr. Julian Bell, interviewed by Malcolm Adcock. Young men are ordained to the office of deacon in the Church's lay priesthood.

The Manchester conference reminded British Latter-day Saints that they were part of a global community—an international church. Arnold Jones, whose mother was baptized during 1932 in South Wales, remembered,

> What I think that did was made us feel part of a global church. We'd had district conferences and we'd had large congregations in a chapel, but we'd never seen anything on that kind of scale. So, it made us feel part of something much, much bigger. . . . It was a stepping stone.[7]

John Tate, baptized in 1961, recalled, "The impressions were the Church [was] expanding. We came from a little ward [congregation] of about 30 or 40 people, something like that, and there were hundreds of people, all Latter-day Saints."[8]

Seventy years earlier, Smith had served his two-year mission in England; however, despite his dedicated service, he did not baptize a single convert.[9] Returning to address the Saints in 1971 at Belle Vue, Manchester, he was thrilled with the Church's progress worldwide over the intervening years, and especially in the British Isles:

> It is a matter of great satisfaction to me, and I am sure to my Brethren, that the Church has now grown to the point that it seems wise and necessary to hold general conferences in various nations. And what could be more appropriate than to begin this new advancement here in the British Isles, the place from which so much of the strength of the Church came, in the early days of this dispensation.[10]

When the British area general conference was announced several months earlier, a total of 69,458 Latter-day Saints lived in the British Isles (with thirty-nine percent of Church members in regionally based stakes led by local leaders who were mature and settled in the faith).[11] Smith, himself a grandnephew of the Prophet Joseph Smith, asserted that "the Church is coming of age in Great Britain and is being built up and strengthened here among some of the best people on earth."[12] Rowland Elvidge, who later became president of the London Temple, was impressed that Smith "spe-

7. Arnold Jones, interviewed by Fred E. Woods.

8. John Tate, interviewed by Malcolm Adcock.

9. Joseph Fielding Smith Jr. and John J. Stewart, *The Life of Joseph Fielding Smith*, 91.

10. *British Area General Conference*, 5.

11. *British Area General Conference*, 55.

12. *British Area General Conference*, 176.

Rowland Elvidge (then Bishop of St. Albans Ward) and Barbara Elvidge, 1976. Rowland would later become president of the London Temple. Courtesy Rowland Elvidge.

cifically emphasized the importance of Saints staying in this country and building Zion up in the British Isles"[13]—continuing the instructions given by President David O. McKay to remain in one's homeland in order to establish the Church abroad. Following this theme, Smith told the assembled Saints that the Church is just as British as it is American: "Thus the Church is not an American church except in America. In Canada it is a Canadian church; in Australia it is an Australian church; and in Great Britain it is a British church. It is a world church; the gospel is for all men."[14]

Other Latter-day Saint leaders speaking at this special conference reinforced the concept of gospel universality and the sense of British identity. President Spencer W. Kimball—then Acting President of the Quorum of the Twelve Apostles and two years later President of the Church—referred to Britain as a "holy land" and described how his grandfather Heber C. Kimball was told by the founding Prophet Joseph Smith that "some of the

13. Rowland Elvidge, interviewed by Fred E. Woods. Elvidge was president of the London England Temple 2004–2007.

14. *British Area General Conference*, 6.

holy men of God had traveled in that region and had dedicated the land, and that he, Heber, had reaped the benefit of their blessing."[15] President Kimball added, "I should like to think that the whole of this great land is blessed and still carrying a blessing from our Heavenly Father from great and holy men who have walked upon its shores. It is fitting that we should have this great conference here in Manchester. It has been a center of many church activities through the years."[16]

Another member of the Quorum of the Twelve Apostles, Elder Gordon B. Hinckley—a committed Anglophile who would also later lead the Church—was kindly to his audience:

> You, to use the phrase that Dickens used concerning a group of Latter-day Saints long ago, are "the very pick and flower of England," and, I should add, of Ireland and Scotland and Wales. God bless you that you may know that sweet joy which [H]e has promised those who, even though they labor all their days to bring one soul into [H]is kingdom, shall know an eternal joy.[17]

These words from modern apostles who the Saints revere as "prophets, seers, and revelators" evinced a deep, abiding, prophetic vision and a commitment to practical plans. Building up the Church further in the United Kingdom, with a missionary zeal, would require additional key elements flowing from the Christian enthusiasm of the Church membership. Apart

---

15. *British Area General Conference*, 21. The link between nineteenth and twentieth century Britain and biblical times resonated with many new Church converts. For example, Michael Danvers-Walker—a London-based English actor who joined the Church in the 1970s—was spiritually motivated by this theme of the British Isles' link with ancient Israel and also the related Latter-day Saint teaching that the Lamanite people described in the Book of Mormon are descended from the house of Israel. He described how he was drawn inside London's Hyde Park Chapel in early 1975 after spotting a big poster on this theme. "I was walking along Exhibition Road one day towards Knightsbridge and I passed the church and there was a large poster. In those days they used to have big posters and things outside, and there was [a Native American], with of course, the feathered headdress, and it said, 'Are the [Native Americans] parts of the Lost Tribes of Israel?'" Michael Danvers-Walker, interviewed by Malcolm Adcock. Danvers-Walker's parents had been eager for him to have a Christian upbringing and supported this new interest that led to his baptism three months later. (Bob Danvers-Walker, Michael's father, was a prominent newsreel commentator and broadcaster.)

16. *British Area General Conference*, 21.

17. *British Area General Conference*, 162, extra capitalization used.

from the physical infrastructure of chapels being built and eventually dotting the land—a critical ingredient and a natural consequence of the British response to missionary outreach from mostly American missionaries—there needed to be further investment in faith-based leadership development. Brits needed to serve missions themselves and apply the skills and spiritual maturity they learned on their missions to subsequent lay leadership positions in the Church back home. This service would ensure them the spiritual depth needed to help guide others in the faith.

There was an appeal to the existing British leaders to prepare the youth to serve as missionaries and a rallying cry to young people themselves to create a tradition of missionary service. "The youth of Great Britain need to qualify to do the missionary work here and to help in other areas," said Smith.[18] As the prophet shared "some stirring missionary stories," he "challenged the members to increase the number of British missionaries from seventy-five to seven hundred."[19] Smith declared, "[Y]ou are the future bishops and stake presidents, the future mission presidents and temple presidents here in Great Britain. You are the future leaders, and because of the great work that lies ahead for you, you have a special obligation to stand true and steadfast."[20] The British Saints took this to heart, and in the subsequent decade, more and more Saints from the United Kingdom started to serve missions. In 1975, this number included 109 young men and 48 young women, and by 1983, there were over 400 British youth serving missions.[21]

In addition to sermons from leaders of the Church, fifteen hundred Saints sang in the choirs, two hundred cultural performers participated, and several Latter-day Saint youth spoke, some as young as twelve. Derek A. Cuthbert, serving as a regional representative at the time, recognized that this was an important era and told conference attendees that "this is the second century of Mormonism in Great Britain. *We are making the history*."[22]

Cuthbert later shared details of behind-the-scenes planning for the conference. "There were some headaches and anxieties," he said, but having the prophet and many of the senior Church leaders in Britain "was more than sufficient compensation."[23] Cuthbert found out about the anticipated event when one of the recently called Apostles, Elder Boyd K.

---

18. *British Area General Conference*, 48.

19. Derek A. Cuthbert, *The Second Century: Latter-day Saints in Great Britain*, 1:113.

20. *British Area General Conference*, 48.

21. Anne S. Perry, "The Contemporary Church," 436–37.

22. *British Area General Conference*, 168; emphasis added.

23. Cuthbert, *Second Century*, 97.

Packer, phoned him the previous October from Salt Lake City "with an interesting request" regarding potential conference halls and logistics.[24] The following February, there was "mounting enthusiasm from the British Saints" after the official announcement.[25]

The tabloid *Daily Mirror* was impressed by the conference, referring to it—in the newspaper's usual style—as

> the biggest evangelical wing-ding in this country since Billy Graham wowed 'em at Wembley [Stadium]. . . . It was a historic occasion. . . . For the first time since founder Joseph Smith had his vision in a secluded wood, the church leaders were holding a general conference outside the United States.[26]

The *Mirror* added, "Joseph Fielding Smith, 95-year-old 'prophet, seer and revelator presiding,' and descendant of his church's founder was there." The newspaper underlined that so were 12,000 Britons, everyone a doorstep convert, everyone the net result of a knock on the door and a sermon on the garden path. Mormonism is the fastest growing religion in Britain, it said.[27]

The BBC broadcast its network documentary *Come, Come Ye Saints*, featuring aspects of the conference, on national television at 10:30 p.m. the night before the great conference gathering.[28] This high-profile media coverage, in itself greatly significant, was the precursor of close media attention and intense scrutiny during the rest of the 1970s. The public's interest in the conference was further mirrored by special conference guests, including Member of Parliament Ezra W. Owen.[29] Respect for Latter-day Saints from British Parliamentarians was to gain further momentum as the decade rolled on, and the Church's outreach to media and elected politicians was an important part of its strategy for growth and acceptance.

The influence of the conference was felt well into the decade and beyond. Conference speakers espousing a visionary purpose in personal and Church growth spurred on British members who had to grapple with the often gloomy economic challenges of the 1970s. (In popular culture, this period is characterized as one of high inflation, power outages plunging cities into darkness, and industrial decline.) Some Latter-day Saint con-

---

24. Cuthbert, 97.
25. Cuthbert, 105.
26. *Daily Mirror*, August 30, 1971, quoted in *Out of Obscurity*, 218–19.
27. *Daily Mirror*, August 30, 1971.
28. Cuthbert, *Second Century*, 111.
29. Cuthbert, 121.

gregants even faced financial sacrifices in traveling to worship services, with transportation costs to and from church meetings in many parts of London being, on average, as much as a tenth of wages.[30]

Yet, by the end of the decade, the general population had greater access to consumer goods, including telephones and cars,[31] making it easier for Latter-day Saints to get to church meetings and go about their outreach efforts toward local membership and others interested in learning more about the faith.

Church Programs Bring Spiritual Strength to UK Youth

Converts to the Church were encouraged to continue acquiring gospel knowledge and applying Christian principles in their daily interactions. To assist in this, spiritual and scriptural education for younger Church members was given a boost with the introduction of part-time gospel study programs new to the United Kingdom: seminary (for younger teenagers) and institute (for young singles eighteen and over). David Cook, an employee of the Church's educational system, pioneered these initiatives in Britain and in other nations. Looking back at the results of these efforts decades later, Cook happily reports: "[M]ore of the young people are reading and studying the scriptures than ever before. . . . That's what our job was, to have the students understand the scriptures and gain a testimony of them. And they did it."[32]

The young people's commitment to serious gospel study was linked to an increase in missionary service by young British Latter-day Saints. Dennis A. Wright, who was serving in the England East Mission at this time, relates his experiences of talking with younger Church members during this period:

> [A]ll of a sudden all of these kids are now in Seminary and they are studying the gospel in the home study [and] in the early morning. And then . . . we are going to have Institute. . . . In the early part of my mission, you were hardpressed to find a young man who was preparing to serve a mission, meaning a Brit. A British youth just did not think of missions. That is something American elders did. We would say, "Why don't you go on a mission?" They would say,

---

30. Cuthbert, 129.

31. By 1981, sixty percent of British households had access to one or more cars or vans, compared with 52 percent in 1971, and just 31 percent in 1961. See Department for Transport, *Road Use Statistics Great Britain 2016*, 11.

32. David Cook, interviewed by Malcolm Adcock.

The team of pioneering Seminary staff, Hyde Park Chapel, 1978. Courtesy Craig Marshall.

"Well, I could never do that." Well, part of it was money, because you know things were tough. And part of it was . . . just tradition. Once Seminary starts, then kids start going on missions, then they come home prepared to be leaders, and they have families, and they are married in the temple.[33]

In addition, countrywide gatherings for young single adults were initiated in the 1970s. In 1972, the Latter-day Saint Student Association was set up, helping serve the needs of the increasing student membership. The Association had its own national convention in Edinburgh during August 1972, attended by Elder Marion D. Hanks (a General Authority serving as Assistant to the Quorum of the Twelve Apostles).[34] The next year, the

---

33. Dennis A. Wright, interviewed by Fred E. Woods. Wright is professor emeritus of Church history and doctrine and was an associate dean of Religious Education at Brigham Young University.

34. Cuthbert, *Second Century*, 135.

Seminary students visiting Sherwood Forest, England, 1969. Courtesy Craig Marshall.

first British Young Adult convention weekend was held at Loughborough University beginning August 31, 1973. Over three hundred joined the event. Harold B. Lee, then President of the Church, attended and said, "It was a most memorable experience and a delight to be with these young people."[35] Elizabeth Clark, one of Manchester's young Latter-day Saint leaders at the time, recalls a "hearty breakfast" and then being divided "into five groups in which we were able to ask questions to the various leaders, including the Prophet of the Church."[36] Future Apostle Elder Jeffrey R. Holland, then Director of the Melchizedek Priesthood MIA,[37] was thrilled: "I returned home physically but I confess my heart is still

---

35. Quoted in *Out of Obscurity*, 287.

36. *Out of Obscurity*, 285–86.

37. The Church's program for single adults.

in the 'Land of Hope and Glory.' . . . The conference was an unqualified success and sets a marvellous precedent for the future."[38]

To assist in these endeavors, in 1972 the Church opened administrative offices in Lichfield, Staffordshire, with a range of church departments all under one roof. Five years later, it further opened a substantial office building in Solihull, West Midlands. For much of the time, the Solihull office also housed the presiding ecclesiastical leadership overseeing multiple nations.[39]

Family History Work Helps Unite British Saints with Their Ancestors

Connecting the generations through family history is dear to the hearts of millions of people globally and especially to members of The Church of Jesus Christ of Latter-day Saints, who believe that eternal spiritual benefits can be obtained through family connections. Apart from its own doctrinal motivations, the Church is also driven to make records available through extensive online archives so others—of any faith or none—can research genealogical lines and potentially feel closer to their ancestral family. Latter-day Saint genealogical efforts have long been a priority of individual members and of the Church as a whole.

Family history work was stepped up in earnest in 1969 when church employee Jeffrey F. Packe started directing the microfilming of genealogy archives in the British Isles. This began with tracking down christening, marriage, and death records, and motivating their keepers, often Anglican parish priests or senior clergy, to have them microfilmed for posterity.[40] By 1974, the Federation of Family History Societies, a nonprofit organization, had been established in Britain, providing a groundswell of support for record preservation and wider sharing of family history information among enthusiasts and anyone interested in tracing their own family tree. Importantly, irreplaceable records in old parish-based storerooms were at

---

38. Quoted in *Out of Obscurity*, 285–88.

39. Perry, "The Contemporary Church," 426. Administrative and other functions once based at the Solihull offices were relocated to Frankfurt, Germany, and to areas in the United Kingdom from 2008 onwards. The Solihull building was used by the Church until December 21, 2018. In April 2022, it was announced that the headquarters of the Church's newly-formed Europe North Area would be UK-based

40. At this time, there was widespread misunderstanding about the Church's motives for wanting to copy these records.

risk of being damaged by moisture, flood, or vermin, and so archivists lobbied the UK Government and pressed for strict laws to support records preservation. By 1979, the Parochial Records Measure 1978, requiring parish documents to be deposited in central records offices, came into law. More doors opened, despite what some archivists saw as the "shortsightedness" and resistance of some members of the clergy during that era.[41]

Mixed Reactions about Church Membership from Family and Friends

Latter-day Saints in the 1970s tended to receive mixed reactions from family and friends regarding their Church membership. Jeremy Dick, who joined the Church at age twenty in 1975, said that most of the population had little idea what the Church and its members were all about:

> [T]he vast majority of people would be totally ignorant of the Church's existence. . . . [M]y initial reaction was one of skepticism and a little bit of suspicion. . . . The first reaction of anybody to think of the Mormon religion would be to think of it as a sect, and perhaps slightly, possibly dangerous. . . . [I]f anybody knew anything about the Church they would immediately think, "American, polygamy." [On] the whole, people would be ignorant of other aspects of the Church.[42]

Julian Bell believes the Latter-day Saints were "a misunderstood minority" during his childhood and says he used to receive a fair degree of persecution from classmates because he was a member of the Church, with one incident particularly etched in his memory:

> [T]hey actually burnt a Book of Mormon in front of me. I don't know how they managed to get ahold of a Book of Mormon but they cruelly, as children are, decided that it would be hurtful to me and my brother to burn this Book of Mormon in front of us. And yeah, we were upset by it. It was not pleasant. So I think you did feel somewhat alone and different. We were the only members of our church in our schools, me and my brothers.[43]

One Church member found that support can sometimes come from surprising quarters. Marie Hunt, raised a Catholic, was baptized as an eighteen-year-old in 1979. She recalled, "I was actually in the Liverpool Stake when I got baptized. . . . I lived in a very strong Catholic town. All the schools were Catholic, everybody I knew was Catholic. And so, when the missionaries came to my sister's door, my parents were not impressed

---

41. Perry, "The Contemporary Church," 432, 433.
42. Jeremy Dick, interviewed by Malcolm Adcock and Fred E. Woods.
43. Cllr. Julian Bell, interviewed by Malcolm Adcock.

at all." The initial reaction to Marie's baptism was that she was "in big trouble" with her family: "They thought it was some sort of cult. They still talked about a tunnel under the River Mersey, they were going to take us all to be brides in Utah." Marie's mother very soon got in touch with the local parish priest for guidance, but his response was the opposite of what her mother expected:

> He said, "There are many roads to God." Which was not what my mother wanted to hear. She wanted the priest to say, "We'll do this, we'll intervene, we'll jump in.". . . . I don't remember my mother ever going to a priest for anything before. . . . I realized that she really was terrified what was going to happen [to] us.

It has now been over forty years since Marie and her sister joined the Church and missed all the Catholic milestones; however, her family's reaction to her conversion has changed. "Their kids didn't get christened; their grandkids didn't get christened. They didn't have all of the rites and things that they would've had if their grandkids had stayed Catholic. But if you talk to my mother now on a good day, she will tell you it was the best thing that we ever did."[44]

Increased Public Prominence of Saints

The 1970s saw some high-profile events and press coverage about Latter-day Saints that helped increase name recognition. In 1973, as the singing Osmond family and the associated "Osmondmania" brought Latter-day Saints further national attention (see the following chapter), another singing group, the Mormon Tabernacle Choir, was featured on network television. At 6:30 p.m. on Christmas Eve, TV presenter Steve Race introduced BBC Two audiences to "The Joy of Christmas."[45] The program had been recorded at Central Hall, Westminster, when the choir was on their European tour during the summer. Conducted by Richard P. Condie, who was seen as the person bringing the choir into the mainstream media, the program featured the Westminster Ensemble and the Tabernacle's world-renowned organist Alexander Schreiner.

And in print, the media often reported on the goodwill and good works of the Latter-day Saints, especially their emphasis on traditional family life. "Be Content: Talk It Over with the Family" was the headline

---

44. Marie Hunt, interviewed by Malcolm Adcock and Fred E. Woods.
45. "BBC Two TV listings."

in the *Romford Recorder* on May 2, 1975, with the article telling its readers: "Thirty minutes with your family . . . that's the new catchphrase for the Mormon church, centred at the [C]hurch of Jesus Christ of the Latter Day Saints, Butts Green Road, Hornchurch."[46] It also quoted a local missionary: "'We know that our families are worth more than 30 minutes,' said elder [sic] Mike. 'Yet often we let a day, or a month go by without any real time with those we love the most.'"

Area Conferences Lift British Saints

Another advance for the Church in the United Kingdom—internally and externally—came June 19–22, 1976, with three area conferences held simultaneously in London, Manchester, and Glasgow. With the 1971 Manchester conference as the model, Church President Spencer W. Kimball used meticulous planning to attend gatherings across the three venues.[47] Latter-day Saints' commitment to missionary outreach was an oft-repeated theme during the meetings, and, in front of 10,000 people at the London event,[48] Kimball thanked the media for bringing up the subject at a press interview:

> The other day when the press interviewed us, one young man said to me, "President Kimball, why do you send American missionaries here to England? We have a lot of fine boys here. Why don't you use British boys for your missionaries?" And of course that pleased me very much. And then I said, "It is because we didn't have the British missionaries that we sent the American missionaries, but now we have turned the corner. From today on we are going to have many, many missionaries in this area." There are many young people who have thought they were not obligated to go on a mission, that that was an American job. We would like to emphasize very strongly at this time that it is not an American job. It is a British job, and it is a Norwegian job, and a Brazilian job.[49]

The *Times* carried a four-page special supplement coinciding with the London conference, written by Clifford Longley (Religious Affairs Correspondent) and Peter Strafford (New York Correspondent).[50] Veteran religion writer Clifford Longley opined, "The Mormons' attractiveness to

---

46. "Be Content: Talk It Over with the Family."
47. "United Kingdom Area Conference Reports," 77.
48. David Croft, "3 Conferences Held in England, Scotland," 3–5.
49. *Official Report of the First London England Area Conference*, 37.
50. Clifford Longley and Peter Strafford, "The Mormons," 29.

converts, therefore, lies less in the credibility of their origins than in their lifestyle."[51] He cited, "Western middle-class values par excellence, but with the added strength of being founded upon an explicit creed and code." Longley predicted growth ahead for the Latter-day Saints: "The British, in turn, have yet to accustom themselves to the presence and influence of this new religious minority, but they can be encouraged by the American experience to believe that it will present no difficulties." There would be some "spirited rivalry" with the mainstream denominations with potential for "a tonic effect on British church life."

Conference speaker Thomas Hill, president of the London England North Stake, picked up on the vital need for The Church of Jesus Christ of Latter-day Saints to be seen as a British church as much as it is seen as a North American church within North America. He related an experience when a young man from his area underwent a pre-mission medical examination.[52] The doctor had written on the assessment form that the young person intended "[t]o serve a mission for an American church." Hill implied that the reputation of being an American religion was a fact of life because the Church was still "pioneering" in Britain. But, he added,

> [W]e will continue so to do until the doctor puts on the form, "To serve a mission for the Lord's Church," or perhaps even for a British church. When we have got them to do that then we will begin to make the sort of headway that will bring the Church to that peak where the Lord surely desires to see it here in this land.[53]

One national British newspaper underlined the expansion that had taken place in just two decades. In an article during the conference weekend, the *Daily Telegraph* noted, "A membership drive by the Church of Jesus Christ of Latter Day Saints (Mormons) opened in London yesterday. Twenty years ago, there were 10,000 Mormons in Britain. Today there are 100,000."[54] At this same time, a North East London weekly newspaper, the *Waltham Forest Guardian*, reported on the conference's cultural activities: "The Battle of Britain and British ballet were just two aspects of the British scene acted out at a pageant during the three-day Mormon Conference held at Wembley Pool."[55] The same publication also noted the

---

51. Clifford Longley, "Mormons: Second Flowering of the Church in Britain," 1.
52. *London England Area Conference*, 38–39.
53. *London England Area Conference*, 39.
54. "Mormon Drive," 13.
55. "Mormons Get Together."

nature of the Church's local lay leadership, relating how a college lecturer became a "Mormon Bishop": "A production engineering lecturer at North East London Poly Precinct, Walthamstow, has become a President in the Mormon Church. Raymond Kemp, 39, was ordained by Apostle of the Mormons Mark Peterson for the Romford-England stake which is equivalent to a diocese."[56]

Despite some public ambivalence, the Church and its members were indeed coming of age as their global leader President Joseph Fielding Smith had underlined at the beginning of the decade. The media were fascinated by the high-profile religious phenomenon of the Latter-day Saints. And the Church's growth in the 1970s was buoyed too by a family of singers who were a show business sensation.

---

56. "Mormons Get Together."

CHAPTER 7

Osmondmania

The boys love the Lord even more than show business.
— George Osmond

Osmondmania intensified in London when the Osmond family band from Utah arrived in October 1973. The boys were Alan (then 24), Wayne (22), Merrill (20), Jay (18), Donny (15), and little Jimmy (10), accompanied by their sister, Marie (14).

Their father, George, had told a correspondent for the *Sunday Times Magazine*, "We're just a plain, simple family. We're all members of the Mormon faith and it is that, more than anything else, that has held us together. I can tell you the boys love the Lord even more than show business." Scattered throughout the United Kingdom were *weenyboppers*, exuberant fans who produced "screams of ecstasy" and did not seem to care what these handsome lads believed. The reporter notes, "Most of them are aged between 12 and 14, howling for a sight of the idols and shrieking at the Heavies. . . . The girls scream and sob on the very brink of hysteria."[1] At the start of the Osmonds' 1973 tour, it was reported that 10,000 shrieking fans met the Osmonds at Heathrow Airport, and shortly thereafter part of a wall on the airport's balcony collapsed, adding to the dramatic experiences of these crazed devotees.[2]

By the spring of 1975, both the Heathrow and Gatwick airports closed to the Osmonds' chartered aircraft due to widely publicized previous problems, such as "several policemen [who] were injured" by mobs of fans and damage from "hundreds of stampeding girls" that cost thousands of pounds to repair. Two years later, hotels also closed to the band, necessitating a temporary house rental.[3] Osmondmania had certainly not subsided. One British woman admitted nearly fifty years later to an obsession with Donny Osmond in her early teen years. Not only did she have a purple duvet on her bed because purple was Donny's favorite color, but she also had a picture of Donny in her bedroom that she kissed each night,

---

1. "The Osmonds," 20–21.

2. A report from the *Daily Mail* notes that the near tragedy at Heathrow took place in October 1973. Roderick Gilchrist, "Osmonds Barred from Two London Airports," 1.

3. Gilchrist, 1.

Osmond Brothers in outfits made by Elvis Presley's costume designer. Courtesy Donny Osmond.

and she wore fragrant perfume at bedtime in the event that her fantasy might come true and that he would come through her bedroom window.[4]

In a May 1975 article, "Osmonds' Girl Fans Riot," the *Daily Telegraph* reported that "[p]olice had to remove hysterical girls who tried to break through cordons and barriers to mob the Osmonds pop group in Eaton Square." The report continued, "The girls were clamouring. . . . After a few minutes of 'pandemonium,' 10 girls were carried away in a state of collapse. With tears streaming down their faces, girls kicked and clawed." Such was the Osmond craze that struck the United Kingdom in the early 1970s.[5]

Looking back nearly half a century later, Alan Osmond recalled,

> They were going wild and so we went over to see them and it was fabulous. It was very dangerous after a while. In fact, we had so many fans come in and find out where we were and they would bombard the hotel and ran over some of the lady policemen.

He added, "We were barred from that one [hotel when] we tried to come . . . later to England." Alan shared that at the time of their reentry to

---

4. A woman wishing to remain anonymous recounted these facts to the author (with her smiling sister looking on), May 21, 2019, while passing through the Medley Manor Farm, Oxford.

5. "Osmonds' Girl Fans Riot," 15.

Donny Osmond, who was frequently the center focus of Osmondmania.
Courtesy Donny Osmond.

The Osmonds arrive at their next destination in the United Kingdom. Courtesy Merrill Osmond.

Britain, the BBC had used the word "Osmondmania" and the newspapers read "Osmonds Go Home." Said Alan, "They thought that we were there just for the money. We were just there for the music."[6]

More than Music

Though their musical talent and charisma drew immense attention, there was more beneath the Osmonds' sound and performance both on and off the stage that caused reverberations among British citizens, especially with those who investigated the Osmonds' faith. Denise Sim, a 1970s Church convert from Hertfordshire, recalled, "If it hadn't been for the Osmond family, I would not [have] known about the Mormon church and its teachings." She adds, "The Osmonds have had a great influence and have been missionaries in their own rights. Through their example and living true to their beliefs and through their music they have brought numerous people to the understanding that we are children of God."[7]

---

6. Alan Osmond, interviewed by Fred E. Woods and Martin L. Andersen.

7. Email response from Denise Sim to Fred E. Woods, May 21, 2018; Denise Sim, interviewed by Fred E. Woods.

One staff member assisting the Osmonds, Carol Oldroyd, observed their exemplary behavior in all seasons. For Oldroyd, the Osmonds treated their employees as if they were part of the Osmond family, which left an indelible impact on her. Oldroyd recalled that those working for the Osmonds adored them: "They would do anything for them [the Osmonds] as I would . . . because they were so kind to me and respectful. It wasn't like I was their employee, it was more like I was their older sister. Olive and George, we called them Mother and Father Osmond. We were kind of like a family, and all the employees that I worked with felt the same way."

This benevolent treatment was likewise extended to British fans, whom the Osmonds regarded with love and respect. Oldroyd remembered,

From the minute we stepped off that airplane . . . the Osmonds were the kindest people to the fans of England. They cared about them, they talked with them, they gave them all the time they needed to tell them their problems. The Osmond brothers were very kind to the people of England and I think that's the reason why they loved them so much.[8]

Even after the Osmonds returned to the States, Mother Osmond (Olive) continued to write columns via her *Spotlight Magazine* articles aimed at giving motherly counsel for young UK girls in need. Marie Osmond remembered a time when she returned home and found her Mom writing an article for *Spotlight*. Referring to the other popular "teeny-bopper magazines," Olive said, "They have no substance! We need to give the girls some substance." Marie said that her mother "would write . . . about faith and family and self-worth and hard work and . . . stuff like that." Marie also recalled with a smile, "I remember one day I went in there and I [said], 'You love the fans more than you love me!' And she looked at me and she goes, 'You know I love you, but I love them, too, so get over it!'"[9]

Dennis Wright, an American Latter-day Saint and former missionary to Britain, also acknowledged the Osmonds' kindness:

[T]he Osmonds were very talented, but they were just nice people and I think something in Britain wanted that at that particular time. . . . [I]t had the Beatles and the Rolling Stones and it had all this stuff, and all of a sudden, these people come on stage who are just as talented, but who are nice people. And I think that appealed to a wide cross section of British youth.[10]

---

8. Carol Oldroyd, interviewed by Fred E. Woods and Martin L. Andersen.
9. Marie Osmond, interviewed by Fred E. Woods and Martin L. Andersen.
10. Dennis A. Wright, interviewed by Fred E. Woods and Martin L. Andersen.

They were not only nice people; they also had a high standard of virtue. Carol Oldroyd explained, "They never sang a song that had off-color lyrics, and so I think that the fans looked at them as wholesome and kind people and they wanted to be like them. . . . [M]issionaries had to have it much easier because of the Osmond family. I personally believe that the Osmond family [were] the single biggest, best missionaries the Church has ever had."[11] Journalist Lee Benson explained, "In almost every way imaginable in the entertainment world, the Osmonds were different—a clean-living, clean-talking, clean-performing bunch that didn't drink, do drugs, curse or complain, all while singing rock 'n' roll and praising the Lord."[12]

Ron Clark, the Osmonds' road manager for fourteen years, was an eyewitness to their tremendous influence, particularly Donny's. Clark recalled,

> Donny was synonymous with starship, fame, everything that you can possibly imagine a young, gifted artist being in the imagination, mind, and heart of a young girl, a teenage girl, he was that icon. And what kind of an icon was he really? He was founded on faith in the Lord Jesus Christ, he had a testimony of that Master. He had a testimony and a great knowledge of His teachings. He knew how to look upon young women with respect and reverence. There was nothing that any parent ever needed to worry about with their child, this precious daughter, having a fixation on any one of the Osmonds because they were non-threatening. All they did was be an example for goodness and as a result of that, these girls start reading the Book of Mormon, they start reading the pamphlets that the missionaries would bring to the home. We had referral cards inside each Book of Mormon that was given away at the concert sites. And they could fill that out and they could send it to the local mission home, and the missionaries would call by. I had no idea how many teaching appointments and how many convert baptisms came into the Church by the Osmonds alone.[13]

Famous Encounters

Not only did the Osmonds influence their fans by performing a high caliber of wholesome music, but they also caught the attention of famous rock groups who were performing in Britain during this same era. For example, Donny recalled that Paul McCartney came to the Osmonds' lodgings in

---

11. Carol Oldroyd, interviewed by Fred E. Woods and Martin L. Andersen.

12. Lee Benson, "Jay Osmond Talks Writing Musical Play that Will Tell 'True Unvarnished Story' of Osmond Family."

13. Ron Clark, interviewed by Fred E. Woods and Martin L. Andersen.

France one day with his young daughter Mary and requested an autograph for her. McCartney spoke softly with his distinct "Liverpudlian" accent:

"Could I get your autograph, please, for my daughter?" and I said, "Yeah," and he hands me a picture of me. He says, "Put it to Mary, please," so I put, "To Mary, love, Donny Osmond," [and] gave it to Paul. He gave it to Mary, [and] she was so excited, and he said, "Thank you very much." I said, "You're welcome," and the door closes, and I'm thinking, "Hold on, that was Paul McCartney! Just asked me for my autograph!" So years later I'm in London at this television studio editing one of my music videos, and Paul was in the adjacent studio, and I thought, "I gotta verify this story, maybe I dreamt it or maybe I made it up or something, I don't know," so I walk in, I say, "Hey Paul." He said, "Hey Donny, how are you?" and we started talking a little while. I say, "Paul, I've gotta verify something," so I related the story . . . and I say, "Did that happen, or did I dream it?" and he said, "Donny, not only did it happen, but your autograph is one of the few autographs I've ever asked for in my entire life."[14]

Donny's older brother Alan was quite impressed by McCartney's visit. He remembered, "We got a phone call early in the morning saying Paul McCartney is down here and would like to meet you. I said, '*The* Paul McCartney?' . . . When we opened the door, there was Paul McCartney, the legend, our hero. But more importantly it was Paul McCartney the father. He brought his little daughter to get our autograph and that said more to me than anything."[15]

But McCartney was not the only British performer who took notice. Elton John once asked the Osmond boys to come to a British party, but after he was told the band members were "milk-drinking Mormons from Utah," he phoned back and withdrew the request.[16] Alan vividly recalled this memorable event:

[W]e were in California and got a call from MGM records [saying] Elton John wants to meet the brothers. I said, "Oh, yeah, I'll go over." So Merrill and I went over and there was Elton with a little pink flower in his ear and we had the best visit. Wonderful visit, talked, just great. [Elton said], "Hey, listen, why don't you come to a party tonight?" He said, "Here's the address. We'll see you." We said, "Okay, we'll see you." As soon as we left, we were driving home and we got a call from his manager, and he said, "Elton started thinking about it, and there will be some people there that may be embar-

14. Donny Osmond interview.
15. Alan Osmond interview.
16. Paul H. Dunn, *The Osmonds: The Official Story of the Osmond Family*, 7.

rassed if you are there, too. So we would like to uninvite you." That was the best compliment he could have told me.[17]

Donny Osmond said, "One of the things that kept us from the 'in crowd,' as we'll call it, of the music industry, is the fact that we never did go to the pot-smoking, drinking parties and stuff where all of these people would congregate and become kind of like colleagues and cohorts and things like that. We avoided all that kind of stuff." Looking back with hindsight, Donny added, "But . . . people kind of respected the Osmonds for not indulging in those kinds of things, because it is a slippery slope, and a lot of people have fallen off. A lot of people I've respected over the years have thrown their lives away, literally, through drugs and alcohol. So I think there is a kind of a secret respect in that."[18]

One of several popular rock bands in Britain at the time was the electric band Led Zeppelin. There was a mutual admiration between some of these famed performers and the Osmonds, who were one of the original boy bands. Donny recalled a memorable exchange that occurred at an event held in Earl's Court during the early 70s:

> Led Zeppelin . . . invited us to go backstage before the show was over, and before their encore they were playing frisbees with their kids, and we were playing backstage with Led Zeppelin. . . . Just before they went on to do their encore, they said, "Why don't you come onstage with us? Well, not on with us, but just stand off to the right." And I'll never forget it. We're standing there stage right, watching Led Zeppelin play "Stairway to Heaven." It was unbelievable.[19]

Another person of unrivalled prominence that the Osmonds met was Queen Elizabeth. Donny explained this unusual encounter, which occurred in the spring of 1972.[20] For him, it included a humorous moment as well as a spiritual memory of his mother's courage and spiritual conviction:

---

17. Alan Osmond interview.

18. Donny Osmond interview.

19. Donny Osmond interview. Donny noted he was friends with Michael Jackson, and the Osmond family knew Elvis Presley, who let them stay in his Las Vegas suite when they performed there. In fact, Donny noted, "My mom had a great relationship with Elvis Presley because Elvis wanted to be a preacher and he would call my mom every once in a while and talk about the gospel because he loved gospel music."

20. According to Dunn, this event took place in May 1972. Dunn, *The Osmonds*, 1.

One of the first memories I have of going over to England was to perform for Her Majesty The Queen, at [the London Palladium]. And after the show it was quite funny because everybody was so nervous. You have to stand there, you can't raise your hand to shake Her Majesty's hand unless she raises her hand to shake yours. I mean the protocol was just out of this world. . . . [M]y brother Merrill . . . had cottonmouth, he was just so nervous. And just as Her Majesty walked up to Merrill he licks his lips and somebody took a picture of it, and that was the cover of the paper the next morning . . . my brother Merrill sticking his tongue at the Queen of England.[21] . . . I remember shaking Her Majesty's hand and it was such a cool moment, but what I took out of that experience was the fact that my mother [gave] the Queen a Book of Mormon. . . . Years later, I [learned] . . . the Queen still has that Book of Mormon in the Palace.[22]

Musical Missionaries

Although the Osmonds met with distinguished and well-known British citizens on occasion, they were also always conscious of their everyday fans and looked for ways they could encourage them. Jay Osmond explained,

One of the things we've always wanted people to know is that we got into show business not because we wanted to be famous or make a lot of money—you know, that fame and fortune thing. We got into this business because we felt we can maybe help families, lift families. And it was always a

---

21. Concerning this humorous occasion and the expected protocol, Merrill recalled, "You're told never to speak to her unless she wants to speak to you, and you never reach out to shake her hand unless she wants to shake your hand. So everybody was nervous. So here she comes down the line, everything's fine with Alan, she's getting to Wayne, they're talking, and . . . I'm wetting my lips, but she comes to me and I say, 'Hello, Mrs. Queen,' and that didn't work, but they start taking pictures of me as I was wetting my lips. . . . [T]he next day in the newspaper it showed 'Osmond Sticks Tongue at Queen.' They caught that one picture. . . . I didn't do it on purpose, obviously, but I was hated per se in the press for a long time." Merrill Osmond, interviewed by Fred E. Woods and Martin L. Andersen.

22. Donny Osmond interview. All the Osmond family were thrilled about this rare meeting with the Queen, with the exception of Marie. Marie, with a wry smile and chuckle, recalled, "When we met the Queen in England, . . . everyone was so excited to meet the Queen. I was so excited. In their excitement, they left me in the room. And I never got to meet her!" Marie Osmond interview.

mission first. I think that's what's kept us grounded through all this up and down rollercoaster of show business.[23]

Carol Oldroyd likewise observed, "[T]he Osmonds always tried to go to firesides [informal church meetings] or to church whenever they could and so they set an example to the people of England."[24] Donny recalled these spiritual events, which the Osmonds always did for service and were not paid for:

> I remember doing firesides over in the UK, and in hindsight I realize and appreciate what my parents were actually doing. We weren't trying to shove the gospel down anyone's throats, we were just living our religion. We were not being hypocrites, because that's what our lifestyle was back at home. We'd go to church on Sunday. But it was a great example for others who were saying, "What keeps this family together? They're going to church on Sunday and they worked really hard Saturday night in a show. Let's check it out."[25]

One British young woman who decided to "check out" the Osmonds was Lorraine Wheeler. She recalled,

> I was curious about the back-story to the Osmonds ever since they burst onto the British music scene in the early 70's when I was just 13 years old. What was behind those white jumpsuits and impeccable dance move synchronizations . . . let alone the amazing harmonies and their genuine personalities that just drew you in. That is what I was most curious about. There had to be something behind all of that. I never thought the answer lay in a religion!

Wheeler's father was not pleased that she was interested in The Church of Jesus Christ of Latter-day Saints, and he did not want her to consider having anything to do with the Church until she was twenty years old, which she agreed to. Wheeler also committed to herself that if she were ever proposed to by a Latter-day Saint, she would sincerely investigate the Church before moving forward with any serious plans. Shortly after her twentieth birthday, such a proposal came, and she began to take another look at the Church. She ended up going to a fireside in Westminster in late January 1979 where she heard every single Osmond family member talk about the Church. Wheeler recalled that special night: "There I sat with thousands of others and the only way I can describe the feelings I felt was as if magic dust was being sprinkled over me. . . . [L]ittle did I know that those feelings were the whisperings of the Holy Ghost witnessing to

---

23. Jay Osmond, interviewed by Fred E. Woods and Martin L. Andersen.
24. Carol Oldroyd interview.
25. Donny Osmond interview.

Donny Osmond speaking at a Church devotional meeting, Central Hall, Westminster. Courtesy *Church News*.

me that the things I was hearing were good." Two months later Wheeler was baptized, and four decades later she began working as the Executive Assistant for Marie Osmond and has now been a friend of the Osmond family for many years.[26]

Looking back on this period, Merrill Osmond shared the process of what was going on with the UK fans as he saw it:

> I think the fans heard the music first. I think they liked the music—we were different. And of course, all of the fan magazines would promote Donny and the brothers, and so the music, the image started it out. But then they wanted to know what we were about. And that's when the tide started to turn . . . very spiritual. . . . We weren't out to convert anybody. But we were out there to tell our story. And the more we told our story, the more interest became in the Church. I look back and I see that was one of the really solid impacts that we had for the Church, was to bear testimony when we had that opportunity to.[27]

Merrill's brother Alan explained how they could further tell their stories in the many firesides they held:

> [T]here in England we would try to share our testimonies. . . . We would sing a few songs, but they were gospel songs, and we shared our testimonies

26. Lorraine Wheeler, email communication to Fred E. Woods, , May 21, 2019.
27. Merrill Osmond Interview.

and talked about what we believed, why we believe, why we do the things we do, why we don't drink, . . . and the fans came . . . and that's what really opened doors. We invited the missionaries to be there and encouraged them [the fans] if they had questions. Who are you? Why are you here? And what are you doing and where are you going after this world? . . . [W]e loved to do shows for the fans and the firesides.[28]

Such devotional meetings not only provided an opportunity to strengthen the British Saints, but they also provided a venue for young Saints to bring their friends and introduce them to their faith. These settings sparked interest on many occasions, which yielded much fruit and thousands of baptisms.

Merrill remembered that people were really affected by the Osmonds' 1973 album *The Plan*, which offered a glimpse into the Latter-day Saint view of the purpose of life. At firesides, the Osmonds permitted the audience to ask about the "plan of salvation," and Merrill was amazed by the questions asked. He stated, "I remember one fireside where the Spirit was so strong that literally people who were not LDS would stand up in the middle of our fireside and start bearing their testimonies of what they were hearing. I mean, we're talking hundreds and hundreds of people would get up over time and just want to bear that testimony."[29]

Decades later, the Osmonds continued to hear accounts of Brits touched by their efforts. For example, Donny tells a story of what happened after a more recent show with his sister Marie in Las Vegas:

This really tall, burly man came up to me and I thought . . . he is a rock and roller and he is forced to be here because his wife dragged him here. But he said, "I have a story to tell you. I am a member of the Church and I want to thank you for it. . . . My mom was a fan over in England and she joined the [C]hurch because of you." . . . What a compliment, that is better than a gold record.[30]

Heeding Prophetic Counsel

The Osmonds' international influence came to the attention of Church President Spencer W. Kimball, who requested that they come to a dinner in their honor. Osmond road manager, Ron Clark, explained this unique occasion:

---

28. Alan Osmond interview.
29. Merrill Osmond interview.
30. Donny Osmond interview.

It was 1977 and we were invited to Salt Lake City for a dinner by none other than Spencer W. Kimball and his wife, Camilla. . . . [He said], "Well, George and Olive, . . . I have some news that I would like to share with you." He says, "It's come to my attention that this past year, through the missionary department referral system, you remarkable Osmond family are responsible for over 28,000 convert baptisms this year alone." ... And he says, "Brother and Sister Osmond, I would like to extend an invitation to you and your children tonight in this very special setting to be missionaries of The Church of Jesus Christ of Latter-day Saints worldwide. And it will be my pleasure and my honor to set you apart individually in that calling." And before the night was over, they had been set apart as full-time missionaries in the Lord's service.[31]

This was not their first encounter with a Latter-day Saint Church President. In 1972, several years before the special meeting with Kimball, the Osmond family was given counsel by President Harold B. Lee, Kimball's predecessor. Jay Osmond recalled the sacred setting when Lee provided this inspired counsel to his family: "Whether it's the places you go, the things you do, the friends you keep, always choose that decision, [that] option[,] that will bring you closer to God." These words sunk deep in Jay's heart. He noted, "I'll never forget that. And when we walked out of that boardroom, down the stairs, our family changed. I felt a big change. I was just a brand-new teenager and I felt a heavy weight on our shoulders."[32]

The Osmonds did not take their spiritual charge casually; they tried to make good daily decisions and bring light into every performance. In fact, each of the Osmonds would tell you that one of the keys to their success was that they never performed before an audience without having prayer together.[33] This tradition continues to the present day. For example, looking back over the Donny and Marie shows of the past decade, Donny noted, "[S]till we pray before every show, even in Las Vegas. We'll have a little circle of prayer—our dancers, Marie and myself, . . . and we let the dancers pray. And you know, it's not traditional Church of Jesus Christ of Latter-day Saints prayer, but it's beautiful, and it brings such a wonderful spirit to what we're going to do for the next 90 minutes on that stage."[34]

The Osmonds maintain that prayer has made a meaningful difference throughout their career, including their launch in the United Kingdom fifty years ago. One American Latter-day Saint who served a mission in

---

31. Ron Clark interview.
32. Jay Osmond interview.
33. Dunn, *The Osmonds*, 199; Ron Clark interview.
34. Donny Osmond interview.

Britain felt that the early 1970s was a turning point for the Church. He learned firsthand how much influence the Osmond boy band wielded on the British public opinions toward the Church:

> I did have an opportunity to sit behind a lady at an Osmond concert who was from England and we chatted and she was just crazy [about Donny] and I said, "What is going on?" and she said, "We love Donny Osmond." I said, "Well, you are a Mormon?" "No. I am not, but I love the Mormons because I love Donny," and it was just a phenomenon that just seemed to be part of this package. It was as if the Lord was putting his finger on a land and saying, "It is your turn, wake up."[35]

Osmond fan and Latter-day Saint convert Denise Sim remarked, "They were absolutely popular, very, very, very, popular . . . and produced a lot of number one records in the UK." She added, "They'll always be remembered for their entertaining. . . . [I]t's over 50 years of entertaining people now, and I still think they would be received today even though it's been many, many years since they have been together as a group, that they would still be very influential today."[36]

Mutual Admiration and Family Connections

Although the original band that performed during the 70s no longer performs as an entire group on a regular basis, there have been occasions when they all perform together for special engagements,[37] and some of the Osmond brothers still continue to perform in the United Kingdom. In fact, Jay and Merrill Osmond gave concerts in 2019, and their younger brother Jimmy has performed in the United Kingdom on a regular basis. Further, in interviews, both Donny and Marie mention with delight how the British fans continue to come to their shows on the Strip, listed as the number one show in Vegas in recent years.[38] Donny tenderly recalls:

---

35. Dennis A. Wright interview.

36. Denise Sim, interviewed by Fred E. Woods.

37. One of those special events took place on the Oprah Winfrey show in November 2007 when Oprah paid tribute to the Osmonds and their fifty successful years of entertainment. All of the nine children were shown on the show and over one hundred of the Osmonds' posterity. Unfortunately, George Osmond, then age 90, died days before the show was broadcast. See "An Osmond Family Tribute," Oprah.

38. Marie Osmond interview; Donny Osmond interview.

President Spencer W. Kimball with Donny and Marie for the Osmond Studios Dedication, November 1, 1977, Orem, Utah. Courtesy Donny Osmond.

> The UK has always had a soft spot in my heart because of the fans. You cannot be in show business, even for a short period of time, unless you have a fanbase. But what was interesting, and this just happened a couple years ago, I did an arena tour over in the UK and it sold out like crazy. I mean, the screaming was reminiscent of the 70s, although we were a lot older [and] the screams were coming from middle-aged women rather than little teenagers, but it was phenomenal. The loyalty that I felt, and other people told me that not a lot of people enjoy this type of loyalty from a fanbase, so the UK has always had such a very, very soft spot in my heart, and a very good place for my career, because it really was the UK that launched us into stardom.[39]

From the start, British fans fell in love with the Osmonds, and the Osmonds loved them back. It doesn't hurt that the Osmond family roots reach back to the British Isles. Alan Osmond said, "Osmondmania came out of . . . England. Our ancestry goes back to England with my father and great-grandfather." He recalled,

> When we'd go to do the tours we were interested in our genealogy. We would say from the stage, "Hey cousin, how are we related?" So many [from] England, you know, our roots go back there. . . . We had free DNA [tests] for them if they thought we were related. We found several, several cousins that

---

39. Donny Osmond interview.

were related with those people, and, in fact, we . . . went so far doing DNA [that] we found that our ancestors came from there. [There were] . . . three brother Osmonds that came from England. But one of them we couldn't find where he was or where he went. And after a lot of DNA study, and also prayer for . . . inspiration and blessings, we found that he had married a Maori girl and went from England down to New Zealand, and we found 622 Osmonds down there for our genealogy and they all came out of the England area.[40]

Donny noted, "We have such a great, loyal fanbase in the UK and I think a lot of it has to do with the fact that I'm from the UK, and not too far back. It was my great-great grandfather [that] . . . came over from England. . . . I think there is a connection there, not just with the music, . . . we're British. . . . That's the origin."[41]

Jay also spoke about this relationship: "My mother [Olive Davis] is mostly Welsh and [my] father is mostly English so we have that heritage. . . . And when our parents were on a mission over there . . . so many doors open[ed] up to them in finding the genealogy. . . . I think there's a strong connection, and they've said the Welsh voice is in our family. . . . [T]here is a definite connection from our English and Welsh history."[42]

Merrill also mentioned that from his UK travels, he learned that "the Welsh love to sing. . . . In these little gatherings . . . the Welsh want to sing us a song." He added that one influential Welsh ancestor of the Osmonds (John Parry) was asked by Brigham Young to form the Mormon Tabernacle Choir. Merrill noted, "So I think the whole ancestors of the Osmonds, that singing stuff, I think really affected the Osmonds."[43]

That "singing stuff" is not slowing down anytime soon, and the Osmond legacy continues into the twenty-first century. In fact, Jay Osmond produced a musical about the story of the Osmond family. *The Osmonds: A New Musical* opened to audiences in February 2022 and was scheduled to be performed at thirty-two theaters in the United Kingdom and Ireland.[44] Jay noted that he wanted "to tell the true unvarnished story of how it really was growing up, the obstacles we faced, and how we stayed together through the journey of our show business life." He takes his production

---

40. Alan Osmond interview.

41. Donny Osmond interview.

42. Jay Osmond interview.

43. Merrill Osmond interview.

44. Jay Osmond, email message to Fred E. Woods. Tour dates were amended due to COVID-19 regulations.

The Osmond family getting together to reach out to their fans. Courtesy Donny Osmond.

very seriously. In fact, Jay and his wife, Karen, moved to Chester, England, just south of Liverpool, to be closer to the scriptwriters. If the musical goes as well as planned, Jay also intends to have his show performed in the States. Interest in the Osmonds has remained robust in the United Kingdom for several decades, "Stronger than America, for some reason," Jay notes.[45] This mutual interest and warm relationship between the Brits and the Osmonds has now extended back a half a century. Their substantial influence is probably best summarized by Donny:

> Throughout the years, a lot of people have thanked the Osmonds for changing the face of the Church in the UK. . . . [P]rior to the 70s, the Church kind of had a weird outlook. . . . We didn't show up with horns and we weren't polygamists, and we weren't this cult. They were Christians; it was a family. They smiled, you know, they had a good time, they're loving life. So this isn't what all these rumors were about what Mormons were. . . .
>
> I am ever grateful to have been in that position that the Lord would trust us that much. . . . To be the face of the church over in the UK in the early

---

45. Lee Benson, "Jay Osmond Talks Writing Musical Play that Will Tell 'True Unvarnished Story' of Osmond Family"; Merrill Osmond added, "The UK has accepted the Osmonds a lot greater than the United States, it's a different thing over in the UK[,] its more about the Osmonds as a family[,] in the United States its more about Donny and Marie and then the family." Merrill Osmond interview.

70s, to thwart all of the bad rumors and the bad thoughts, and the outlook that people had on The Church of Jesus Christ of Latter-day Saints. Because of the Osmonds . . . it put a little bit of normalcy in the gospel, the restored gospel of Jesus Christ. This is something not to be afraid of. . . . We are not weird. The Church of Jesus Christ of Latter-day Saints is such a wonderful organization that brings families together and that is the message the Osmond family brought to the British Isles.[46]

---

46. Donny Osmond interview. A portion of this chapter was highlighted in Fred E. Woods, "Osmondmania in the United Kingdom," 40–41, 43–44, 47–50.

CHAPTER 8

Public Communications Comes to Britain

*He said this missionary had disappeared, the police felt that he
had been kidnapped. . . . Well the media picked up on this very,
very quickly.*

— Michael Otterson

With the mounting press interest in the 1970s, the opening of the Church's Public Communications office in London's Hyde Park Chapel in 1975 was a significant initiative for the global faith. Salt Lake City–based Public Communications Department staffer and educator Dr. Lorry E. Rytting was the trailblazer for this new office. He began making connections with media, trained local church volunteers in media outreach (a new program for the United Kingdom), and searched for a full-time British replacement in his job role. In doing so, Rytting helped open the way for Liverpool newspaperman Michael Otterson, later global Public Affairs managing director, to take over the efforts on September 1, 1976. "I remember getting off the train from our home in Southport and walking to my work in the *Liverpool Daily Post* office and having this really intense feeling that I just wanted to spend the rest of my life working for the Church," Otterson recalled.[1] "Sometime about the late summer of 1976 I got a telephone call from Wendell [Ashton] who said the First Presidency (the Church's governing council) had approved the setting up of a permanent office and, 'Would I be interested in coming to work for the [C]hurch?' That was not a difficult decision to make."[2] Over the next three years, the Church would receive major attention from the British media—some of the coverage was very sensational.

Bringing Light Out of Darkness

Otterson recounts, "In 1977, that's a year I will never forget. . . . I'm going to say 'all hell'—and I'm going to put that in quotes—broke loose. Because several things happened in '77 that absolutely consumed

---

1. Michael and Cathy Otterson, interviewed by Malcolm Adcock and Fred E. Woods.

2. Wendell J. Ashton was then the worldwide managing director of the Church's Public Communications Department.

me and consumed the work. One of those things was the kidnapping of a missionary." The dramatic series of events surrounding the kidnapping of Latter-day Saint missionary Elder Kirk Anderson on September 14, 1977, outside the Church's meetinghouse in suburban Epsom, Surrey, were of great concern to the police and—needless to say—to the Church's members and leaders.

Otterson was alerted to the missionary's disappearance in a late-night phone call from Church headquarters.

> It was about one o clock in the morning, and I got the call from Wendell [Ashton]. Wendell had a wonderful knack of when he called you at one in the morning, the first question was, 'Mike, what time is it there?' And I always thought he should ask that question *before* he picked up the phone. So I said 'Well, it's about one in the morning.' . . . 'Oh ok, Mike!' Anyway, he told me that there was a young missionary called Kirk Anderson. 'Now, Kirk is still alive. . . . We obviously want to be really sensitive about this.' . . . He said this missionary had disappeared, the police felt that he had been kidnapped, it had been reported as a kidnapping, he was concerned that the media would get a hold of this, I needed to be aware of it and prepared. And he told me that there's been some history here . . . there's a woman that was pursuing him before his mission, and that he'd been assigned overseas a long way away [so] she could [not] find him, because she was kind of a stalker, we'd use the term stalker today, they didn't use that term back then. So I needed to be aware. Well the media picked up on this very, very quickly of course, they follow police reports and the police were looking for this young man.[3]

The missionary had been abducted at gunpoint and driven to a remote country cottage where Joyce McKinney forced him to have sex while he was chained to a bed.[4] Thankfully, Elder Anderson was able to get away three days later, at which time he contacted police and explained to his ecclesiastical leaders what had happened; they, along with the police, believed his account. The perpetrators, former model and Wyoming beauty queen McKinney, and her accomplice, Keith May, were soon arrested and taken to court—only to jump bail through devious means (including using ingenious disguises). For the Church in Britain, this was to become one of the twentieth century's most high-profile cases, mainly because of the story's many bizarre twists and turns. Recalling the nonstop media attention the story received, Otterson said, "The media publicity was absolutely unbelievable. It was intense! It was in the dailies day after day,

---

3. Michael and Cathy Otterson interview.

4. Under English law, forced sex is only considered rape if committed by a man.

Michael Otterson (left) with Elder Mark E. Petersen, President Spencer W. Kimball, and Sister Camilla Eyring Kimball. Courtesy Michael Otterson.

after day, after day, for a period of months. I mean *everyone* knew about this story."[5]

Press clippings of the time include the following:

The Sun September 17, 1977

Mormon Kidnap: Hunt for a Girl he Jilted

Police last night were hunting a rich, love-sick girl who may have had missing missionary Kirk Anderson kidnapped.[6]

Daily Express October 21, 1977

Fear of Mormon Revenge

American beauty queen Joyce McKinney lives in fear of Morman [*sic*] vengeance because of her passion for a missionary sworn to celibacy, a court heard yesterday.[7]

---

5. Michael and Cathy Otterson interview.
6. Robert Traini, "Mormon Kidnap: Hunt for a Girl He Jilted," 7.
7. Michael O'Flaherty, "Fear of Mormon Revenge."

Observer April 16, 1978

Mormon Girl Vanishes

Police have issued an alert to all British ports after the disappearance of the two people on bail in the Mormon kidnapping case—Joyce McKinney and Keith May.[8]

The Sun April 18, 1978

Mounties Join Hunt for Joyce

Canadian Mounties last night joined the hunt for runaway Joyce McKinney and her boyfriend Keith May.[9]

Understandably, there was worry among Latter-day Saints in Britain about the impact of the saga. In the eyes of many Church members, the situation was exacerbated when national newspapers printed front-page pictures of the Latter-day Saint temple garment.[10] The *Sunday People* banner headline "How the Mormons Lock out Lust" with the subheading "Chastity Suit Revealed" did not convey how Latter-day Saints regard the clothing: as sacred and personal. The article did, however, quote Otterson's clarification: "The garment is not a chastity belt. It is a reminder to the wearers to keep themselves away from immoral situations such as promiscuity, and to keep as morally clean as possible."[11]

Otterson's initial reaction to the McKinney saga, in terms of the Church and its reputation at that time, was "alarm." But he began to see what was happening. "Good will come out of this," Otterson would reas-

---

8. "Mormon Girl Vanishes."

9. Peter Bond, Robert Traini, Peter Game, "Mounties Join Hunt for Joyce," 1. The extraordinary story of Joyce McKinney's escape from justice using multiple identities made the *Daily Mail* front page, which reported that McKinney and her accomplice Keith May had traveled across the Atlantic disguised as "deaf mute" mime actors (see "The Mounties and the FBI Join in Big Hunt, Not So Dumb!," 1). The night before McKinney skipped bail, she had even put on an evening dress and posed for press photographers at a world movie premiere in London's West End (see Victor Swain, "48hr Delay in Bail Alert for Mormon Girl," 3). Fifteen months later, the FBI caught up with McKinney and May and they were held in a North Carolina county jail. Speaking for police in the UK, Scotland Yard's response was, "We are not seeking her extradition" (Peter Burden and Shaun Usher, "Yard Doesn't Want Sex-in-Chains Girl," 17). These were the sensational backstories about the kidnapper of a Latter-day Saint missionary.

10. Modest white underclothing worn by adults who are practicing followers of the faith to remind them of their covenants [promises] to God.

11. Clive Entwistle and Dan Wooding, "How the Mormons Lock Out Lust," 1.

sure others. The media fervor had given him access to the "typical tabloid press that you wouldn't normally deal with but once we had those contacts and we had the relationships with those journalists, it was so much easier to have conversations with them over other things that they might be interested in,"[12] including—notably—reporters at the *Sunday People*.

The Church's raised profile and its media response, driven by Otterson, produced proselyting success. Otterson remembered: "I saw a JAK Cartoon, he was a famous cartoonist at the *London Evening Standard*, and it had the little church, and then it had a long line of people waiting to get into the church. Then right at the end, it had a little cleric, a little clergyman, a Church of England minister speaking to somebody else saying,'Is this the line to join the Mormon church?'"[13] He continued,

> Frequently when the missionaries would knock on a door, people would say, "Oh, do you know that missionary? Do you know that Kirk Anderson?" Sometimes they'd mention him by name, and they'd want to talk about it. The missionaries would say, "Yeah, we do. But we're not here to talk about that, but we'd love to tell you why we're here and we'd love to tell you what our message is." Now it was *amazing* the success they had. Up till then, we were having about 2,000 baptisms a year, that particular year we had 4,000 baptisms.[14]

This membership spike was reported in the press:

The Daily Telegraph January 9, 1978

'Chains' Case Boosts the Mormons

Mormon Church leaders believe that recent publicity over the alleged kidnapping of the Mormon missionary, Mr Kirk Anderson, who was said to have been chained in bed, may eventually help the Church.

A public survey carried out under the direction of one of Mr Anderson's fellow missionaries, Mr Richard Eyre,[15] a marketing consultant, shows that nearly half the general public is now more aware of the Church than they were six months ago.

More than a quarter of the 1,038 people interviewed claimed they now understood more about the beliefs and standards of the Church of Jesus Christ of Latter Day Saints, the Mormons' full title.[16]

---

12. Michael and Cathy Otterson interview.

13. Michael and Cathy Otterson interview.

14. Michael and Cathy Otterson interview.

15. Richard Eyre was president of the England London South Mission, where Elder Kirk Anderson was serving.

16. "'Chains' Case Boosts Mormons," 13.

Media coverage referencing the Church on other topics was sometimes a mixed bag, reflecting as it did from time to time on events in the United States, with little relevance to the lives of British Latter-day Saints. One example was the Gary Gilmore case. Gilmore, convicted of murdering a motel manager in Provo, Utah, was the first person to be executed in the United States for almost ten years, after the death penalty was controversially reinstated by the US Supreme Court. This would have been shocking to some in the United Kingdom, where the last judicial hanging took place over a decade before the Gilmore execution. The *Observer* reported:

Death Wish Could Start a Bloodbath

The resolve of the condemned murderer, Gary Gilmore, 35, to die before a firing squad this week could start a virtual "bloodbath" of executions around the United States. That is the fear of American opponents of the death penalty, and especially black opponents. It is also the hope of many in this stronghold of Mormon justice.[17]

An altogether less somber subject attracted the attention of television viewers and newspaper readers in the run-up to Easter 1977. Jewish impresario and media owner Lord Grade commissioned and screened the British-Italian faith-based TV film epic *Jesus of Nazareth*. The £11 million drama was a big hit with audiences and critics. It was televised in the United Kingdom over two episodes—2 hours 45 minutes on Palm Sunday and 3 hours 15 minutes on Easter Day. Wendell J. Ashton, Church Public Communications managing director, was reported to have told Lord Grade, "We all should be most grateful . . . congratulations."[18] British Latter-day Saints were encouraged by the Church to view the programs with their families and—at a time when VCRs were not truly mass market—Sunday worship service schedules were even adjusted to accommodate this.

Saints Depicted on Television

Another media success was the rise of travelogue-based television shows. The programs might include wide vistas of the Western United States—"cowboy country" and "Mormon country"—as well as interviews

17. Charles Foley, "Death Wish Could Start a Bloodbath." Latter-day Saint church leaders at the time publicly stated their support for capital punishment in murder cases. The Church today distances itself from suggestions that it calls for execution as the morally right punishment for murder. See "Capital Punishment," The Church of Jesus Christ of Latter-day Saints.

18. Ronald Hastings, "How Lord Grade Decided to Do the Life of Jesus," 19.

with fascinating individuals. BBC Television featured veteran broadcaster Robert Robinson, who retraced "one of the world's great journeys—the Pioneer Trail west across the USA." Robinson followed the route of the Saints who were driven from their Illinois township on the Mississippi River in 1846 and crossed the plains to establish Salt Lake City. One viewer wrote to the BBC TV and radio listings magazine about the legacy of the Latter-day Saint pioneers, "Surely the perseverance with which its citizens succeed in making their gardens blossom amid the desert—not to mention the absence of juvenile delinquency in the city—has something to say about the pioneers and why they made the journey?"[19]

Not to be outdone, the rival television channel ITV carried a full-length documentary three weeks later in the *Whicker's World* series (*Whicker's World* was one of the longest-running programs on UK television). Alan Whicker's presentational style in the ITV show was much more tabloid than the BBC's conservative approach. *TV Times*, the TV guide, declared that in addition to Whicker's interviews with the Church's then prophet Spencer W. Kimball, the Osmond family, and Robert Redford's wife, Lola, Whicker "penetrates the forbidden nuclear blast–proof vaults where billions of names gathered from around the world [for family history purposes] . . . are kept on microfilm." The publication stated that Whicker also "meets the armed man who has been married 16 times and still has 12 wives, and the happier polygamist who declares: 'I only have two wives—I'm just a peanut in this business.'"[20] Needless to say, the polygamists would not have been members of The Church of Jesus Christ of Latter-day Saints. Despite some confusing juxtapositions within the show, the program provided the opportunity for some good press coverage that would have done the Church no harm. In an interview connected with *Whicker's World*, Otterson said, "We're a very family-orientated Church and one of our practices is to set aside every Monday, or one special day of the week, for the whole family to be together."[21]

Priesthood Ban Lifted

In a letter to the world presented on June 8, 1978, the First Presidency announced an important change to the Church's racial policy. Among other things, the letter stated that God "has heard our prayers, and by

---

19. Letter from Isabelle Bradley, "Salt Lake City Blues."
20. Ken Roche, "When Religion Costs You 10 Per Cent of Your Pay."
21. Roche, "Religion Costs."

revelation has confirmed that the long-promised day has come when every faithful, worthy man in the Church may receive the holy priesthood. . . . Accordingly, all worthy male members of the Church may be ordained to the priesthood without regard for race or color."[22] This announcement reversing its policy that excluded persons of African descent from priesthood ordination and temple worship made international headlines, including in Britain. The *Daily Telegraph* reported a few days later:

> The Mormon Church has lifted its ban on blacks serving in the priesthood, an increasing source of embarrassment in recent years. A direct revelation from God has led to the policy change, according to the Mormon's president, Mr. Spencer Kimball, [age] 83.[23]

The Church has long emphasized its doctrine that all humankind are children of a loving Creator. For example, the Book of Mormon affirms, "[God] denieth none that come unto him, black and white, bond and free, male and female; . . . and all are alike unto God."[24] However, the policy relating to people of African descent that appeared to run counter to this doctrine was an increasing challenge within multiracial societies and in the face of an expanding international missionary effort.

Otterson has vivid memories of the moment he found out about the Church's change. He was working late in his office on a Friday evening when the phone rang, and he immediately had the feeling that Salt Lake City was calling. When he picked up the phone, Wendell Ashton was on the line:

> "Mike, I want you to take this down verbatim," he said. Nobody said anything about the Priesthood, but I *knew* it was going to be revelation on the

---

22. "Official Declaration 2," The Church of Jesus Christ of Latter-day Saints.

23. Ian Brodie, "Mormon Ban on Black Priests Ends," 13.

24. 2 Nephi 26:33. In 2013 the Church published an essay on its website entitled "Race and the Priesthood" that provided a quick overview of the history of this policy. "Race and the Priesthood," The Church of Jesus Christ of Latter-day Saints. This essay also notes, "The structure and organization of the Church encourage racial integration. . . . The Church's lay ministry also tends to facilitate integration: a black bishop may preside over a mostly white congregation; a Hispanic woman may be paired with an Asian woman to visit the homes of a racially diverse membership. . . . Despite this modern reality, for much of its history—from the mid-1800s until 1978—the Church did not ordain men of black African descent to its priesthood or allow black men or women to participate in temple endowment or sealing ordinances. . . . Over time, Church leaders and members advanced many theories to explain the priesthood and temple restrictions. None of these explanations is accepted today as the official doctrine of the Church."

Priesthood before he even opened his mouth. . . . I just grabbed a piece of scrap paper, shoved it in the typewriter and I was typing with the phone between by chin and my shoulder, so there's all kinds of mistyping in it, but I've still got the piece of yellow paper that I typed [which] is now recorded as the formal revelation in the Doctrine and Covenants.[25]

Otterson deliberately made no effort to publish the story in the United Kingdom and instead left it to US news agencies to carry the reports to British national media outlets along with background explanations.

Church members of African descent were ecstatic following the announcement. George Rickford, a longtime faithful Latter-day Saint who was born in British Guiana (now Guyana) and settled in the United Kingdom, had found the pre-June 1978 policy extremely difficult to swallow. He reacted strongly when he heard about the policy from the missionaries: "I had a very hostile reaction," Rickford recalled. "I became very aggressive and after some heated discussion I kicked them out. . . . I gave them a real verbal tongue-lashing about discrimination and racism and all those kinds of words."[26] However, following a remarkable experience, Rickford overwhelmingly felt that he should make a leap of faith and be baptized into the Church:

My investigation prior to my baptism was such a challenging thing and my faith was tested so deeply, especially by the fact that I could not hold the priesthood. . . . But having conquered that and having had my answer from the Lord, a very personal answer for me, I was left with no doubt at all. I describe it as going on raw faith.[27]

Previous struggles were now history for Rickford. He was overjoyed when he found out he could be ordained to the priesthood. In fact, Otterson's first call after receiving the news was to Rickford to read him the official statement. Rickford struggled at first to process what he was hearing because the news was so unanticipated. He remembers, "As he [Otterson] read, the implications of what he was reading dawned on me and I just felt goose bumps coming all over. . . . He finished and he said, 'Are you still there?' I said, 'Does it say what I think it's saying?'"[28]

---

25. Michael and Cathy Otterson interview.

26. Elizabeth Maki, "I Will Take It in Faith: George Rickford and the Priesthood Restoration." The article includes references to George Rickford and June Rickford, interviewed by Matthew K. Heiss, 9.

27. Maki, "I Will Take It in Faith."

28. Maki, "I Will Take It in Faith."

The change was also greeted with overwhelming rejoicing from the majority of Latter-day Saints who realized that it opened the way to truly global outreach and closer Christian brotherhood and sisterhood. Yet, it has been a long haul—into the twenty-first century—for perceptions of the Latter-day Saint stance on race to be understood and embraced by advocacy groups. For example, the *Economist* (headquartered in London) described the recent (as of 2018) and growing relationship between the National Association for the Advancement of Colored People (NAACP) and the Church's senior leadership as "an improbable breakthrough." The publication underlined, "One of its early manifestations reflects the LDS ethos of self-reliance: in four inner cities the church is offering free courses on how poor people can manage their money. . . . These exercises amount to a cautious rapprochement between segments of American society that remain very different."[29]

Latter-day Saint Lifestyle Draws Attention

When it came to the Latter-day Saints' approach to clean living, some commentators were skeptical. Polly Toynbee's 1977 article in the *Guardian* cynically asserted, "Mormons don't smoke, drink or take tea or coffee. Statistically, they claim, they are the healthiest people in the world. Their most prized converts are young families. The missionaries are at their most lyrical when extolling the virtues of family life. It's so sugary that it sets your teeth on edge."[30]

A defense of Latter-day Saints' lifestyles—but not their theology—came quickly from York's Labour Member of Parliament Alex Lyon, who said,

> I am sorry Polly Toynbee . . . should have been quite so scathing about the Mormons. I once spent three days in Salt Lake City trying to understand them. Their theology is bad; the Book of Mormon . . . is absurd; their religious paintings and architecture are distressingly naïve. But they have one all-redeeming quality. They practice what they preach.[31]

---

29. Erasmus, "Overcoming the Mormon Legacy on Race: Building Bridges Between an Anti-racist Movement and a Conservative Faith."

30. Polly Toynbee, "Mormons Don't Smoke, Drink or Take Tea or Coffee. Statistically, They Claim, They Are the Healthiest People in The World. Their Most Prized Converts Are Young Families. The Missionaries Are at Their Most Lyrical When Extolling the Virtues of Family Life. It's So Sugary That It Sets Your Teeth on Edge," 9.

31. Alex Lyon MP, "Mormon Spirit."

It was the faith's "practical religion" that pundits noted and often extolled. The 1978 Church-produced film *Mormons: Fact and Fantasy* portrayed—in just under half an hour—a church whose members were beginning to make their mark on British society and impress opinion leaders. Interviewees were Lancashire-born Rhodes Boyson MP, Conservative Member of Parliament for Brent North; Canon Gordon Bates, Canon at Liverpool Cathedral and a radio journalist; and Lord Thomson of Fleet, *The Times* owner who became Canada's richest businessman. The film was narrated by BBC newsreader Richard Baker and put together in a current-affairs style. Shot in Britain and produced in Canada, it was designed to be an "honest, uncontrived documentary."[32] The film itself got press attention and was faith-affirming for impressed British Church members.

Baker's narration began, "American, extremist, misunderstood—a few of the labels popularly tagged to this remarkable religion which is probably Britain's fastest-growing faith. . . . The Mormons' ability to combine religious faith with a practical lifestyle, especially their passionate attachment to the ideal of family life, seems to have special appeal for the British." Canon Bates compared and contrasted theological differences between The Church of Jesus Christ of Latter-day Saints and mainstream Christian churches. He emphasized, "One of the things which I admire certainly about the Mormon Church is their belief that Jesus Christ is the Savior and that people really come to belief through the acceptance of Christ through baptism for the remission of sins and through the laying on of hands." He added that "the Mormon Church" has a "real commitment to the family which . . . we would see as part of the great Christian tradition." He encouraged members of the established churches "to meet Mormons and to talk with them about the things they have in common," which would result in "more and more Christians in this country" beginning "to accept Mormons as fellow Christians." But he underlined, "I think it's equally important that the members of the Mormon Church begin to meet other Christians from other denominations and begin to see them as Christians too."[33] Bates was wise in his assessment. Interfaith interactions between The Church of Jesus Christ of Latter-day Saints and other

---

32. "People Around the World 'Meet the Mormons'—in Their Own Language," 78–79; Interview with John G. Kinnear. *Mormons: Fact and Fantasy* (1978) was directed by Karl Konnry.

33. Canon Gordon Bates interview, in *Mormons: Fact and Fantasy*.

Christian faiths were taking place to some degree in the 1970s, but such activity was certainly in its infancy.

A Pragmatic Approach to Religion

The physical infrastructure of the "British Zion" was still being established by local congregants. Between 1973 and 1982, a new Latter-day Saint chapel was completed in Britain every seven weeks.[34] This reflected the rise of convert baptisms, which increased British membership from 67,849 in 1970 to 87,776 in 1980.[35] Local Saints contributed both time and money to the building efforts, and by the late 1970s, a fifth of new chapel building costs were typically being raised through local member contributions. Much of the work for each meetinghouse was done by a few dozen worshippers who often committed to provide many hours of on-site labor weekly (overseen by the Church's full-time building supervisors who were assigned to work locally). For example, by 1975, the Enfield branch (less than ten years old) in north London enjoyed steady growth and was preparing to construct a new meeting house with the direct help of its nearly 300 members. The faith journey of more recently baptized members was taken up by the press. The Enfield branch president at the time had been a member for just four years and reflected on the new converts joining the Church. The local newspaper reported that he and his wife, who had two young sons, "were converted after visiting some American relatives. . . . They brought back a niece with them and through her, became interested in the Latter-day Saints and eventually joined."[36] The branch president "used to go to church and was Church of England but he always felt something was missing."[37]

Mormons Suggest Farm Job Instead of Dole

This faith-based, pragmatic approach to religion had potential benefits for wider society. This attracted the media spotlight, especially with

34. Derek A. Cuthbert, *The Second Century: Latter-day Saints in Great Britain,* 1:184.

35. V. Ben Bloxham, James R. Moss, and Larry C. Porter, eds., *Truth Will Prevail: The rise of the Church of Jesus Christ of Latter-day Saints in the British Isles, 1837–1987,* 442.

36. "Mormons Plan Chapel in Enfield."

37. "Mormons Plan Chapel in Enfield."

the Church's approach to helping people improve their lives during economic hard times. As the United Kingdom faced greater joblessness, British Church leaders said that they had a novel alternative, and the press picked up the story:

> The Mormons' alternative system to the dole queue, which it is claimed will save the Government £6 million a year, was outlined in Norwich last night. Mr. Kenneth Johnson, Norwich stake president covering East Anglia, told a missionary meeting at the Central Library that the church was also at present looking in East Anglia for a 1000-acre farm to buy. . . . Mr. Johnson said that three per cent of their church members were drawing benefits as against six per cent of the population. By taking that three per cent off they would be saving the Government £6 million.[38]

In the words of the (London) *Times* publisher Lord Thomson of Fleet, the Latter-day Saints had ambitious but achievable aims, wanting to be as self-reliant as possible with the goal of good schooling for their children too:

> With a special dedication to self-improvement, to hard personal endeavor, and frankly lofty objectives—they aim high in anything they seem to wish to do. . . . [O]ne of the most beneficial things they can do for their children is to confer upon them the tools with which to be happy and successful in their lives, and I think they feel that education plays a very important role in that future for their children.[39]

These were to be key principles for the many multigenerational Latter-day Saint families that made their way within British society and the world. This increasingly visible faith and its growing membership continually drew the attention of the British media in a predominantly positive way during the decade of the '70s—and that attention would only continue to grow.

---

38. "Mormons Suggest Farm Job Instead of Dole," 3.
39. Lord Thomson of Fleet interview, in *Mormons: Fact and Fantasy* (1978).

CHAPTER 9

The 1980s and 1990s:
Spaghetti Cans and Lancashire's Legacy

I think we like them very much and we always did like them,
but we like them better now.
— Lord Clitheroe, Downham, Lancashire

Pictured on the front page of the thought-leading *Sunday Times Magazine*, a fair-haired man in a suit sits confidently on top of hundreds of cans of Heinz "spaghetti in tomato sauce." What is the point of such a quirky image, seemingly poles apart from anything at all religious? This *tableau vivant* was depicted on the November 15, 1987, issue with the intriguing caption, "This man is a Mormon. His church is growing faster than Sainsbury's. So why does he need all the food?"[1]

Bryan Grant, who the magazine notes is "the Mormons' public relations chief in Britain," was the man in the photograph. The story context was summarized just inside the front cover: "The saints come marching in. Never underestimate the Mormons—they work hard, love their families and always know where the next meal is coming from."[2] The magazine photo was both an attention-grabbing cover for the publication's weekend readers and an iconic image for the Church and its Public Affairs people (composed of staffers and field volunteers).

Cans of food were also used as props for other public outreach, emphasizing the Church's principles of caring for the needy and self-reliance. Just before the dawn of the 1980s, soon after Margaret Thatcher became Prime Minister, Michael Otterson delivered several cans of "Deseret" brand vegetables to 10 Downing Street—the brand produced by Church welfare operations that money literally could not buy.[3] It was a simple goodwill gesture, and several food cans were also sent to media outlets. For security

---

1. Front page photo and caption to story by Keith Wheatley, "The Saints Come Marching In," 54–61.

2. Wheatley, 3.

3. Deseret-branded commodities are available from Church-owned bishops' storehouses, which are sometimes compared to "supermarkets without tills." Needy people receive a written requisition from their congregation leader and have opportunities to work for what they receive, according to their ability.

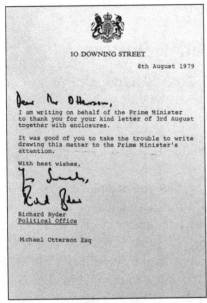

10 DOWNING STREET

8th August 1979

Dear Mr Otterson,

I am writing on behalf of the Prime Minister
to thank you for your kind letter of 3rd August
together with enclosures.

It was good of you to take the trouble to write
drawing this matter to the Prime Minister's
attention.

With best wishes,

Richard Ryder
Political Office

Michael Otterson Esq

Thank you letter from the Prime Minister's office, 10 Downing Street. Supplied by Michael Otterson.

reasons, the end of Downing Street was sealed off, but the police let Otterson through, and then through the front door of Number 10 where his brown paper package was inspected and then accepted.

"The can did indeed make it to the Prime Minister," Otterson said. "I still have the thank-you letter [from Margaret Thatcher's office] in my journal."[4]

The Church's theme of caring for your own and for your neighbor was to continue. Two significant developments took place in 1980 that would assist the Church in helping others: the purchase of a 305-acre farm in Worcestershire that included dairy and meat-producing herds, and the creation of the first UK bishops' storehouse in Birmingham (with "mobile bishops' storehouses" to follow) that provided food and home essentials.[5] The Church's holistic approach to Christianity soon led to the Church opening employment centers, forming an adoption agency, and providing counseling services.[6] Five years later, these efforts would take a global but focused scale as many Church members worldwide, including in the United Kingdom, went without food for special fasts and made special donations—raising over $11 million to provide aid for those caught in the devastating Ethiopian famine that had caused so much suffering.[7] (Nearly two decades later, in 1999, Church-owned farms in Eastern England donated

---

4. Michael and Cathy Otterson interview. The letter from Downing Street was dated August 8, 1979, following Otterson's covering note to the Prime Minister dated August 3, 1979, along with the food cans.

5. Baugh, "The Church in Twentieth-Century Great Britain: A Historical Overview," 237–59.

6. Anne S. Perry, "The Contemporary Church," 429.

7. "The Origins of Latter-day Saint Charities," *Latter-day Saint Charities Blog.*

over £307,000 to charitable causes, including help for a women's refuge center in Birmingham and overseas flood and hurricane relief.[8])

Church membership continued to grow throughout the decade, along with the organizational growth of more places of worship and additional programs to help members and friends with personal development and family solidarity. As the children of Latter-day Saints baptized during the 1960s began to have families of their own, a second and third generation of Church membership—many hundreds of whom had been missionaries themselves—contributed to the rich tapestry of life within town or city congregations and in the wider community.[9]

Making Their Mark in Serving the Community

The older stalwarts also made their mark as Saints. Jack Watson had joined the Church in 1961 and worked as a train driver for his day job. He was also a busy Latter-day Saint bishop in Dunfermline for over a decade, between 1982 and 1995, and a chairman of the neighborhood council. According to his son Daryl Watson, Jack was even getting invited to community lunches held by the town's funeral directors, which helped Latter-day Saints get noticed and serve more effectively in the town:

> Dad really believed in looking outward and being part of the community.
> . . . [The] local funeral company, which was having annual luncheons and dinners, they'd never invited a Mormon bishop. So Dad said, "Why am I not invited to this? Why can't I come along?" So, lo and behold, [the] first Mormon bishop gets an invite to go along to the local funeral parlor annual luncheon. What does that start to do? It starts to break down barriers. It starts them actually saying, "See those Mormons? They're actually okay, they're good people. They're actually doing things in the community, and their values are really positive, and they're making a difference, and they want to serve, and they're actually doing things that are good and they're contributing."[10]

During the 1980s and 1990s, it became increasingly common for stakes and bigger congregations to engage in large-scale days of service to benefit the community.[11] For example, "Make a Difference Day" gave

---

8. "Church Farms Provide Aid," 2.

9. "The Origins of Latter-day Saint Charities." In 1983, Great Britain provided over 400 full-time missionaries.

10. Daryl Watson, interviewed by Fred E. Woods and Martin Andersen.

11. During the early '90s, this increased focus on community bridge building was emphasized in the Church's Public Affairs program, which became broader

Jack and Margaret Watson and children, Dunfermline, Scotland, 1960s.
Courtesy Daryl Watson.

Latter-day Saints an opportunity to mobilize their membership and "make
a difference" with en masse service on one designated day in the area—
whether it was clearing overgrown weeds, painting fences, or cleaning up
graffiti. This was the beginning of large-scale community service that was
later to become known as "Mormon Helping Hands."[12]

---

based in its scope. Public Affairs UK office staffers trained regional volunteers on
this type of outreach.

12. In various countries during the 1990s, especially in South America,
this type of well-received activity began to come under the "Helping Hands"

In 1987, the Church's London-based young single adults congregation, with many other young people from the London area and beyond, linked up with top entertainment stars for an event supporting seriously ill children, in association with the charity Dreams Come True. Peter Moore, Town Crier of London, welcomed around three hundred children from across Britain who were excited to meet their idols.[13] The celebrities turned out in force—singers Bob Geldof, Paul Young, Rick Astley, and Dave Stewart, together with boxer John Conteh and a host of other celebrities.[14] Singing star Rick Astley performed his hit single "Never Gonna Give You Up" to a delighted audience.[15] Two hundred and fifty young Latter-day Saints supported the event that was planned to bring joy to the hearts of sick children. The gathering attracted national publicity, including a front-page photo in *The Sunday Times*.[16]

Among British Latter-day Saint humanitarians of the late twentieth century, Carol Gray stands out—for her personal strength, courage, and sheer determination against the odds.[17] In 1992, this visionary Relief Society president of her Sheffield congregation was moved to act after witnessing television news reports of extreme suffering during the civil war in the former Yugoslavia.[18] Soon, her own selfless, single-minded efforts would receive media attention. For much of the 1990s, Gray organized dozens

umbrella. Church members in the UK took up the initiative in the 2000s and donned the yellow, highly visible "Mormon Helping Hands" vests. "Helping Hands" became the official program for the Church's Europe West Area from September 2004. The program soon became well established: "In September 2006 members in the Bristol England Stake worked within their community to improve a struggling community farm. In one day, members were able to work on a wheelchair access path; paint; dig; clean; and build educational toys, bird boxes, and feeders for the farm. More than 2,500 hours of service were given, and the improvement was noticeable. The local mayor visited the farm, expressed his gratitude, and said how impressed he was with what had been accomplished." See "Mormon Helping Hands Completes First Decade of Service."

13. LBC, London radio broadcast, September 27, 1987.

14. "A Dream Come True," 104.

15. "Dreams Come True." Malcolm Adcock stood next to the stage as Rick Astley sang.

16. Photo caption on front page, "High, you up there," 1. This book's coauthor Malcolm Adcock supported media outreach.

17. See Carol R. Gray, *Miracles Among the Rubble: Bringing Convoys of Humanitarian Aid, Hugs, and Hope to a War-torn Region.*

18. Kate Holbrook, "Housewife in a Foreign War Zone."

of convoys of relief supplies to war-torn areas across Croatia, Kosovo, and Bosnia, personally leading on-the-ground efforts in the Balkans at least thirty-four times.[19] One Christmastime, due to lack of funds to cover all transportation costs, it was touch-and-go whether a large number of donated seasonal gifts would make it to children in refugee camps and orphanages. Gray reflected stalwartly, "But the children were waiting for us . . . we must use our faith."[20] Her Christian convictions shined through then and during all the darkest hours. "I know that doors and even the heavens have opened to help me," she said.[21] Gray received numerous accolades and awards including, in 1998, Britain's Woman of the Year Award.[22]

Seminary Makes Its Mark in Britain

The Latter-day Saint program of daily—often early morning—religious education for young people (seminary) helped Church youth get grounded in Christian living, and it caught the media's attention as well. The *Times Educational Supplement* (*TES*) reported in 1998 that "more than 2,600 teenage British Mormons . . . follow the church's education programme."[23] David Cook, then Area Director (Europe North) for the Church Educational System, was quoted as saying that seminary is "a missionary preparation course in the broadest sense of the word,"[24] as it helped the individuals enrolled gain confidence in sharing the gospel. The *TES* also highlighted seminary's role in teaching principles of parenthood and emphasized that it helps young people solidify commitment to their faith: "The education programme teaches Mormon teenagers to resist the temptations found outside the church."[25]

According to Cook, one seminary group even met in a school (at Rawtenstall, around twenty miles from Preston, England) in the mornings before main school classes began for the day: "[A]ll of the young people who were members of the Church [in that area] happened to go to the same

---

19. Gray, *Miracles Among the Rubble*. Gray died in 2010, following a final battle with cancer. In the preceding years, she had extended her humanitarian influence to Ghana.

20. Gray, *Miracles Among the Rubble*.

21. "Bound for Bosnia," The Church of Jesus Christ of Latter-day Saints.

22. Gray, *Miracles Among the Rubble*.

23. Sarah Cassidy, "Ready to Knock on the Door of Adult Life."

24. Cassidy, "Adult Life."

25. Cassidy, "Adult Life."

high school."[26] The class was taught by a member of the Latter-day Saint congregation who was on the staff of the high school. Cook later found out that the request to hold seminary there had to go to the highest level at the Department of Education and Science in London to gain approval.

For individual students in other areas who could not meet face-to-face because of distance, and long before Zoom and video call capability, seminary organizers set up telephone conference calls. Cook explained:

> They conducted it as if they were present. "We'd like to welcome you to seminary this morning. Are you there in such and such a home?" "Yeah." "Good morning. Would you pray for us? And then we've got the [brief] spiritual [message] here." And then interact, and other interaction as if they were in the room. . . . [T]hey were probably in their pyjamas still, but they had the scriptures in front of them and they made contributions. And the teacher would invite them to participate as if they were in the room. It was a wonderful experience.[27]

More Experienced Lay Leadership

The 1980s and 1990s also saw greater ecclesiastical integration at the congregation level and regionally, through experienced British lay leadership who were becoming less dependent on direction from Church headquarters. Sometimes there were cultural differences between American mission leaders and British ecclesiastical leaders (with the latter on occasion questioning new converts' level of commitment to their newfound faith).[28] But responsibility for missionary work and the integration of recent converts was increasingly emphasized as a joint responsibility—shared between local leadership and the mission president and his missionaries.

There was also a need to understand the application of Church programs in the context of the British cultural experience. "British reserve," where Brits are less likely to share private feelings including about religion, may militate against evangelization by some Latter-day Saints within their friendship groups. Yet, the greater prominence of the Church in the UK

---

26. David Cook, interviewed by Malcolm Adcock.

27. David Cook interview.

28. See Madison H. Thomas, "The Influence of Traditional British Social Patterns on LDS Church Growth in Southwest Britain," 1–11. The author of this essay was president of the England Bristol Mission (1982–1985) and afterwards served a public communications mission in New York City.

public sphere during this time gave its members greater confidence in referring to their membership during informal conversations with friends.

Opposition and Positive Outcomes

Despite the increased positive attention the Church was receiving, it was not free from opposition in the UK public square. In 1985, the anti-Mormon film, *The Godmakers*, made its way to British shores. Produced by campaigners from the United States and made widely available on videocassette, the film was a sensational exposé of Latter-day Saint beliefs and practices that attempted to marginalize their theology and portray the Church as being in opposition to Christianity. The full-time Public Communications Director in the United Kingdom, Bryan Grant, and the London mission president, Harold Goodman, were both interviewed by the filmmakers under false pretenses.[29] Although the film had limited cinema showings in the United Kingdom, its American evangelical framing likely had little resonance for the majority of British people. The greatest impact of the film may have been to preserve stereotypes of Latter-day Saints in certain parts of the Christian community.

As had been the case since Latter-day Saint missionaries began preaching in Britain a century and a half earlier, some local newspapers continued to report negative views about the Church during this era. One reader's letter to the *Surrey and Hants News* from September 1981 was contemptuous of "the smooth-suited young men with the short back and sides seen in town centres locally waylaying passers-by to peddle their own particular brand of philosophy as Mormons."[30] Within days, a retort appeared in the *Camberley News*:

> I have no connection whatsoever with the Mormon Church. Having studied Mormon beliefs in some detail, I would have to admit, if pressed, that I find them strange and impossible to accept. However I have always been deeply impressed with the Mormons I have met – both in this country and in North America. Without exception they have proved themselves polite, courteous, generous and friendly.[31]

Both printed letters are indicative of the continued attention Latter-day Saints attracted on television and in the tabloid press. In 1981, ITV's cleverly titled program "The Mormon Conquest," with its wordplay on

---

29. Bryan Grant, conversation with Malcolm Adcock, 1983.
30. Anne S. Perry, "The Contemporary Church," 435.
31. Perry, 435–36.

the "Norman Conquest" of the eleventh century, was aired on the main commercial television channel. At least thirty-one people decided to join the Church after Latter-day Saint missionaries invited them to watch the show.[32] There were also headlines in the popular *Sunday Mirror* referring to the teetotal habits of Fred Bishop MBE, the Latter-day Saint firefighter who rescued Cabinet minister Norman Tebbit following a terrorist bomb. The government minister had sent Bishop a bottle of whisky as a token of appreciation, presumably unaware that he was "on the wagon," and the newspaper declared that it is the "[t]hought that counts, Norm."[33]

Other Latter-day Saints in the public eye included broadcaster David Fewster, one of only a few Church members in the United Kingdom who worked in the media. The first voice that was aired on Viking Radio in Hull (the local commercial radio broadcaster) at its launch in March 1984 was Fewster's; he was to become the station's director of programming. "I consider this a privilege and an honor to represent, in a sense, Latter-day Saints in the media," he said.[34] Fewster further commented, "My Church membership is well known at the [radio] station, and I frequently get into very positive discussions about the Church with staff members."[35]

For the filming of one BBC TV program in October 1988 about Latter-day Saints, twenty-two-year-old Kevin Johnson "stood in a circle of light, surrounded by darkness."[36] Inquisitors from the studio audience "emerged in turn from the shadows to fire questions at him and then disappeared again into the darkness." This was all part of the BBC's approach to youth culture for its series "A–Z of Belief." It was a grueling experience for Johnson, but he was robust in his responses. At least four people reportedly joined the Church through baptism after viewing the show, again demonstrating the positive repercussions of Church representation in mainstream media.

---

32. Perry, 436, referencing the *Church News*, October 24, 1981, 5. A program with the same name, *The Mormon Conquest*, was also broadcast on BBC Radio 4 on July 21, 1987, compiled and presented by Ian Bradley (see also Ian Bradley, "Living by the Book," 13).

33. Perry, "The Contemporary Church," 436, referencing the *Sunday Mirror*, August 18, 1985.

34. Bryan J. Grant, "David Fewster: Sending a Clear Signal," 58–59. David Fewster later worked in senior roles with the Church's Public Affairs Department, including in the UK as Director of the Europe West Area.

35. Grant, "David Fewster: Sending a Clear Signal."

36. Lesley Baxter, "Church Member Appears on BBC TV Series."

Annie Across America was a 1992 ITV network series presented by Belfast-born television travel journalist Anne Gregg, combining tourism and religion with its focus on "Christianity in the United States."[37] Referring to the religious diversity the show explored, Gregg had said she was fascinated by "the totally oppos[ing] views of people who all profess to be Christians,"[38] and one commentator described *Annie Across America* as being about "odd religious sects."[39] It made sense then that The Church of Jesus Christ of Latter-day Saints was featured in the series with a visit by Gregg to the Church's headquarters in Salt Lake City. In that episode it was clear that Gregg was impressed by her family discovery experience at the Church's Family History Library, and her coverage of the "Mormons" had a fairly warm approach.

A few years later, Latter-day Saints would again be the focus on British television, when full-time missionary Elder Mark Dundon and his associates in the Church's London Mission were part of a technically groundbreaking program in the BBC's well-respected *Everyman* religion series in 1995.[40] The episode "Knocking on Heaven's Door" used a specially designed set of spectacles with a built-in mini camera so the missionaries' doorstep conversations could be captured for the show's five million viewers. An underwater camera was also used to film a simulated baptism. The program received high critical acclaim.

Church Sesquicentennial in Britain

The year 1987 was a landmark year, marking 150 years since the first Latter-day Saint missionaries docked in Liverpool. A three-day celebration was held July 24–26 throughout Britain, and global Church leaders traveled the land, including Church President Ezra Taft Benson, First Counselor Gordon B. Hinckley, four other Apostles, and many other Church leaders. This visit by the Church's international leaders was a time for them to interact with the Saints both one-on-one and in large gatherings. "Flocking to hear a 'prophet of God'" was how a British newspaper characterized a two-hour gathering at Wembley Arena, where members

---

37. "Anne Gregg, Travel Journalist and Broadcaster," *Independent*.

38. "Anne Gregg, Travel Journalist and Broadcaster."

39. "Anne Gregg," *Press Gazette*.

40. "Knocking on Heaven's Door," 81. The program was broadcast September 24, 1995.

were on a "pilgrimage to Wembley."[41] The visit also presented an opportunity for Church leadership to engage with British government representatives and other opinion formers. For example, to commemorate the anniversary of missionaries arriving in Britain, the Church provided anniversary celebration gifts for the Queen and the Prime Minister: the newly published pocket edition of Latter-day Saint scriptures and a reproduction of an early edition of the Book of Mormon that had been presented to Queen Victoria and Prince Albert in 1841.[42]

Peter Trebilcock related how as bishop of the Preston ward—the Church's longest continuous congregation globally—he came to invite President Hinckley (who had served as a missionary in Great Britain from 1933 to 1935, including in Preston) to be part of their Preston ward reunion and other memorable events in the area for the 150th anniversary year. On assignment from the stake president, Trebilcock wrote to Hinckley directly and did not really expect a response; however, a response did come a few evenings later when he received a phone call from Hinckley:

> "Hello Bishop, how are you?"
> "I was alright until you phoned, President."
> "I've got your note, what's the plan?"
> When I could remember what the plan was, I said, "Well, President, we're going to have a whole day of celebration in Preston. We're going to tour the historic sites, the River Ribble where the first converts were baptized, where the missionaries lived. We're going to hold a conference" (in the biggest facility that we could hire in the day). "We'd love you to come out, we're going to finish off with a ward social in the chapel."
> He said, "It sounds good. I'm going to come."
> Wow. "Thank you, President."
> "Cheerio," he said.
> "Tara," to be English kind of.
> So he came. He came in July 1987.[43]

During his visit, Hinckley dedicated a commemorative plaque in Avenham Park near the banks of the River Ribble to mark the first British baptisms on July 30, 1837. Trebilcock spent the whole day at President Hinckley's side:

---

41. "Flocking to Hear a 'Prophet of God.'"
42. "Scenes of the 150th Anniversary Celebration."
43. Peter Trebilcock, interviewed by Malcolm Adcock and Fred E. Woods.

When President Hinckley arrived at the station, I had an itinerary planned. . . . He said, "Yes, that's fine, but I'm going to show you somewhere." And he told the driver to go right, go left. . . . He said, "I'm going to the chapel." He said, "I'm going to the River Ribble." And ended up at his house, 15 Wadham Road. He said, "Bishop, this was my first place. This is where I lived when I was a missionary." He got Sister Hinckley out of the car; he had the temerity to go to the front door. A little old lady answered the door and I was out of earshot, but he told this later in conference. . . . He said, "Well, I rented one of the rooms." She said, "Would you like to come in?" "Oh, please." And they went in. "Which room was it?" "It was upstairs." "Would you like to go upstairs?" "Yes, please." . . . "Which room?" It was the front bedroom. She said, "You can go in the bedroom but please don't get in the bed!" "Okay, okay." But it was in that room that he wrote that letter to his father. And it was in that room that he opened up his scriptures with his companion where they read, "Lose yourself in the service of others."[44] And he said, "I made a pledge in Preston." You could tell it [was] a very special place. It was a turning point in his life. And of course what a great life of service. And he shared with us those thoughts.[45]

The next day, 12,000 members of the Church packed into the National Exhibition Centre near Birmingham, and Hinckley expressed that "he had never dreamed he would return to participate in such a historic celebration."[46]

The Mormon Tabernacle Choir Stirs Hearts

On June 14, 1998, at London's Royal Albert Hall, the Mormon Tabernacle Choir moved some audience members to tears after the Choir's associate director Craig Jessop invited them to stand and join in with the patriotic hymn "Jerusalem," from English poet William Blake's writings.[47] The Sunday morning performance in the iconic hall was recorded by the BBC for rebroadcast on the popular *Songs of Praise* Christian music program. The show's presenter, Welsh tenor Sir Harry Secombe, said, "The Tabernacle Choir is like four Welsh choirs combined." He added, "The

---

44. At a time of great discouragement, accompanied by severe hay fever, the young Elder Hinckley wrote to his father and received a short reply. "Responding as both father and stake president, Bryant Hinckley sent a reply that was brief and to the point: 'Dear Gordon, I have your recent letter. I have only one suggestion: forget yourself and go to work.'" See Sheri L. Dew, *Go Forward with Faith*, 64.

45. Peter Trebilcock interview.

46. See Dew, *Go Forward with Faith*, 452.

47. Gerry Avant, "Choir Begins Europe Tour in Famed London Hall," 3; the song "Jerusalem" is England's unofficial anthem.

choir is fantastic. It has that same sort of spiritual feel. They're not just singing the words, they feel them. That's what Welsh choirs do."[48]

Special Announcement Opens the Way for a Second British Temple

An extensive remodeling of the London Temple had been completed in 1992 with the temple open for public tours for the first time in thirty-four years, as pointed out by *The Independent*.[49] During rededication services at the temple held October 18–20, 1992, President Gordon B. Hinckley recalled his own life as a missionary in Britain during the 1930s and how, as a newly called Apostle at the time of the original 1958 dedication services, he lived with his family in a home on the temple grounds for a month.[50] Now, as First Counselor in the Church's governing First Presidency, he reflected on the faith and heritage of the British Saints over decades of history. Reading from an address he had originally delivered thirty-four years previously at the first dedication, Hinckley said,

> All of the sacrifices of all who have gone before are a part of the price, of the cost, of this house of the Lord in which we worship today. . . . This building cannot be reckoned alone in terms of pounds sterling; it must be reckoned in terms of struggle and sacrifice and devotion and loyalty and love and faith and testimony and conviction. What a price it has cost! But it has been worth every farthing because it now offers to the people of this and other lands the wholeness of the everlasting gospel of Jesus Christ.[51]

In total, over 13,000 people attended the ten rededication sessions. As well as the spiritual uplift from the special events, there was some very good news for the faithful. On October 19, Hinckley announced that the Church had bought land and would build a second British temple, this time near Preston in Chorley.[52] He had been involved in the selection of the fifteen-acre temple site and, as it turned out, had a hands-on interest in the project as it progressed.[53]

Two years later, on June 12, 1994, Hinckley returned to conduct the groundbreaking ceremonies for the Preston England Temple, and four

---

48. Avant, "Choir Begins Europe Tour."

49. "The London Temple of the Church of Jesus Christ of Latter-Day Saints."

50. Gerry Avant, "Temple Rededicated, Lives Renewed," 9.

51. Avant, "Temple Rededicated, Lives Renewed."

52. Avant, "Temple Rededicated, Lives Renewed."

53. Baugh, "The Church in Twentieth-Century Great Britain: A Historical Overview," 251.

years after that he returned again (this time as President of the Church) to preside over the dedication of the Preston England Temple, which took place over fifteen dedicatory sessions between June 7 and June 10, 1998.[54] The temple site incorporated a missionary training center, a retail distribution center, a stake center, a family history center, and housing for temple patrons and temple workers. As thousands had joined the Church in this region during the mid-nineteenth century, so thousands of Latter-day Saints would now travel to Chorley for temple worship.

But around the time that the Church first announced the Preston Temple project, some residents expressed opposition. Disinformation spread in the vicinity, including from a trifold pamphlet distributed via an Anglican-run primary school. "It was 'anti-Mormon' literature," according to Latter-day Saint volunteer Public Affairs worker Marie Hunt. "My five-year-old came out of school one day and she had in her hand an envelope. And she said they said to give this to you. And it contained a pamphlet that they had given to every child in the infant and in the junior school which was calling out the Church for being a sect."[55]

Bernard Walsh, who served as a Latter-day Saint bishop in the area, said that during this time there was "lots of misinformation" being promoted in Chorley about the Church: "plural marriage, all of those things. . . . People were very negative about that, baptisms for the dead, for instance, they thought that we had dead people in the temple." [56]

Apart from this theological platform adopted by some ministers in the town, the local council in Preston was not impressed with the temple development either. By this time, Trebilcock was working for the Church-appointed architects. "[T]he first thing we did was to go and see the local council, the city officials who would need to give consent. And we went with some pictures of some temples of the Church and said we'd been commissioned to design this work. And you know what they said to us? 'Go away. We don't want a temple.'"[57] Discouraged, Trebilcock wrote to Hinckley and told him about the opposition. Hinckley wrote back and said, "Brother Trebilcock, we're delighted you're involved. We have every confidence in you."[58]

---

54. See the dedicatory prayer offered by President Gordon B. Hinckley in Appendix B.

55. Marie Hunt interview.

56. Bernard Walsh, interviewed by Malcolm Adcock and Fred E. Woods.

57. Peter Trebilcock interview.

58. Peter Trebilcock interview.

Preston England Temple. Courtesy Europe Area Communication Department.

With that prophetic message, Trebilcock and his team got to work and went back to the municipal council with other pictures and images, but council officials insisted, "The local councilors have landmarked this land for business use. For employment, for hotels, for bars, for offices, and you want a temple? That's not going to employ many people, so please would you ask the Church to reconsider?"[59] Still undeterred, Trebilcock and his team got together with Church members and knocked on the doors of municipal councilors, one of whom was the late Councilor (Cllr.) Ralph Snape MBE, Mayor of Chorley, who worked with a recently converted Church member (his Church membership was initially unknown to the mayor). Trebilcock explained that the mayor had "seen a change in this man's life, and he said 'Well, okay, let me tell you something. Last Christmas Day, I had two missionaries in my home [for] Christmas dinner. And I've also visited Salt Lake City and your people are the salt of the earth. You've got my support.'"[60]

However, when Trebilcock phoned an influential councilor for his view, it appeared there was another roadblock. He was again told, "[Your church] bought the prime piece of real estate in the whole of Chorley and

59. Peter Trebilcock interview.
60. Peter Trebilcock interview.

I want jobs, not a temple."[61] Prospects changed for the better, though, after they were able to meet with local residents:

> [S]omebody asked a question that changed the entire course of the events. They asked what the quality [of the temple] would be like. . . . I was prompted to ask and invite, "Has anybody in the group ever visited a temple site?" [A reply came from a resident,] "I have visited one of your temple sites," and he didn't say which one, "But the grounds were just beautiful, the quality was first-class, and it was absolutely wonderful," and then, without prompting, he pointed to his neighbors and said, "Look, this will be the best neighbor that you will ever have."[62]

When it came to the night of the vote at the council, the first person to speak was the influential councilor who had wanted an economic development rather than a temple. He announced that he had reversed his stance: "I've looked into this. It will be a wonderful development. . . . It will be a landmark for our town and a wonderful neighbor to have and I say we should support this temple one hundred percent."[63] There was not one vote of opposition, and plans for the temple went ahead. Previous Chorley Mayor Cllr. Snape, who admired the loyalty of Latter-day Saints, reflected on the episode decades later. "We won the day!" he declared, adding that he and his wife Cllr. Joyce Snape were delighted to attend community events and join the congregation for public worship: "[W]hen we were finished, we went in and we went to the services."[64]

With the building of the temple, many Latter-day Saints moved into the area from other parts of the country. Bernard Walsh explained that, at one point, this was a mixed blessing because some moving to the area were rather less than saintly, showing lack of respect for the government housing they rented from the municipality and in attitudes to their neighbors. Walsh leveled with the council, which understood that "not all 'Mormons' were perfect" but "the majority of them are good people, and that's what the community wanted."[65] Overall, the impact of move-ins to Chorley was positive for both the Latter-day Saint congregations in the district and the community as a whole. The number of regular congregants has grown

---

61. Peter Trebilcock interview.

62. Peter Trebilcock interview.

63. Peter Trebilcock interview.

64. Ralph Snape, interviewed by Malcolm Adcock and Fred E. Woods. Cllr. Snape passed away on September 15, 2019, aged 90. He was elected Mayor of Chorley in 1992.

65. Bernard Walsh interview.

almost twenty times—from 50–75 before the temple was announced to up to 1,000 today, with four congregations in Chorley and two in Preston. New converts contributed to the increase, as well as people moving into the neighborhood. This area now has the largest concentration of Latter-day Saints anywhere in Europe.[66]

The current Speaker of the House of Commons (as of 2022) and Chorley's Member of Parliament, Sir Lindsay Hoyle, was a Chorley councilor who initially opposed the temple being built. "I was worse than skeptical. I was rather annoyed, because here we are, a prime piece of real estate that could create jobs, it could have created lots of jobs because it's on the motorway junction," Hoyle recalled.[67] However, he changed his view, and currently in his work as an MP, he very much sees the Church's contribution to the area but thinks that Church members are perhaps still hiding their light under a bushel:

> The Church will come along and put support in and make a difference. Also collecting food for people who can't afford to feed themselves, people who have been homeless. They are [there] to support. And it's that good work that we need to remind people [of], this is done by people from the temple. And I think that's why I get disappointed and very frustrated . . . when I say, "Please, don't be shy about telling people about the good work you do!"[68]

Lord and Lady Clitheroe, prominent landowners in the picturesque village of Downham, Lancashire, also appreciated the Latter-day Saints' care for their community. "They are very helpful. They come quite often, [doing] all sorts of useful, boring things like picking up litter in country lanes, . . . tidying up gravestones. Very personal, very friendly,"[69] said Lady

---

66. Peter Fagg, interviewed by Malcolm Adcock and Fred E. Woods; Jason and Marie Hunt interview; Bernard Walsh interview. Matthew Lyman Rasmussen compares that modern-day gathering to the nineteenth century when Saints migrated to Nauvoo and Salt Lake City where temples were built. He points out that while it enlarged the population of the Chorley and Preston areas dramatically, it has weakened areas where the Saints have gathered from. Finally, Rasmussen suggests that more research is needed on the impact the Preston as well as the London Temple have had on "congregational dynamics." Rasmussen, *Mormonism and the Making of a British Zion*, 190–91.

67. Lindsay Hoyle, interviewed by Fred E. Woods and Martin Anderson.

68. Lindsay Hoyle MP interview.

69. Lord and Lady Clitheroe, interviewed by Fred E. Woods. Latter-day Saint leaders and congregation members from Lancashire have deeply valued their close links with the village of Downham and with Lord and Lady Clitheroe. For example,

Clitheroe. And Lord Clitheroe's overall impression of Church members? "I think we like them very much and we always did like them, but we like them better now," he quipped.[70]

John Maxwell, who served as Preston Temple President between 2003 and 2006 and was previously a member of the Europe North Area Presidency, pointed out the practical blessings that the new temple brought to Church members on the isles off Scotland's "mainland" and other far-flung places. "It's a long way to London if you live on the Hebrides or the Shetland [Islands]. The people from Shetland used to come once a year [to the London Temple], and they'd come for a week. But it'd be a fourteen-hour boat trip to Aberdeen, and then from Aberdeen to the temple. So, it was much better for them and all the people up in the very North, and also in Ireland, to be able to get to [the Preston Temple]."[71]

The Preston Temple draws on a very substantial spiritual heritage. The construction of a temple there is a tribute to the nineteenth-century Latter-day Saint pioneer emigrants who worked Lancashire's fields and cotton mills before leaving for America—often at huge personal sacrifice—to build up Zion in the New World. Now, the Saints were also building Zion in Britain and worshipping within God's temple in their native land.

Membership Growth and Proactivity in Public Life

United Kingdom Church membership was over 149,000 in 1989 and stood in excess of 173,000 a decade later—more than 24,000 Brits had joined the Latter-day Saints in that ten year period.[72] When Church President Gordon B. Hinckley was asked by a London broadcast journalist about the Church's growth, he said that the faith offered "an anchor in a world of shifting values" and that its aim to strengthen families "satisf[ies] a human need and offers hope to many, many people who are desperately looking for something as fathers and mothers."[73]

a choir from The Church of Jesus Christ of Latter-day Saints sang at a fundraiser for a new organ at St Leonard's Church in Downham, and the stake president made a donation at the event on behalf of the Latter-day Saints. See "Choir Raises Funds for 1000 Year Old Chapel," The Church of Jesus Christ of Latter-day Saints.

70. Lord and Lady Clitheroe interview.

71. John Maxwell, interviewed by Malcolm Adcock.

72. Official statistics provided to the authors by The Church of Jesus Christ of Latter-day Saints.

73. Dew, *Go Forward with Faith*, 580; "Interview with Lawrence Spicer."

As well as experiencing numerical growth, the Church saw Latter-day Saints become more active and influential in wider society as individual citizens. For example, many Church members supported the campaign to keep Sunday shop opening hours to a minimum, in the spirit of what they saw as respecting the Lord's day. In a 1991 interview, UK-based Area [multi-country] Public Affairs Director Bryan Grant said members aimed to preserve the spiritual quality of life in their communities.[74]

The growing Church membership in the United Kingdom soon began to be reflected in British politics. Terry Rooney was elected to the British Parliament in 1990, the first Latter-day Saint to join the UK House of Commons. Two years later, David Baxter ran as a parliamentary candidate for the Norwich South constituency.[75] Many other members of the Church have run in elections for the UK House of Commons—as representatives of their political parties. In 1999, biochemist and Latter-day Saint Brian Adam was elected to the first Scottish Parliament in modern times and represented constituencies in North Western Scotland. Adam became widely respected and influential in Scottish political circles.[76]

Furthermore, academic study of The Church of Jesus Christ of Latter-day Saints was given a boost on October 23, 1990, when the first Mormon Studies research collection to be established at a major UK university began at Nottingham, funded by the Clifford R. Hodgett bequest.[77] The founding of the center was proposed by Douglas J. Davies, then professor of theology at Nottingham University, and David Cook, Church Educational System Director for the United Kingdom and Ireland.

In 1997, the 150th anniversary of the arrival of Latter-day Saint pioneers in the Salt Lake Valley presented an opportunity for the Church to

---

74. Don L. Searle, "Two-way Window on the World." Bryan J. Grant passed away on November 30, 2015, aged 71.

75. Elder David S. Baxter was sustained as a General Authority Seventy of The Church of Jesus Christ of Latter-day Saints on April 1, 2006.

76. Brian Adam became Chief Whip for the Scottish National Party (2007–2011) and was later appointed Minister for Parliamentary Business. He died of cancer on April 25, 2013, in Aberdeen, Scotland, aged 64. His obituary paid tribute to a man of faith: "That Adam was more of a behind-the-scenes man than a tub-thumper was shown by the fact that his Mormon faith was never something he thrust at you. He was truly committed to the Church of Jesus Christ of Latter-day Saints, and thus drank neither coffee nor alcohol, but otherwise wore his faith lightly." Martin Hannan, "Obituary: Brian Adam MSP, politician and biochemist."

77. "Mormon Studies Centre Founded at Nottingham University," 81.

provide educational materials for schools. Throughout England, schools were given copies of the *Faith in Every Footstep* CD-ROM, with background on the pioneer trek and other Church beliefs. Many British schools used a game produced by the Church Educational System, involving "students in making the kinds of practical decisions pioneers made as they prepared for and carried out their trek to Utah."[78]

Greater participation by Latter-day Saints in public life was evident as an evolving change in social makeup took place within the Church's congregations, going from an essentially working-class church to a faith that reflected society's demographics more widely. Writing in 1987, a former mission president argued, "The LDS church in Britain has for the most part been a working-class church. Few members are from upper classes, reputedly because such members are not accepted and feel uncomfortable out of their own class."[79] Although British working-class people who became converts demonstrated a strong personal conviction by often giving up a social life centered on "pub culture" (an especially strong pull in working-class communities), missionaries found it harder to find and teach wealthier individuals. Interviewed in the late 1980s, former regional ecclesiastical leader (stake president) Warrick Kear expressed,

> You've got the middle classes who literally are obsessed with making money to pay for their very high mortgages. And the Church comes along and says to them, "We want to take 10 percent of that away. And as well, you've got to give up all your social friends, or a lot of them," because there again it revolves around the pub, weekends for drinks, holidays in France, and just keeping up with the Joneses.[80]

Despite all the things that working-class individuals had to give up, they often did so willingly and joined the Church. Wealthier people had been less responsive.

But after the 1970s, the Church in the United Kingdom did start to see a social transition, as described by Simon Gibson CBE DSc DL:

> Since the '70s, the Church has profoundly changed in the UK, but not enough. When I joined the Church, you could have counted the amount of professional people in its membership, probably on two hands for the whole of the UK. Professional people don't tend to join the Church, but the children of converts become well educated and move into society and begin to make a contribution.

---

78. Don L. Searle, "The Church in the United Kingdom and Ireland," 45.
79. Thomas, "LDS Church Growth," 107–17.
80. Warrick Noel Kear, interviewed by David J. Whittaker, 32–33.

And then their children. Very few people in the '70s in the Church had been to university. Now we've got professors, we've got post-graduate populations, we've got people in all walks of life, in terms of professions and civil responsibilities. That didn't exist 40 years ago. So that's a profound change.[81]

Keith Bishop, a former senior church leader in Britain, discussed the long view of church members' changing economic and educational backgrounds:

Although sometimes it's difficult to convert people from, shall I say, higher classes of society, people who don't feel a need for anything (they feel they've got what they need), I think that the Church gives people a mission and a vision to progress. I think that over two or three generations, the third generation often climb higher in their education and in their vocational achievements so that they are moving up social strata. The people in the Church today, I'm sure they are a more educated membership than we had 50–60 years ago.[82]

Daryl Watson, who served as the Church's National Communication Director for Great Britain, referred to "a great, solid foundation through the '60s and '70s of good people" leading to a second generation of British Latter-day Saints doing "great things into the '90s and into the early 2000s." He said Church members became much more visible and influential within society: "We saw lawyers and politicians and people who were standing up for their beliefs."[83]

Strategic Insights from a British General Authority

British-born global leader Elder Derek A. Cuthbert made ten key observations about reasons for the advancement of The Church of Jesus Christ of Latter-day Saints in the United Kingdom and Ireland (referring to the period until 1987, but many points are also relevant for later years). His views reference practical steps and what he saw as heavenly intercession:[84]

---

81. Simon Gibson, interviewed by Malcolm Adcock and Fred E. Woods.
82. John Keith Bishop, interviewed by Malcolm Adcock.
83. Daryl Watson interview.
84. Thomas, "LDS Church Growth," 106–18; Derek A. Cuthbert, "Church Growth in the British Isles, 1937–1987," 13–26. The body of our own text is an analysis of Elder Cuthbert's observations from his appendices (pp. 23–26), with directly attributed words in quotes.

1. Divine blessings: "These islands have a divine destiny, and the quickening during the past half century is indicative of greater things to come."

2. UK-based investment in sharing the gospel: "The setting up of the Missionary Training Center within the precincts of the London Temple is an important development in the training of British and European missionaries more effectively."

3. Greater temporal and spiritual self-sufficiency: "[T]he British and the Irish are proud peoples, and their quest for self-sufficiency has made significant strides in recent years, in both financial self-sufficiency and self-sufficiency in missionary and temple work."

4. Stemming the flow of emigration from the United Kingdom to the United States: The United Kingdom was now maintaining local membership and building up the local missionary force composed of congregational members.

5. The impact of temples: "[T]he London Temple has been the means of raising up a covenant people in the British Isles, a people committed to living righteously and serving their fellow men and women. . . . [T]he British Saints can look forward to a second temple in the coming years."

6. Increased visibility: "Over two hundred beautiful new chapels now dot the country. Furthermore, the appointment of a full-time director of public communications in 1978 has intensified these efforts."

7. Setting up temporal offices in Britain, supporting needs of Church members: "All of the necessary supplies and services are now within two or three hundred miles instead of six thousand miles away."

8. The calling of Regional Representatives in the British Isles.[85]

9. The watershed first area conference of the Church (1971): "President Joseph Fielding Smith's statement at that time that the Church was

---

85. Regional Representatives (a Church position that has been superseded by that of Area Seventy) were previously called as "part-time lay officers of the Church that are called by the First Presidency, [and who] receive general instructions from the Quorum of the Twelve Apostles and serve under the direction of the area presidency." See Douglas L. Callister and Gerald J. Day, "Region, Regional Representative," 3:758.

'coming of age' was a landmark in the growth of the Church in Britain."

10. Emphasis on ordaining lay members to the office of elder: "[T]he future of the Church in the British Isles is very bright as missionaries and members work together to baptize men who will hold the . . . Priesthood and lead their families to the temple."

These were all evident in the decades of the 80s and 90s—a period in which the Church continued to come out of obscurity in Britain. And they would pave the way forward as The Church of Jesus Christ of Latter-day Saints had its "Mormon Moment" in the two decades that would follow.

CHAPTER 10

The Church of Jesus Christ in Modern Britain

As far as we know, no sitting Prime Minister has had the good fortune of ever meeting an apostle before.

— Stephen Kerr MP

I t is described as a Punch-and-Judy show—the weekly bare-knuckle bout where the British Prime Minister metaphorically slugs it out with their political opponent across the floor of a heaving House of Commons, while Members of Parliament (MPs) cheer and jeer.[1] Prime Minister's Question Time (PMQs) is more than just a theatrical sparring display—heavy blows can be inflicted, perhaps giving the lie to the stereotype that the British are unfailingly polite. Here, MPs reciprocate insult with insult, and the presence of some distinguished ecclesiastical guests would soon provide a "time out" for the head of the British government.

Elder and Sister Holland Visit Parliament

On November 21, 2018, UK Prime Minister Theresa May faced Labour Leader Jeremy Corbyn eye-to-eye in heated interactions about Brexit (the plan for the United Kingdom to leave the European Union) inside an electrically charged, chock-full Parliamentary chamber. Watching from the public gallery above were Elder Jeffrey R. Holland, a member of the Church's Quorum of the Twelve Apostles, and his wife, Patricia T. Holland. On this of all days, with countless political deadlines looming, Rt. Hon. Theresa May MP was about to personally host Holland ahead of her urgent *tête-à-tête* in Brussels with European Commission President Jean-Claude Juncker. The London meeting with the Hollands provided May with a kind of breathing space after the rowdy Parliamentary exchanges.

The Hollands came bearing a meticulously researched and beautifully bound five-generation family history for May, as well as a framed pedigree chart—a practice that had become customary when Church leaders met with dignitaries. (May's predecessor, Prime Minister David Cameron,

---

1. See Ayesha Hazarika and Tom Hamilton, *Punch and Judy Politics: An Insiders' Guide to Prime Minister's Questions*. Members of Parliament represent their local constituents in the national Parliamentary chamber.

received his own family history from the Church three years earlier on February 4, 2015.[2]) Holland related how the conversation went with May:

> I said, "Given the kind of day that you had and the week that you are having, this is meant to be a kind of a respite." And she said, "This is a true interlude. This is a happy moment." She smiled about that. I think it was nice for her to have somebody who was not shouting in her face or shaking a fist over some element of Brexit.[3]

Elder Holland held Britain very close to his heart. As a young man, he was a missionary to the United Kingdom, and that experience was clearly on his mind as he sat in on Parliament:

> We have never had a day in Parliament like today. . . . You do not get many meetings with Prime Ministers. As a 19-year-old missionary here, I wanted to get in any door at all. I never thought a day would come when I would get in the door at Parliament or to the office of the Prime Minister.[4]

The event in Parliament was also attended by Latter-day Saint MPs Stephen Kerr and David Rutley, as well as Kerr's wife, Yvonne Kerr.[5] Reflecting on this remarkable day, Kerr said:

> As far as we know, no sitting Prime Minister has had the good fortune of ever meeting an Apostle before. Today, Theresa May, at a most critical moment in her time as our Prime Minister, and probably in her life, met someone who

---

2. Other government heads presented with family histories from the Church include former US President Barack Obama; New Zealand Prime Minister Jacinda Ardern; previous Australian Prime Minister Julia Gillard; and former President of Germany Johannes Rau. Helping people with their family roots is very much on the Church's radar—the Church runs over 120 family history centers in the United Kingdom, which are open to the public at no charge.

3. Tad Walch, "An Apostle in England: British Prime Minister Theresa May Pauses from Brexit to Meet with Elder Jeffrey R. Holland."

4. Walch, "An Apostle in England."

5. Stephen Kerr became a Conservative Member of Parliament for Stirling, central Scotland on June 8, 2017. He was unseated in the snap general election of December 12, 2019. On May 8, 2021, Kerr was elected as Scottish Conservative and Unionist MSP [Member of the Scottish Parliament] for Central Scotland and was soon appointed as his party's Chief Whip in the Scottish Parliament. David Rutley was appointed Parliamentary Under Secretary of State (Minister for Welfare Delivery) at the Department for Work and Pensions on September 17, 2021. He was a Government Whip from June 15, 2017, to September 16, 2021, and was previously Parliamentary Under Secretary of State at the Department for the Environment, Food and Rural Affairs from September 3, 2018, to July 27, 2019.

British Prime Minister Theresa May (right) receives her family history from Elder Jeffrey R. Holland (left), accompanied by Stephen Kerr MP (center), November 2018. Courtesy Intellectual Reserve, Inc.

could bring her something very special [through] a handshake and through a few words.[6]

The Book of Mormon in the Legislature

The presentation of Theresa May's family history was not the only noteworthy event for the Church in the United Kingdom that day. As Holland walked through oak-paneled corridors of the nine-hundred-year-old Palace of Westminster, he had with him several bound volumes of the Book of Mormon that had been commissioned for selected individuals and institutions. May was presented with her personal copy, and then heading for the House of Commons Library, Holland met Philippa Helme, Principal Clerk of the Table Office (who sits berobed at the Table of the House within the House of Commons chamber during sessions), and Hannah Russell, Head of Operations and Engagement at the House of Commons (based at the Commons Library). Helme commented that the edition of the Book of Mormon the House of Commons then owned was "a little elderly" and welcomed the brand-new copy from the Church that would be used for swearing in new Latter-day Saint MPs. Then House of Commons Deputy Speaker Rt. Hon. Sir Lindsay Hoyle MP, Member of Parliament for Chorley where the Preston Temple is located, was delighted to also be presented with his own copy of this specially bound scriptural edition, exclaiming, "It's beautiful!"[7]

An Improving Image

For the combination of experiences, this was a very significant apostolic visit, highlighting how much things have changed for Latter-day Saints since missionaries arrived in 1837. The meeting showed that respect for the Church was increasing in the United Kingdom, with the perception of Latter-day Saints elevated among the populace, in the media, and among elected representatives. The Church doesn't back political parties or get dragged into partisan political frays, but its leaders greatly value relationships and contact with government figures in sharing common religious values and in standing for matters of ethical principle.

Many events, over decades, incrementally helped open the door for a serving British Prime Minister to spend time with an apostle. In July 1987, Latter-day Saint President Ezra Taft Benson attended a big event

---

6. Walch, "An Apostle in England."
7. As noted by the author.

in London with former British Prime Minister Edward Heath. The four-hundred-person dinner at London's Savoy Hotel, funded by donations from US Church members in appreciation for their British heritage, marked 150 years since Latter-day Saint missionaries arrived in Great Britain.[8] The banquet included a videotaped message of congratulations from United States President Ronald Reagan, who underlined the "immense" contribution the Church made to British life.[9] Former cabinet minister Rt. Hon. Sir Rhodes Boyson MP—known in Britain for his social and political conservatism—noted Latter-day Saints' emphasis on "self-discipline, cheerfulness, tolerance, education, civic duties, the tithe, and the primacy of religion."[10] The event was attended by Canadian newspaper magnate Rt. Hon. Lord Thomson of Fleet. The Trumpeters of the Life Guards—who perform on ceremonial occasions for the Royal family—provided a rousing fanfare based on the Latter-day Saint hymn "Come, Come, Ye Saints." President Gordon B. Hinckley—at that time First Counselor to Benson—gave the keynote address.[11]

Nearly two decades later and well-across the Atlantic, former UK Prime Minister Baroness Margaret Thatcher was hosted in Utah, where the headline in the *Deseret News* highlighted that she had endeared herself to the Utah audience: "Thatcher Focuses on Faith, Families."[12] During her visit Thatcher was awarded an honorary doctorate from Brigham Young University in front of 22,000 people.[13] Her level of engagement with the Utah-based audience was well-nigh perfect as she spoke about the Pilgrim Fathers and how the United States was founded on the basis of religious

---

8. The *Sunday Telegraph* anticipated the event thus: "eminent figures from the worlds of politics, business and the arts on both sides of the Atlantic will sit down to an extraordinary dinner at the Savoy Hotel. The host will be 84-year-old former member of the Eisenhower Administration, Ezra Taft Benson by name, who is regarded by more than six million people as a prophet receiving direct revelations from God." (Ian Bradley, "Living by the Book," 13.)

9. "British Saints Celebrate 150th Anniversary," 70. Correspondents in Great Britain Bryan J. Grant, John Ashmead, Peter J. Trebilcock, Kathleen A. Penny, Alan Brown, Margaret Cumming, Rory McCune, and Kevin Fingleton. The 150th anniversary events are also referenced in Francis M. Gibbons, *The Expanding Church: Three Decades of Remarkable Growth Among the Latter-day Saints, 1970–1999.*

10. "British Saints Celebrate 150th Anniversary," 71.

11. "British Saints Celebrate 150th Anniversary," 71.

12. Sharon M. Haddock, "Thatcher Focuses on Faith, Families." Opinions on Thatcher's visit would have been divided in Britain, including among Church members.

13. Margaret Thatcher, "The Moral Challenges for the Next Century."

liberty, shunning complacency in the work of espousing fundamental human rights,[14] and the strong spirit of western pioneer Brigham Young, the Latter-day Saints' second Church President ("So often the hour produces the leader," she said).[15] Responding to her remarks, Hinckley (now Church President during this time) commented that "some might wish that she would run for the office of President of the United States."[16] In addition, as reported by the *Deseret News*, Hinckley emphasized the importance of the audience's British heritage and urged them to "not forget that from England came the Magna Carta, the King James Bible, poets, philosophers and people who helped put in place the underpinnings of liberty."[17]

Church Family Values Awards

Beginning in 2003, the Church has offered "Family Values Awards" in the United Kingdom to "honour members of the community in the public eye whose work and influence have a significant impact on family life within UK society."[18] These awards have underlined the Church's aim to be part of the chorus in identifying with people of other faiths—people who Latter-day Saints may not always agree with theologically but who share a common interest in family values. Recipients have included government cabinet ministers, people of influence in the third sector, and faith leaders.[19] As evidence of the awards' appreciation, the tradition of holding the award events at the United Kingdom Parliament building soon became firmly established.

Awardees include the Reverend (Revd.) Canon Ann Easter, then-Chaplain to the Queen and a well-known voice on BBC network radio, who received the Family Values Award in 2014, alongside David Burrowes MP. In 2015, senior NGO workers (and husband and wife) Dr. Husna Ahmad OBE and Saif Ahmad received the awards along with parliamen-

---

14. Thatcher, "Moral Challenges."
15. Thatcher, "Moral Challenges."
16. Haddock, "Thatcher Focuses on Faith."
17. Haddock, "Thatcher Focuses on Faith."
18. "Family Values Award."
19. They include Rt. Hon. Lord Paul Boateng; Rt. Hon. Frank Field MP; the Marriage Foundation founder, Sir Paul Coleridge; Edmund Adamus, previously Roman Catholic Diocese of Westminster's Director for Marriage and Family Life; Baroness Scotland, then Attorney General for England and Wales; and Mary Crowley OBE, President of The International Federation of Parenting Education.

Dr. Husna Ahmad and Saif Ahmad after receiving their Family Values Award. They are joined left to right by Elder Clifford T. Herbertson, David Rutley MP, and Elder Patrick Kearon, December 2015. Courtesy Intellectual Reserve, Inc.

tary campaigner Fiona Bruce, MP for Congleton in Cheshire. Recipients for 2016 were Jim Shannon, MP for Strangford in Northern Ireland (also chair of the All-Party Parliamentary Group (APPG) for International Freedom of Religion or Belief), and Revd. Prebendary Rose Hudson-Wilkin, then Chaplain to the House of Commons Speaker and a Chaplain to the Queen.[20] Nola Leach, CEO of prominent Christian campaigning group CARE, received the award in October 2018, where she referenced a stark trend of "a child . . . now [being] more likely to have a smartphone than to have a father."[21]

Despite all this, Stephen Kerr MP felt that more can be done by the Church across its congregations as it engages with the community:

> For example, we recently invited a prominent Labour member to receive the Family Values Award. And although she's been a member of this place [the

20. Revd. Rose Hudson-Wilkin MBE is now Bishop of Dover, the first black woman to become a Church of England bishop. She was one of several clerics to lead prayers at Prince Harry's wedding to Meghan Markle, Duchess of Sussex, on May 19, 2018. See "Rose Hudson-Wilkin: First Black Female Bishop Consecrated," BBC News.

21. According to Ofcom, 83% of 12–15-year-olds have their own smartphone. See "Children and Parents: Media Use and Attitudes Report 2019."

House of Commons] for nearly 30 years, she couldn't accept the award because she's never actually visited the congregation that she had in her constituency. And I felt sad about that because I would've thought that we would have invited the Member of Parliament to come to something over 30 years.[22]

Progress over these years in including local government leaders to Church events has been made though. For example, hundreds of Church members from the areas around Coventry have attended the annual Rotary Club charity event held at the stake center, where the Member of Parliament has been hosted.[23] In London's Hyde Park building, Lady Victoria Borwick, MP for Kensington and former Deputy Mayor of London, met with the Latter-day Saint children as part of her Sunday visit.[24] One MP received a voucher for 100 hours of volunteer service within his constituency.[25] Similarly, MPs have toured family history centers and received copies of their own genealogy,[26] and government ministers have also met with local Latter-day Saints to thank them for their community relief efforts, including in response to floods.[27]

Latter-day Saints in British Government

Further improvements of the Latter-day Saint image in the British mind can be seen in the growing number of Latter-day Saints participating in British government. At the 2015 UK general election, no fewer than fourteen Latter-day Saints stood as candidates in parliamentary constituencies—four Conservatives, one from the Labour Party, and nine from UKIP (UK Independence Party).[28] One of the UKIP candidates, Nathan Gill, was unsuccessful in the 2015 United Kingdom Parliament election

22. Stephen Kerr, interviewed by Malcolm Adcock.

23. "Local MP Attends Coventry Christmas Carol Concert," The Church of Jesus Christ of Latter-day Saints.

24. "Kensington MP Visits Hyde Park Children," The Church of Jesus Christ of Latter-day Saints.

25. "Toby Perkins, MP, Receives Community Voucher for Staveley Cemetery," The Church of Jesus Christ of Latter-day Saints.

26. "Daventry MP Receives Personal Family History," The Church of Jesus Christ of Latter-day Saints.

27. "Government Minister Meets York Helping Hands," The Church of Jesus Christ of Latter-day Saints.

28. No current evidence exists that these numbers for parliamentary candidates (four Conservatives, one Labour Party, and nine UK Independence Party) were reflective of Latter-day Saints' voting intentions at the 2015 general election.

Festus Akinbusoye's swearing in ceremony as Bedfordshire Police and Crime Commissioner, May 13, 2021, at Bedfordshire Police Headquarters. Courtesy Festus Akinbusoye.

but had been successfully elected as a Member of the European Parliament (MEP) the previous year.[29] Festus Akinbusoye, Parliamentary candidate for West Ham, East London, during 2015, was in May 2021 voted in as Bedfordshire's new Police and Crime Commissioner. Effectively the public overseer for the county's police service, he is the first ever black person to be elected to this office anywhere in Britain.[30]

Despite the common perception that Latter-day Saints are an ideologically conservative homogenous group, involvement in British government by Church members covers the spectrum of political thought just as it does in the United States (where, for example, in 2012 both the Republican candidate for the US President Mitt Romney and the Democratic President of the Senate Harry Reid were Latter-day Saints). In the United Kingdom, Julian Bell is a Church member who is a "Labour man" through and through. In fact, he was long-term Leader of the

29. Nathan Gill resigned his membership of UKIP in December 2018. See also "Mormon Faith Is Important to Me, Says UKIP's Nathan Gill," BBC News.

30. Dipesh Gadher, "First Black Police and Crime Commissioner: I've Been Stopped and Searched but I Back It."

Council at the London Borough of Ealing (one of the capital's thirty-two boroughs, population 342,700).[31] He admits that there may well have been raised eyebrows from some Church members in reaction to Latter-day Saints being elected to represent left-of-center parties. However, he is not alone. An example is Terry Rooney's 1990 milestone polling victory for the Labour Party in Bradford North, West Yorkshire. Rooney was the first member of the Church to be elected to the British House of Commons, and he represented his constituents as their MPs for nearly twenty years.[32] He was jokingly called the "orange juice king"[33] by his political associates because of his conspicuous teetotaling habits as a Latter-day Saint.

Rooney was followed by three more Latter-day Saints who became Members of the UK Parliament (all members of the Conservative Party), beginning two decades later. There may still be an internal challenge, however, to political involvement by Church members. Latter-day Saints tend to lead very full lives, including church assignments—a busyness that layers over the regular time demands of modern life. For Bell, his faith was a contributing reason to get involved in politics. Referencing Joseph Smith's teachings, he said, "If you love mankind, you'll [range] throughout all the world.[34] And [there is] no better place to do that than in public service."[35]

---

31. Cllr. Julian Bell was Leader of Ealing Council for eleven years, until May 2021.

32. "Church Member, Elected to British Parliament," 80. Terry Rooney was elected with the seat's largest-ever majority until that time, receiving 18,619 votes, compared with 9,105 for his nearest rival.

33. Rooney related how his teetotal lifestyle led to temperance meetings at the Westminster Parliament. "I was almost instantly christened 'O.J.' for Orange Juice. Because I didn't drink. And at that time, there were only two known Members of Parliament who didn't drink. So that was one thing. And because of that, there's an organization in Britain called United Kingdom [Temperance] Alliance, which is from the Temperance Movement, and they're about 100 years old, and they made contact with me, and I facilitated lots of events for them in Parliament and built a great relationship with them. We used to do lectures, we used to get 150–200 school kids from around London and talk to them—not lecture, talk to them, about drugs, alcohol, tobacco, in a friendly sensible way. Not a lecture. And that was great. That was one of the most enjoyable parts of my time in Parliament." Terry Rooney, interviewed by Martin Andersen and Fred E. Woods.

34. Joseph Smith stated, "A man filled with the love of God, is not content with blessing his family alone, but ranges through the whole world, anxious to bless the whole human race." "Letter to Quorum of the Twelve, December 15, 1840," 2.

35. Cllr. Julian Bell interview.

Doing Good

It was within this context of Latter-day Saint public engagement that Elder Jeffrey R. Holland became the first member of the Latter-day Saints' Quorum of the Twelve Apostles to address a gathering at the Houses of Parliament, three years prior to his meeting with Prime Minister Theresa May. There he spoke before the APPG on Foreign Affairs in the House of Lords at the UK Parliament on June 10, 2015, addressing the topic "Religious Conflict: Can Humanitarian Aid Help?" [36] Holland followed Rowsch Shaways, Deputy Prime Minister of Iraq, who also addressed the gathering, along with a representative from global charity AMAR International and Sharon Eubank, president of LDS Charities (now Latter-day Saint Charities).[37] Baroness Emma Nicholson, AMAR's Founder and Chairman, had previously been hosted by the Church in Utah and personally invited Holland to Parliament, despite a little bit of initial "stuffy" resistance, as she candidly explained:

> The first time Elder Holland came, I received some unpleasant emails and silly people, unhappy people who said some quite unacceptable things. So, I wrote straight back and said, "Sorry you've got the wrong end of the stick. You can come and discuss it with me, if you like, but you are not allowed to say that again." And it took about a year, but that completely faded out and [went away].[38]

"These members of Parliament, particularly in the House of Lords, are interested in what we're doing," Holland said in an interview. "They're doing many of these same kind of things, and I believe now they see us [the Church] as a significant partner, a significant contributor, and I think they want to build that relationship."[39]

After the humanitarian partnership between The Church of Jesus Christ of Latter-day Saints and AMAR—and with her continuing rela-

---

36. Jeffrey R. Holland, "Religious Conflict: Can Humanitarian Aid Help?" The APPG on Foreign Affairs is an informal group where Members of Parliament, faith leaders, charities, and academics examine issues of foreign policy to stimulate wider policy discussion among parliamentarians. Addressing the meetings is seen as an honor because the APPGs play an influential role in the workings of Parliament.

37. Sharon Eubank became the First Counselor of the General Relief Society Presidency in April 2017.

38. Baroness Nicholson of Winterbourne, interviewed by Malcolm Adcock.

39. "Mormon Apostle Addresses All-Party Parliamentary Group in UK House of Lords," The Church of Jesus Christ of Latter-day Saints.

Baroness Emma Nicholson and Elder Jeffrey R. Holland outside Parliament, 2015. Courtesy Intellectual Reserve, Inc.

tionships at BYU—an event at Windsor (just west of London) was held in September 2016 to continue to foster humanitarian relationships and discussions. Constable and Governor of Windsor Castle, Admiral Sir James Perowne KBE, welcomed the guests to Queen Elizabeth II's castle estate. Attendees included leading Anglican clerics, humanitarians, scholars, and government leaders. Latter-day Saints, Holland told the conference, hit "rock bottom" in 1838 when Missouri Governor Lilburn Boggs issued an "extermination order" against them—they fled by the thousands to Illinois and then later to Utah for refuge. "Religious restrictions not only increase social violence and hostilities but also have been demonstrated to increase forced migration," Holland said. He referred to religious groups forced to emigrate, as have the Yazidi and other minorities surrounded by conflict areas of the Middle East currently. Senior Yazidi leaders listened intently as Elder Holland spoke.[40]

The following year, after meeting again for a second Windsor Castle conference, Baroness Nicholson was awarded honorary membership in the Relief Society, the Church's global women's organization. Sister Sharon

---

40. See Jeffrey R. Holland, "The Mormon Refugee Experience; Religious Persecution: A Driver of Forced Migration Conference."

Sister Sharon Eubank and Baroness Emma Nicholson reflect on their association and friendship, Windsor Castle, September 2016. Courtesy Intellectual Reserve, Inc.

Eubank, who was also First Counselor in the Relief Society General Presidency, cited the Baroness's work in safeguarding families.

The 2018 Windsor events culminated with a gathering in London at the Chatham House think tank, officially known as the Royal Institute of International Affairs. There, Holland advocated a holistic approach to meeting humanitarian needs that respond to emotional and spiritual challenges as well as physical wants.[41] During their interactions in July 2018, Holland, Baroness Nicholson, and Eubank also participated in a discussion hosted by the APPG for the Prevention of Sexual Violence in Conflict held at the UK Parliament.

LDS Charities' work with AMAR was also recognized by Prince Charles, who joined a roundtable with charity representatives in December 2017.[42] Praising the work of AMAR and its supporters, Prince Charles said, "During the past twenty-five years over ten million people in Iraq, Lebanon, Iran and Pakistan have been able to benefit from the healthcare facilities made available through AMAR, with many more benefiting from

41. See Jeffrey R. Holland, "Investing in our Future with Faith."
42. See "LDS Charities Joins Humanitarian Event Hosted by Prince Charles," The Church of Jesus Christ of Latter-day Saints. The event took place on December 13, 2017 at Lancaster House, London.

the educational opportunities that AMAR provides," and he recognized LDS Charities' contributions with a ceremonial citation honoring the organization for its commitment to health and education.

Closer to home, in an effort to support the resettlement of refugees and help them apply their own skills in contributing to society, the Church set up two Friendship Centers in the UK capital—one in Peckham, South East London, and the other in Wembley, West London. Since these sites have opened, many refugees have met there to discuss job opportunities, learn English, work on resumes, and look at the next steps for obtaining an education for themselves and their children. A volunteer instructor at the Peckham Center, Peggy Powell, reflected on how she had helped one student get a job as a teacher's aide: "When she started our [English Language] course, she had been working in England as a cleaner for two years."[43]

On a more grassroots level, teenage Latter-day Saints have joined ranks with Royal British Legion (RBL) "Poppy Appeal" collectors to help make a difference in communities. The RBL is Britain's largest Armed Forces charity, with 110,000 volunteers nationwide providing support to serving personnel, veterans, and their families. One fourteen-year-old Latter-day Saint from the Norwich area even addressed the Royal British Legion's national conference.[44] In addition, Latter-day Saint meetinghouses are opened hundreds of times a year for blood drives with the National Health Service's Blood and Transplant organization. Around four percent of all blood donated in England comes from these blood donation sessions.[45]

---

43. "Changing Lives at Friendship Centres," The Church of Jesus Christ of Latter-day Saints.

44. The young man spoke at the Royal British Legion National Conference, Bournemouth International Centre, May 17–19, 2018 (information known to author Malcolm Adcock about Latter-day Saint community service in Britain). The Royal British Legion (RBL) Poppy Appeals of 2014 and 2018 held special meaning for Latter-day Saint volunteers collecting for the RBL. During those years, the Church in the UK opened up its meetinghouses to commemorate the one hundredth anniversary of World War I, part of Britain's national effort to honor the service personnel who perished and other war dead. The meetings were attended by British opinion leaders and members of local Latter-day Saint congregations and included music and dramatic performances. The Church shared social media content as part of the commemorations.

45. In 2008, nearly 3.9% of all blood donated in England came through sessions held in Latter-day Saint church buildings, with 455 sessions taking place (information known to author Malcolm Adcock, based on numbers supplied by National Health Service Blood and Transplant).

Defending Religious Freedom

As members of a smaller religious sect outside of traditional Catholic and Protestant Christianity—and that has historically seen considerable persecution and restrictions for their beliefs—Latter-day Saints have had a keen interest in defending religious freedom. In 1843, Joseph Smith, the Church's founding prophet, proclaimed:

> I am bold to declare before Heaven that I am just as ready to die in defending the rights of a Presbyterian, a Baptist, or a good man of any denomination; for the same principle which would trample upon the rights of the Latter-day Saints would trample upon the rights of the Roman Catholics, or of any other denomination who may be unpopular and too weak to defend themselves.[46]

In May 2018, Latter-day Saint Apostle D. Todd Christofferson told the APPG for International Freedom of Religion or Belief that "religion or belief is fundamental to societal wellbeing" and that religious faith does not operate in a bubble: "Freedom of religion benefits not only believers, but all of society, whether they know it or not."[47] Christofferson was joined by Dr. Daniel Mark, chair of the United States Commission on International Religious Freedom, and by Margaret Galy, then head of Freedom of Religion or Belief, UK Foreign and Commonwealth Office.[48] Christofferson's Parliamentary visit seemed to have made an impact. According to Stephen Kerr (Conservative Party), a Labour MP "made a beeline for [him] and asked, 'How did you manage to get him to come here? How did you manage to get that to happen?'"[49]

---

46. "History, 1838–1856, Volume E-1 [1 July 1843–30 April 1844]," 1666.

47. See D. Todd Christofferson, "Why Atheists (and Everyone Else) Should Support Freedom of Religion or Belief," 4.

48. The previous year, Christofferson had also expressed to an audience at Downing College, Cambridge, that religious freedom "is the core right in what might be thought of as an 'ecosystem' of freedom." D. Todd Christofferson, "Religious Freedom: The Foundation Freedom."

49. Stephen Kerr interview. Stephen Kerr's Parliamentary speech marking International Freedom of Religion or Belief Day was also an appeal for tolerance: "With this debate, we are talking about something that is fundamental to civilization: freedom of religion or belief. . . . I feel passionately about the subject because I am a member of a religious minority—The Church of Jesus Christ of Latter-day Saints – that has a long history of persecution and misrepresentation." Kerr enumerated extensive human rights abuses against other religious minorities and explained his faith's deep concern for the freedom of people of religious belief or of none. See "International Freedom of Religion or Belief Day," UK Parliament.

To further the cause of religious freedom, the Church continues to engage within the infrastructure of government. Lord Ahmad of Wimbledon, Minister of State at the Foreign, Commonwealth & Development Office,[50] has a record of consulting senior UK Church representatives on religious liberty issues, and the Church is closely collaborating on public-facing events with Fiona Bruce MP, the United Kingdom Prime Minister's Special Envoy for Freedom of Religion or Belief. Recognizing the efforts of the Church, one parliamentary motion signed by MPs from four different political parties, including the sponsoring Member, Dr. Lisa Cameron MP from East Kilbride (Scottish National Party), celebrated the contribution of Latter-day Saints in the community:

> That this House recognizes the work of the Church of Jesus Christ of Latter Day Saints in East Kilbride for over 50 years of service since Elder John Longden, an assistant to the Quorum of the Twelve Apostles, performed the dedication . . . [and] acknowledges the community spirit and dedication that they have shown.[51]

The "Mormon Moment(um)"

While in recent years leaders of The Church of Jesus Christ of Latter-day Saints have asked its members to no longer use "Mormon" or "Mormonism" to reference other members or the faith, that stands at a stark contrast to the first decade and a half of this century when the Church embraced the terms as part of its extensive "I'm a Mormon" campaign. This multimillion-dollar effort involved high-dollar billboards and

---

50. Lord Ahmad of Wimbledon was the Prime Minister's Special Envoy for Freedom of Religion or Belief 2018–2019. "Lord Ahmad of Wimbledon," GOV.UK.

51. "50 Years of The Church of Jesus Christ of Latter-day Saints In East Kilbride." A famously misquoted phrase is that the British Parliament at Westminster is the Mother of Parliaments. The original quotation from Victorian statesman John Bright is "England is the Mother of Parliaments." England—with her British sister nations and other democracies—has nurtured free speech and religious freedom, albeit in an evolutionary fashion, from the seventeenth century onwards. See Bill Cash, *John Bright: Statesman, Orator, Agitator*, 96.

At the United Kingdom's legislature, the National Parliamentary Prayer Breakfast is now on the annual calendar for Latter-day Saint ecclesiastical and Public Affairs leaders. For example, faith and government representatives joined together at Parliament in London for the 2018 event attended by UK Prime Minister Theresa May. See "Church representative joins Theresa May, faith and government leaders in National Parliamentary Prayer Breakfast."

advertising in New York City and elsewhere that highlighted "Mormons" as everyday people and the Church encouraging members to create and share "I'm a Mormon" profiles on its Mormon.org website. It was a time described by commentators as the "Mormon Moment" that largely began with the 2002 Winter Olympics being held in Salt Lake City and reaching its climax with Mitt Romney's 2012 bid for the White House and the opening of the raunchy and satirical *The Book of Mormon* musical.

Seeing it as something broader and bigger than a particular moment, Michael Otterson, then worldwide Public Affairs managing director, described this period as the "Mormon Momentum," as the impact of preceding events and Church initiatives was cumulative: "[L]et's now try to examine where we are today, with the expectation this is not a transitory moment that will end but simply the latest phase in the historic emergence of the Church to a higher level of public consciousness."[52]

Romney's campaign and the religion's response to it in the United Kingdom raised awareness and understanding about the faith to new levels. While the Church went out of its way to remain nonpartisan, the faith's spokespeople on both sides of the Atlantic were well prepared to respond to a press hungry for backgrounders about the religion behind the political candidate. This was an opportunity to enlighten a public and a media largely ill-informed about The Church of Jesus Christ of Latter-day Saints and whose default position was to see the Church's membership as rather eccentric, perhaps even odd.

Overall, media coverage of the Church was balanced. The media would often have probing questions about Romney's faith as it is practiced in Britain. British newspapers especially reveled in the quirkiness of Romney's own Lancashire roots, and the *Guardian* was pleased to reveal details of his family history, writing, "What may be less familiar is the fact that he is descended from one of the first European converts to the new religion in the 1830s; and that this ancestor was an *echt* [genuine] Northerner."[53]

Before Romney's Republican nomination, veteran TV inquisitor Jeremy Paxman gave US pastor Dr. Robert Jeffress a TV grilling on

52. Michael Otterson, "In the Public Eye: How the Church is Handling Increased Global Visibility," 17. As to the origin of the phrase the "Mormon Moment," Otterson notes that it was well before the 2012 Romney campaign: "History has not recorded the name of the journalist who created the phrase, the 'Mormon Moment,' but the earliest reference I have found was a headline in *U.S. News and World Report* in November 2000." Otterson, "Global Visibility," 16.

53. Alan Sykes, "Mitt Romney's 'Lamentable' North of England Roots."

BBC Two's *Newsnight* when the minister leveraged his viewpoint that "Mormonism" is a "cult."[54] Paxman's abrasive interviewing approach had the effect of counterbalancing the story. As every aspect of Romney's lifestyle was microscopically examined in the media, including his white undergarments that were mockingly described as "magic underwear," journalists were looking for stories that grabbed attention. Latter-day Saint scholar Terryl L. Givens provided the context within which the religion had often been pigeonholed in US culture:

> I don't see any fundamental shifts in the way "Mormons" are portrayed or characterized in the mainstream media, or in the way they are perceived by Americans in general. I think the greatest surprise, as a historian . . . has been watching the two Romney campaigns and to realize that what many of us thought were fairly outdated and discredited modes of representation reappeared in the course of those campaigns in venues as prestigious as *The New York Times*.[55]

It was also easy for British journalists to take cues from their North American cousins. Aggressive stereotyping was the exception in Britain, but "old chestnut" mischaracterizations did seep through the cracks.

With the Church receiving media attention, many opinion leaders were enthusiastic to get to know Latter-day Saint leaders. Clearly, American politics had now provided a catalyst for greater dialogue about the Church in Britain. At a meeting held in London's Hyde Park Chapel, one prominent British Evangelical leader made the point that hitherto Evangelicals and Latter-day Saints would rarely meet. Romney's US presidential campaign was to prove hugely significant on the way the Church and its members were perceived for the better, including in the United Kingdom. It is difficult to overstate the impact. J. W. Marriott, the chairman of hotel chain Marriott International Inc., said of the attention:

> There has never been as much positive attention to the church, thanks to the wonderful campaign of Mitt Romney and his family. . . . Today, we see the church coming out of obscurity and we see that 90 percent of what has been written and said . . . has been favourable.

Marriott noted that the media spotlight led to high public expectations of individual Latter-day Saints, "so that of course, now that we're out of

---

54. Robert Jeffress (First Baptist Church of Dallas) interview, interviewed by Jeremy Paxman.

55. Terryl L. Givens, interviewed by Fred E. Woods and Martin Andersen.

obscurity, everybody is looking at us and saying, 'Are you as good as the Romneys?'"[56]

One local Latter-day Saint who entered the media spotlight during this time was Belfast-based Paralympic champion Jason Smyth, who was being lauded for his commitment to religious principles and adherence to the Latter-day Saint health code, the "Word of Wisdom." Indicative of the improved image that others were having of Latter-day Saints, Smyth noted that he has "found people very, very respectful of members of the Church for a number of reasons."[57] And he sees himself shedding "a bit of light" as he shares his beliefs and responds to people's questions. Northern Ireland's *Belfast Telegraph* underlined the importance that Smyth's religion has in his life and how it is a significant factor in his approach to sport. "It very much makes me who I am," Smyth told the newspaper. "I'd regard myself as being honest and with good morals and those attributes translate into sport. At times it can be a bit of a lifestyle which complements what I do in athletics."[58]

The Church's efforts to improve its image were ironically soon to be further supported by another opportunity occurring less than four months after the US election. On February 25, 2013, *The Book of Mormon*, one of the highest-grossing Broadway musicals, opened in London's West End. As his TV crew set up for an interview at the Church's Hyde Park visitors' center, BBC Arts Editor Will Gompertz expressed amazement at the Church's response to the musical. After all, this was a raw and blasphemous production depicting supposedly naïve missionaries assigned to a far-flung Ugandan village. But there were no religious protesters outside the Prince of Wales Theater, no accusatory big-lettered placards. The Church's position was that "the production may attempt to entertain audiences for an evening, but the Book of Mormon as a volume of scripture will change people's lives forever by bringing them closer to Christ."[59]

This understated methodology had proven successful in New York. It was certainly a principle-based "turn the other cheek" approach in response to the musical's over-the-top satirical portrayals. It was also a wise move in reputational terms, running alongside promotions for the pro-

---

56. Ginger Gibson, "Mormons praise Romney's impact."

57. Jason Smyth, interviewed by Fred E. Woods and Martin Andersen.

58. Jerome Taylor, "Team Ireland's Sprint Star Jason Smyth: I'm Not Politically Irish or British, I Don't Really Care."

59. "Book of Mormon Musical: Church's Official Statement," The Church of Jesus Christ of Latter-day Saints.

duction itself in London. The musical's marketers plastered posters with the slogan "The Mormons are coming!" on the sides of red double-decker buses. Hundreds of thousands of commuters picked up free copies of London's *Evening Standard* with wraparound front and back pages advertising the show.

The Church moved up a gear in its own multimedia campaign. The British-based Public Affairs office decided to mailshot key media outlets with what was effectively a video press release—a small battery-powered video screen inside a handheld cardboard box that journalists could easily flip open. The bold question on the box, "I'm a Mormon. What's the Real story?" grabbed their attention. *The Independent* remarked, "The Mormon church's increasingly hi-tech approach to door-knocking has reached new levels of wizardry. . . . Like an iPad crossed with a musical greetings card, it's easily the most elaborate of the hundreds of press releases newspapers receive every day."[60] The writer of the piece did question whether the Church leader featured in the videos was fully aware of the musical's very obscene lyrics; however, he likely was. The videos inside the box also included an interview with London-born Latter-day Saint singer Alex Boyé, who was subsequently probed on BBC World Service radio and asked several tough questions.

Some journalists were demonstrative in not providing the Church with a PR platform. Tanya Gold's feature in *The Sunday Times* was akin to a blatant opinion piece: "Mormons are among the most courteous people I have ever met; and I hope nobody converts to Mormonism after reading this article."[61] But even Gold noted, "The British Mormons, with a pragmatism I will come to recognize, decided to use the musical as a marketing opportunity. Such pragmatism, in dealings with the outside world, is typical of Mormons."[62]

Soon after the musical opened in London, the Church's own "I'm a Mormon" campaign took the London underground by storm. Many of the capital's transport hubs were covered in advertising, paid for by the faith's Missionary Department, inviting busy commuters to find out more about The Church of Jesus Christ of Latter-day Saints. The Church's public outreach in London during this campaign was unprecedented. To travel up an escalator at Oxford Circus or Piccadilly Circus Underground station and see

60. Simon Usborne, "Mormons: Unlikely Hi-tech PR Wizards."
61. Tanya Gold, "God Will Guide Us Through."
62. Gold, "God Will Guide Us Through."

The Book of Mormon musical, Prince of Wales Theatre, London, 2021.

every single available advertising space occupied by a Church advertisement would have left a strong impression on daily commuters. And then, going into the main concourse at Charing Cross station and seeing giant billboards everywhere was doubly impactful. Michael Otterson later reflected,

> In reality, a church that suffers from anonymity or indifference bought all available ad space in England's busiest stations, and cleverly piggy-backed on *The Book of Mormon* musical's own poster campaign also seen on dozens of London buses. That was surely faith-affirming for Latter-day Saints who often feel reluctant even to mention their religion to friends or work colleagues.[63]

The messaging was not couched as an appeal from a religious institution—the approach was person-to-person and aimed to introduce Latter-day Saints as people with interesting lives and deep faith that resonates with everyday life. The parallel digital campaign featured Church members from various parts of Britain. During his trip to the UK, Alex Boyé said the campaign had personal poignance for him because he appeared on the larger-than-life–size posters on the London Underground (subway system):

> I had personal experience because my face was . . . in those Mormon ads. I remember when I went back, and people would be like, "Oh my gosh, that is Alex Boyé, he used to be in a boy band and did that and that," so it was really cool for me. It was a great [conversation] piece with my friends, and it was a lot easier [because] they were like, "What is this about? I see you everywhere now. . . . In the Underground I see pictures of you." I said "Oh yeah, that is my church, I represent my church and we are trying to promote the goodness of our church, and try to let people know what we do, and try to break all the myths that were there." And can I tell you another thing? That was big for the Church in England.[64]

The "I'm a Mormon" theme was the focus for stories on the Church's UK Newsroom sites and on its social media channels. Mainstream media also picked up the theme and spoke to British Latter-day Saints. In a

---

63. Email from Michael Otterson to Malcolm Adcock, February 11, 2021.

64. Alex Boyé interview, interviewed by Fred E. Woods and Martin Andersen, home of Martin Andersen. Boyé was formerly a member of the 1990s British boy band Awesome when he took his own unorthodox and bold initiative in giving a copy of the Book of Mormon to Prince Charles in 1997. Boyé recalled that Prince Charles "looked at it, brought it close to his chest and said to me that he thought it would prove some interesting reading. 'Yes it will,' I responded. 'Perhaps you could read it in the helicopter on your way home.' He told me that he may just do that. And then he left." See Alex Boyé, "Prince Charles and the Book of Mormon." Also recorded in "A Royal Gift," 1.

Major advertising, Charing Cross rail station, London, April 2014. Courtesy Intellectual Reserve, Inc.

major feature, *The Daily Telegraph* quoted Richard Auger (among others), one of the "I'm a Mormon" campaign's faces, who challenged myths about his religion:

> "Obviously there are misconceptions and that is a real frustration," says the 51-year-old former firearms specialist, who was part of the first unit on the scene of the Hungerford massacre in 1987. "They always seem to be the same ones that come up. People who meet Mormons know these things aren't true. We're just people trying to live good lives and bring up families."[65]

Catching the Media's Attention

In the years following the "Mormon Moment," the Church continued to find itself in the media spotlight. In particular, two high-profile court cases attracted national media attention in March 2014. The first was a legal action at Westminster Magistrates Court, begun by a disaffected Latter-day Saint who asserted that the Church's religious claims were untrue and that tithes paid to the Church were thus fraudulent. This resulted in a UK magistrate issuing a summons to the Church's global leader President Thomas S. Monson. As reported by *The Daily Telegraph*, this was "one of the most unusual documents ever issued by a British

---

65. Joe Shute, "British Mormons Take On The Book of Mormon."

The 2013 UK "I'm a Mormon" campaign included advertisements on the sides of London's double-decker buses. Courtesy Intellectual Reserve, Inc.

court. . . . The document . . . demands that Mr. Monson appears in court number six at Westminster Magistrates' Court on Marylebone Road at 10am on March 14 or face arrest."[66] The Church's response was emphatic: "The Church occasionally receives documents like this that seek to draw attention to an individual's personal grievance or embarrass church leaders. . . . These bizarre allegations fit into that category."[67] Senior District Judge Howard Riddle who heard the case rejected the claims brought by the former follower of the faith: "I am satisfied that the process of the court is being manipulated to provide a high-profile forum to attack the religious beliefs of others."[68] According to Robert Pigott, the BBC's Religious Affairs correspondent,

> There has been a long history of reluctance by judges to intervene in theological disputes. . . . The court's verdict will be a relief to Mormons, whose 12th article of faith expresses a belief in "being subject to kings, presidents, rulers and magistrates, in obeying, honouring and sustaining the law."[69]

---

66. John Bingham, "Head of Mormon Church Thomas Monson Summoned by British Magistrates' Court over Adam and Eve Teaching."

67. Bingham, "Thomas Monson Summoned."

68. "Mormon leader Thomas Monson Fraud Case Thrown Out."

69. "Mormon leader Thomas Monson Fraud Case Thrown Out."

Entertainer and singer Alex Boyé featured in an advertisement from the Church within the Book of Mormon musical playbill UK. Courtesy Intellectual Reserve, Inc.

That same month, the European Court of Human Rights (ECHR) in Strasbourg, France, decided on an application brought by the Church about the levying of rates (property taxes) on the Preston Temple. While buildings used for "public religious worship" are exempted from paying property taxes, the Preston Temple was instead being classified as one for charitable use and only given an 80 percent relief. At stake was whether the temple's restrictive admittance for worship precluded it from being a place of public worship.[70] The Church's case was "that the denial of the exemption from business rates, reserved for buildings used for public religious worship, in respect of its temple at Preston, Lancashire, gave rise to violations of its rights" under the European Convention for the Protection of Human Rights and Fundamental Freedoms.[71] The ECHR, however, decided against the Church and concluded that there had been no human rights violation. As reported in the UK's *Church Times*, "Two of the ECHR judges added that tax exemption was a privilege and not a right, and that the application of that privilege did not interfere with the exercise of the right to freedom of religion."[72]

As editorial control always rests with the broadcaster, the best that the Church can hope for is a balanced show, sometimes with opposing—even controversial—viewpoints expressed. Anything more is an added bonus. Yet sometimes independently made media can be a mixed bag. In 2014, the television documentary *Meet the Mormons* depicted the missionary life of a young man assigned to proselyte in the Leeds area.[73] The producers had approached the Church with their proposal to make an inspiring observational documentary that would dispel myths about Latter-day Saints. Although opinions about the show have varied, feedback from observant British Latter-day Saints who had viewed the program indicated that they

---

70. Premises used for charitable purposes typically receive charity business-rates relief, reducing rates payable by 80 percent.

71. The Church of Jesus Christ of Latter-day Saints v. The United Kingdom, European Court of Human Rights (ECHR).

72. Shiranikha Herbert, "Mormon Temple Denied Rates Exemption."

73. *Meet the Mormons* (not to be confused with the Church-produced documentary of the same name), made by independent production company CTVC, broadcast on Channel 4, June 26, 2014. CTVC had previously liaised with Public Affairs on *The Story of Jesus*, BBC One, April 22, 2011 (a positive, faith-promoting program). Not long after *Meet the Mormons*, Channel 4 transmitted a balanced portrayal of "Mormon Helping Hands" volunteers on the peak time program *Double Your House for Half the Money*, September 17, 2014.

generally thought it provided an unbalanced portrayal of the Church and its missionary life—one inconsistent with their own experiences.

However, as in the past, there was also positive and informative coverage of the Church in the media. For example, one program leveraged viewers' love of ornate flower gardens and featured the Preston Temple. The BBC Two series *Britain in Bloom* (2018) followed communities throughout the UK taking part in an annual floral event—Brits are passionate about their well-kept green spaces. When the show came to Chorley, where the temple is located, the beautiful grounds came in for a very special mention, with the Church being "Highly Commended."[74]

Similarly, an episode of *Stacey Dooley Sleeps Over* that aired in 2019— a show in which the TV host spends three days living with a host family—captures the essence of Latter-day Saint family life and missionary preparation. [75] In this episode, Dooley spent seventy-two hours living in the home of Latter-day Saints Lindsay and Mark Preston and their three sons (ages 12, 15, 17) in Ashton-under-Lyne, near Manchester. Highlights of the show include interactions with Adam Preston, who was preparing for his mission, and an interview with a Latter-day Saint convert who became friends with the Prestons, and explained to Dooley how his life had transformed following homelessness and long-term drug dependence. Mark's heartfelt reflection about his and Lindsay's stillborn daughter was the most powerful part of the program and very moving for the TV audience. Dooley was in tears after this loving dad explained the pain of loss but expressed his hope in God's eternal blessings for their family.

The Academic Environment

In the United Kingdom, the strategic influence of global Latter-day Saint Church leaders and scholars, addressing academic groups with a common cause, has helped raise the profile of faith and emphasize its relevance in assisting with the world's challenges (socioeconomic and other).[76] For example, in 2011, the four hundredth anniversary of the King James Bible was celebrated throughout Britain and in much of the

74. Chris Bavin, "Chorley."

75. Stacey Dooley, "Mormons."

76. Brigham Young University promotes positive influence within the British academic and professional spheres via the BYU London Centre, the J. Reuben Clark Law Society (affiliated with BYU), and the BYU Management Society; as well as through the US-based but globally authoritative International Center

world. On May 14, Oxford's Harris Manchester College hosted an event cosponsored by The Church of Jesus Christ of Latter-day Saints. There, BYU Professor John S. Tanner explored the King James Bible's role in the lives of four prominent figures in United States history: John Winthrop ("the Pilgrim"), Joseph Smith ("the Prophet"), Abraham Lincoln ("the President"), and Martin Luther King ("the Preacher"). Emeritus member of one of the Church's Quorums of the Seventy Elder Kenneth Johnson also shared his personal testimony of the Holy Bible. "It has transformed me as I've learned what it teaches," he said. "The Bible bears witness of Jesus Christ as the Son of God."[77]

While once (and sometimes still) reviled for being unorthodox and outside of traditional Christian theism, Latter-day Saint teachings revealed through Joseph Smith's revelations and translated scripture have begun to find an academic home in interfaith dialogue. Revd. Dr. Andrew Teal—Chaplain, Fellow, and Lecturer in Theology at Pembroke College Oxford—has stimulated discussion on how faith can transform the human condition and has progressed dialogue about Latter-day Saint theology, including a November 22, 2018, public discourse with Jeffrey R. Holland that worked toward building theological bridges.[78] One of Teal's arguments is that aspects of Latter-day Saint doctrine, including humankind's potential to become like God and the belief in a spiritual creation prior to the physical one, are consistent with teachings in the early centuries of the Christian Church:

> Athanasius of Alexandria talks about, "He became human that we might become divine," that salvation is understood as divinization. And this is within

---

for Law and Religion Studies. BYU supports and participates in numerous conferences and events, including at Oxford University.

77. "Oxford University and Latter-day Saints Join for King James Bible Symposium," The Church of Jesus Christ of Latter-day Saints.

78. During an event held at Oxford's University Church of St. Mary the Virgin, Revd. Dr. Andrew Teal was in conversation with Elder Holland in a public discussion about Latter-day Saint beliefs. Elder Holland later joined a distinguished panel at Pembroke College, Oxford, which addressed how Christian doctrine can be translated into Christian practice through service. He joined Rt. Hon. and Most Revd. Lord Rowan Williams (a former Archbishop of Canterbury), Professor Lord David Alton (Roman Catholic Independent Crossbench life peer in the House of Lords), and leading Methodist minister Revd. Professor Frances Young. See Andrew Teal, ed., *Inspiring Service: Interfaith Remarks with Elder Jeffrey R. Holland at Oxford.*

the mainstream of the early church. And [an] early Christian called Origen of Alexandria, who was martyred in [around] 250 of the Common Era, he postulated, from the story of Genesis, that there was a spiritual creation and a material one. That all souls were created and were part of the eternal life of God.[79]

Through these efforts Teal has urged Christian theologians to take a new approach to the Book of Mormon and other books regarded by Latter-day Saints as scripture, an approach that sees value in them as tools to help people get closer to God:

> I think people judge the Book of Mormon and The Church of Jesus Christ of Latter-day Saints, I think in a different way than they would do, for example, the Bible. The Bible has got a history of all sorts of scholarship and interpretation from the earliest days. There's as [many] strange things that happen in the Bible if you want to pick [them] out. . . . But actually, we ought to be bigger than that. We ought to say, "What is it then, about the Book of Mormon, and the Doctrine and Covenants, Pearl of Great Price, what's their real scandal?" I think it's because it's saying that God, the real, true God who is the Creator and who loves us and who sent His Son to completely redeem and restore the creation, can be present.[80]

Dr. James Holt, Associate Professor of Religious Education at the University of Chester and a Latter-day Saint, flags the challenge some religious leaders and public bodies have faced in categorizing Latter-day Saints within Christianity and suggests a potential solution: "There are traditionally seen to be three main groupings of Churches: Orthodox, Catholic, and Protestant. However, The Church of Jesus Christ of Latter-day Saints would place itself outside of this traditional typology, perhaps preferring the term 'restorationist.'"[81] However, Holt says that no one—whether Latter-day Saint or not—should overly focus on this issue:

> Sometimes I think in the United Kingdom, we get a little bit too hung up on being seen to be Christian. Because being Christian, and being a Christian myself is great, and I'm very comfortable with who I am, my own beliefs, and that I'm a disciple of Jesus Christ. But if all we ever talk about, is "you're not Christian, or I am Christian" and have that discussion, then the discussion . . . can't go further.[82]

---

79. Andrew Teal, interviewed by Fred E. Woods.
80. Andrew Teal interview.
81. James D. Holt, *Beyond the Big Six Religions: Expanding the Boundaries in the Teaching of Religion and World Views*, 33.
82. James Holt, interviewed by Fred E. Woods and Martin Andersen.

Efforts by Latter-day Saints to engage in productive interfaith dialogue have proven fruitful, and in 2014 The Church of Jesus Christ of Latter-day Saints was accepted into membership of the state-funded Inter Faith Network for the United Kingdom,[83] following tireless work by many Public Affairs volunteers and staffers, as well as extensive lobbying from several faiths. Canon Sarah Snyder, with her background as a special adviser to the Archbishop of Canterbury, welcomed the Latter-day Saints' interfaith outreach and thinks the public should hear more about it: "I think the Church [of Jesus Christ] of Latter-day Saints are doing a huge amount of bridge-building in the UK and I would love other people to know more about that."[84]

Celebrations of Faith

Public engagement by the Church institutionally in the United Kingdom is increasing, and individual members are making their mark as well. Sea Trek 2001, an ambitious project with extensive community results, is one such example. This reenactment of the nineteenth-century European Latter-day Saint emigrants' ocean voyages in tall ships was conceived as a privately organized venture with public benefit—though ultimately a third-party Church affiliate provided what amounted to a financial bailout.[85] The events drew in large crowds, and dozens of news stories were published about the tall ships' arrivals at four UK harbors— Greenock in Scotland, and the English ports of Hull, Liverpool, and Portsmouth.[86] In addition, the BBC broadcast its coverage of the events to millions of viewers on network radio and national television.[87]

---

83. On September 29, 2014, the Church was granted full membership status of the Inter Faith Network for the UK, at their Annual General Meeting. See Andrew Dawson, "Religious Diversity and the Shifting Sands of Political Prioritization: Reflections on the UK Context."

84. Canon Sarah Snyder, interviewed by Fred E. Woods and Martin Andersen. She has contributed to the UK and global faith community as the Archbishop of Canterbury's Special Adviser for Reconciliation Programmes and Resources, as well as founding director of the Rose Castle Foundation.

85. Carrie A. Moore, "LDS Affiliate Pays Off Sea Trek Debt."

86. John and Shauna Hart, "20,000 Line Riverbanks Leading to Hull."

87. Hart, "20,000 Line Riverbanks Leading to Hull." See also John and Shauna Hart, "Sea Trek Gleans Broad Media Attention."

Latter-day Saint missionaries sharing the British Pageant stage, August 2013. Courtesy Intellectual Reserve, Inc.

The year 2013 saw another widely publicized celebration of the Church in the United Kingdom with the British Pageant breaking new ground as the nation's first large-scale Latter-day Saint pageant.[88] In Latter-day Saint tradition, pageants are a celebration of events, people, and places that are important in the history and doctrine of the faith, and they typically have a strong musical element. On July 31, three hundred volunteers of all ages performed the British Pageant on a 480-square-foot stage within a specially built theater on the Preston Temple grounds.[89] The event, entitled *Truth Will Prevail*, told the story of the Latter-day Saints' British heritage and their deep roots in Christianity. There were ten performances, with 17,000 audience members over that period.[90] Three members of the Quorum of the Twelve Apostles attended—Elder Russell M. Nelson, Elder M. Russell Ballard, and Elder Jeffrey R. Holland—along

88. A pageant to mark the centennial of the arrival of the first missionaries to Britain was held at Rochdale Town Hall on July 31, 1937. In attendance was Church President Heber J. Grant and First Presidency Second Counselor J. Reuben Clark. See Linda Jones, "Missionary Memories Link Pageant Past to Pageant Present."

89. "Truth Will Prevail! UK Mormons Honour British Heritage in The British Pageant," The Church of Jesus Christ of Latter-day Saints.

90. David M. W. Pickup, "Church Leaders Attend 'Stunningly Moving' British Pageant."

with community leaders. Nelson, who would begin leading the Church five years later, commented on the great resonance he saw in the event:

> The significance of the British Saints in the history of the Church is without parallel. . . . The pageant is a bridge-building effort to show the reciprocal relationship ebbing and flowing between Britain and America, very vital to the history of the Church.[91]

RootsTech Comes to London

RootsTech is a family history and technology conference held each year in Salt Lake City, organized by FamilySearch International, whose primary benefactor is The Church of Jesus Christ of Latter-day Saints. In October 2019 this family discovery conference was held outside of the USA for the first time, at London's ExCeL Convention Centre. With a total of forty-two countries represented, nearly ten thousand attendees came from across the United Kingdom, continental Europe, the Middle East, and other parts of the world to explore innovative ways to connect with ancestors and celebrate family heritage.[92]

The three-day event featured several prominent speakers addressing the RootsTech London audiences. Dan Snow, British historian and television presenter, was the opening keynote on the event's first day.[93] Paralympic gold medalist Kadeena Cox shared her personal story of determination and perseverance.[94] And Donny Osmond entertained the audience as he shared his personal journey of family discovery.

---

91. Pickup, "British Pageant."

92. "RootsTech Hosts International Conference in London," The Church of Jesus Christ of Latter-day Saints.

93. "RootsTech Hosts International Conference in London," The Church of Jesus Christ of Latter-day Saints.

94. "RootsTech Hosts International Conference in London," The Church of Jesus Christ of Latter-day Saints. Relatable human interest angles about family history can drive the national press to respond to media outreach from the Church Communication Department. A UK tabloid newspaper latched on to the personal story that British TV actress Sunetra Sarker told at the online RootsTech Connect event, held February 25–27, 2021. Sarker, well-known for her roles in television soap operas and other primetime shows, addressed issues of racial identity and family heritage. She acknowledged that learning to appreciate her family history was personally therapeutic: "The defensiveness, the shame I felt at being of Asian origin just went when I realised how incredible my history was." See "Sunetra's 'So Proud' of Her Past," 7.

Donny Osmond at RootsTech London, October 2019. Courtesy
FamilySearch International.

In addition, government, faith, and community leaders were also
hosted. Martin Vickers, Member of Parliament for Cleethorpes on
England's East coast, commented on the significant themes he saw in
Donny Osmond's presentation at the VIP dinner: "It emphasized to me
the importance of family ties and how family is . . . the foundation of society and I think [that's] valuable and it's something that's under threat at
the moment."[95] Addressing the audience of dignitaries at the dinner, Elder
David A. Bednar of the Quorum of the Twelve Apostles outlined what he
described as an "audacious" plan, to compile a family tree of all humankind spanning all history and geography: "Together with the Lord's help,
we will accomplish something that one would think cannot be done."[96]

Special events were also held for the London-based diplomatic corps.
During the RootsTech ambassador reception, Bednar met Nicaragua's
ambassador to the United Kingdom, Her Excellency Guisell Morales-
Echaverry. She later introduced the Apostle to several high-ranking government representatives during his visit to Managua, Nicaragua, where
the Church is building a temple. The Church News reported Bednar's
reflections on his interactions in London and Managua:

---

95. Martin Vickers, interviewed by Fred E. Woods and Martin Andersen.
96. Scott Taylor, "The Big Picture of How London Is the Gateway for
RootsTech's Global Reach."

For 30 minutes during a morning breakfast meeting, Elder Bednar explained what a temple is and why The Church of Jesus Christ of Latter-day Saints is building a temple in Managua, Nicaragua.

Only the Lord could orchestrate a seemingly chance meeting in London with a leader who . . . then would arrange important meetings in Nicaragua, said Elder Bednar, who had been assigned to visit both countries months earlier.[97]

Light the World

In 2018 London was one of two cities to be the first locations outside the United States to host the Church's "Giving Machines" that provided novel ways to give at Christmastime.[98] Using the specially designed vending machines, members of the public could use their credit or debit cards to pay for specific items, whether it be a goat for a struggling family overseas, a meal for a homeless veteran, or a donation to a UK foodbank. These Giving Machines are part of the Church's Light the World initiative that includes an online campaign to promote altruism in everyday life. A year later in 2019, this same approach to charitable giving caught the attention of three hundred UK news outlets through Press Association syndication.[99]

Influencing the Influencers

As well as an improved media and digital profile, much of the change for The Church of Jesus Christ of Latter-day Saints has resulted from the interpersonal relationships between members of the Church and people in the public eye. As Councilor Julian Bell explained,

There's an awful lot of people who don't know any "Mormons" and therefore, they don't have any actual, personal friendships that they can kind of look to, to say well okay, I know Judy or whoever and they're "Mormons" and they're very sound, good people. So, for example, I remember when I first started working for the Labour Party in the mid '90s, I was working in Islington for the Islington South and Finsbury Labour Party as a campaign

---

97. Sarah Jane Weaver, "Central America Is Evidence the Gospel Strengthens Generations Says Elder Bednar."

98. The other city was Manila, Philippines.

99. The Church Communication Department (formerly known as Public Affairs) worked closely on the campaign with Bonneville International Corporation (the media and broadcasting company owned by The Church of Jesus Christ of Latter-day Saints) and its partner agencies.

"Light the World" Giving Machine, London, Hyde Park Chapel, 2020. Courtesy Martin Andersen.

organizer. And it was reported that one of the councilors who later became a London Assembly Member . . . heard that I was a Mormon. And this got fed back to me, but when she heard that I was a Mormon she said, "That can't be right. He's far too sensible to be a Mormon." So I think there is that perception even now that we're not seen as being sensible, unless you actually meet somebody and know them.[100]

These efforts by the Church and its members in the United Kingdom to promote and be examples of Christian living have made an impact on British minds. For example, Canon Ann Easter has recently noted how her own perspective on The Church of Jesus Christ of Latter-day Saints has been modified over the years:

---

100. Julian Bell interview. Bell also related an account where he was intensely questioned about the Church's social attitudes. "When I got the job working for Chris Smith, the Islington South and Finsbury Labour MP in the mid '90s, . . . Chris was at the time [an] . . . openly gay MP [in] Parliament [who] later went on to be a Cabinet Minister, a lovely guy Chris, I got along very well with him. But in my interview when I got the job, I was quizzed about my church's views on homosexuality. And the questioning got quite intense. And I answered the questions as best I could, but [in] the final answer which I gave, which I think got me the job, I said, 'Look, I've grown up in a minority religion all my life. As a result of that I've experienced prejudice . . . and because of that experience, I'm against prejudice wherever I find it.' And that was it, the questioning stopped, and they gave me the job."

I think once upon a time it was most definitely regarded as quite a weird sect. And as such, I wouldn't particularly [have] had much to do with it because in a way one is somehow a bit nervous, frightened. You know, do they take people and make them stay places? Or something like that. . . . As the years have gone by, I think I've come round to a different view and I've come round to valuing the Mormon way of life and the Mormon faith which I do most definitely see as Christian. You know, I don't see how anybody could say that you're not Christians because I believe very strongly that you are.[101]

Moving Forward

There is, however, still much to be done. The modern-day owner of Benbow Farm, Louise Manning, regularly talks to groups about the significance of the farm in Latter-day Saint history, and she believes that "there is still a high level of unawareness" of the Church's activities "by most people in the UK."[102] "[T]here probably is a job to be done to explain in more detail about the Church and what it believes and how it interacts with communities throughout the world." Not only would this help people understand about how the Church is spending resources to assist broken neighborhoods, but the Church's approach could also be replicated in civil society.

The philanthropic ethic is not unique to any one religion, but it is certainly a principle held dear by members of The Church of Jesus Christ of Latter-day Saints. Prominent UK Muslim Mohammed Amin MBE observed:

What I find inspiring about "Mormonism" is, first of all, their strong sense of religious faith and secondly, their commitment to supporting other members of their own community. . . . But on top of that, I see an enormous commitment to making the world better for everyone, and there are so many factors about "Mormonism" which are intensely positive from the perspective of its practitioners.[103]

---

101. Ann Easter interview.

102. Louise Manning, interviewed by Fred E. Woods and Martin Andersen.

103. Mohammed Amin, interviewed by Malcolm Adcock and Fred E. Woods, London. Mohammed Amin MBE's leadership roles have included being chairman of the Council of the Islam & Liberty Network, chairman of the Conservative Muslim Forum, and co-chair of the Muslim Jewish Forum of Greater Manchester.

From this groundswell of internalized Christian faith comes a range of practical ways that individuals can add value to society at large. Simon Gibson CBE DL believes that Latter-day Saints have even more to offer:

> For us to continue to make strides and contribute to society, we need to mobilize our members to do more. There's too few of our members getting involved in society. And sometimes that was historically due to church commitments. You know, they have callings in the Church that take so much time that they don't have time to do civil responsibilities. But you can see the Church now streamlining church, reducing the amount of time we have to spend at church. . . .
>
> We take it for granted our ability to administer things. We teach kids from 8 years old how to run meetings, how to get action plans done. We take that for granted. We have young people go on missions and they learn incredible skills about how to interact with society, they can do it in multiple languages! . . .
>
> I just would say that I think if we can mobilize Latter-day Saints to do more of that, the impact would be profound because they'll have this multiplier effect. They'll be able to inspire more people to do it. But it has to be done with a spirit of doing it for society.[104]

The impact of "doing good" inevitably leads to new, more accurate narratives. The Bible mandates Christians to "let [their] light so shine"[105] so more people can praise God and be brought to the Father of all.[106] There is good evidence that reports of service can result in powerful news copy—even in a media environment where journalists report religious conflict, often covering this at the exclusion of religious good.[107] For example, the Church's own media survey for a submission to a 2020 British Parliamentary inquiry on religious reporting referred to the reader appeal

---

104. Simon Gibson interview.

105. See Matthew 5:16.

106. See Matthew 6:1–4.

107. The COVID-19 pandemic provided many additional opportunities for the Church in the UK to reach out to people in need, and this community outreach attracted media interest. The Latter-day Saint mindset to prepare for emergencies also provided a timely pandemic-related angle for BBC network radio when the broadcaster focused on the Isle of Anglesey, just off the North Wales coast. The reporter was intrigued by the Church's foresight to ready people for unexpected events. BBC Radio 4's promotional material for the program noted that "in 2018, the church even instructed its members to prepare to worship at home. They have felt well equipped to deal with the uncertainty brought by 2020." "Anglesey," BBC Radio 4.

of community and interfaith angles—stories about positive faith-related activities with headlines including "Bishop Saves the Day by Hosting Blood Drives," "Women's Day Marked at Church," [108] and "Aid Worker Shows Support for Flood-hit Communities."[109]

Looking to the Future

Impressions of Latter-day Saints vary widely; there is huge diversity of experience across the range of personal interactions and throughout the public square. Perhaps one theme that has emerged from our research is the imperative for members of The Church of Jesus Christ to be seen as— and to actually be—inclusive, outwardly facing towards their fellow members of British society and to the world. In the past, the time demands in building a British Zion—serving congregational needs—had perhaps understandably caused challenges in this regard. Now, building Zion in practical terms means strengthening congregations *and* supporting local communities. JustServe, the service initiative provided by the Church, has recently been launched in the United Kingdom. It brings organizations and volunteers together so they can do good in the community. Accessing local opportunities is intended to be user-friendly via the JustServe social media app. As well as responding to the needs of others, the "giver" often gains much too, even if it is a temporary respite from dwelling on their own problems. Community service by Latter-day Saints is not new, but JustServe has the potential to be scalable as Church members link with people of other faiths and beliefs.

Actress Savannah Stevenson, a member of the Church, praised Church members for their efforts and encouraged cultural changes from Latter-day Saints themselves:

---

108. The role of women within The Church of Jesus Christ of Latter-day Saints has often been the subject of close scrutiny by external observers including British media, and from some campaigning groups and individuals within the Latter-day Saint community. Women are not ordained to priesthood offices in the Church. But the doctrine that women exercise priesthood authority, even though they do not hold priesthood office, has received renewed emphasis from global Church leadership.

109. All-Party Parliamentary Group on Religion in the Media, "APPG On Religion in the Media Response to Call for Written Evidence: Inquiry into Religious Literacy in Print and Broadcast Media," 6.

I think something that we can do to sort of change the look of [Latter-day Saints] in a more positive light, is to break away the barriers that I think are sometimes in place for people. I think sometimes we can be [in] an "Us and Them" situation and actually we are no better, no different to anyone else. We're all finding our way in the world. I think that if we can lose that part of our culture sometimes, it's wonderful because we create communities, but I think we can reach out more. We can reach out and go "We might not think the same, but we can go get along and we can work together, and we can love each other."[110]

Latter-day Saints have typically wanted to be friends with those around them and to enter dialogue with others. Some cultural attitudes and the use of certain language may, in some cases, have interrupted the conversation. Latter-day Saints are increasingly identifying and dealing with the barriers that they may have even erected themselves. Examples of this exclusionary language include the phrases "non-member" for people who are not baptized members of the Church, or "investigators" for those meeting with Latter-day Saint missionaries. Now, "neighbors" and "friends" are, respectively, emphasized and are becoming more common. Even overly formal missionary clothing can be daunting, especially to millennials and Generation Z. In June 2020, the Church announced an option for more smart-casual standards of attire;[111] this is in tandem with significantly increased online interactions by missionaries, rather than the traditional door-knocking approach.[112]

---

110. Savannah Stevenson, interviewed by Fred E. Woods and Martin Andersen. British actor and writer Michael Danvers-Walker, born in 1935 and baptized forty years later, sees Church discourse with a diversity of groups, including with LGBTQ support groups, as imperative. "It's so important that there is dialogue between all these different communities, because you can live in isolation otherwise, and ignorance and prejudice. And that's unfortunately what does happen, not only in our church but [in] lots of churches. . . . And so I think dialog and understanding and intercommunication is so vital." (Michael Danvers-Walker, interviewed by Malcolm Adcock.)

111. "In approved teaching areas, young men (commonly known as elders) may be able to wear a white or plain blue dress shirt with or without a tie." See "Exceptions to Dress Standards Announced for Young Male Missionaries," The Church of Jesus Christ of Latter-day Saints.

112. For example, an online devotional from the England London Mission was livestreamed on May 3, 2020, reaching more than 32,600 people from forty-five countries. The Facebook page for the event received 3,500 comments. Note that Revd. Dr. Andrew Teal, Chaplain, Fellow, and Lecturer at Pembroke

In addition, social media interaction is often the norm for many initial social contacts across society, especially in younger age-groups. Reaching out about faith in this way is simply reflective of how people increasingly relate to each other. Utilizing social media channels is thus becoming an important aspect of Church communication. (The Church's UK Facebook page has over 100,000 "likes" and is buoyed by frequently updated content.)

As the decades have rolled on, this is now the context surrounding membership within The Church of Jesus Christ of Latter-day Saints in modern Britain and how it is perceived. The religion was once persecuted, even feared. Hateful epithets are now virtually nonexistent. The Church is no stranger to the media spotlight, and indeed its activities are often subjected to microscopic scrutiny. In a society largely ambivalent toward the benefits of any organized religion, this particular faith may sometimes face a skeptical public, and even hostility in the media. But its profile is changing. Theological differences aside, here is a church once at the margins that is now increasingly seen as part of the local religious community as much as any other faith. Its observant members incorporate adherence to a rigorous moral code with integration in British society (and, typically, effectiveness in their professions). The Church will always be a proselyting one, consistent with the biblical commission,[113] but now a complementary and concurrent narrative is developing—here is a group of people aiming to make a difference through organized and spontaneous Christian service, the essence of the gospel they seek to follow.

College Oxford, also spoke at the devotional. "England London Mission's Online Devotional Strengthens Christian Faith Globally," The Church of Jesus Christ of Latter-day Saints.

113. Latter-day Saint leaders' prophetic vision for the Church's future in the British Isles was encapsulated by President Gordon B. Hinckley, immediately before he offered the dedicatory prayer at the Preston Temple groundbreaking. He stated, "Your presence here today, my brethren and sisters, in such large numbers, is evidence that 'truth has prevailed', it will continue to prevail, and whereas there are now thousands, tens of thousands of members of the Church in this wonderful land, there will be hundreds and hundreds of thousands. I have no doubt of that, and do not hesitate in saying so." (Remarks by President Gordon B. Hinckley, Preston Temple groundbreaking June 12, 1994.)

Dedicatory Prayer of the London Temple

Plans to construct the temple were announced August 10, 1953; Church leaders broke ground August 27, 1955; and David O. McKay, President of The Church of Jesus Christ of Latter-day Saints from 1951 to 1970, dedicated the London England Temple on September 7, 1958, with this prayer. Following renovation, President Gordon B. Hinckley rededicated the temple on October 18, 1992.

O God, our Heavenly Father, Thou who hast created all things, whose plans infinite and progressive, ever serve to foster closer relationship between Thee and the human family. We, Thy children, assemble before Thee this day in gratitude and praise. Thou hast said that Thy work and Thy glory is "to bring to pass the immortality and eternal life of man" (Moses 1:39).

Therefore, human beings are engaged in life's highest activity when they cooperate with Thee in bringing about this consummation. Earth with its barren rocks and saline seas, and lifeless planetary systems would be purposeless without the creation of intelligent human beings. Only in their creation and eternal destiny do we find the answer to the question:

"What is man, that Thou art mindful of him and the son of Man, that Thou visitest him?

"For Thou hast made him a little lower than the angels, and hast crowned him with glory and honor" (Psalm 8:4–5). Plainly Thy glory is not in lifeless formations, but in the "immortality and eternal life of man" (Moses 1:39). Temples are but one means of man's cooperation with Thee in accomplishing this divine purpose.

On the occasion of the dedication of this, the fourteenth temple, may we first express overwhelming gratitude just to be alive in this great age of the world. We pause this morning to open our hearts to Thee for this special privilege. No other time in world history has been so wonderful— no other age wherein Thy secret powers have been more within human control; in no other era hath Thy purposes been nearer human comprehension. Help us, O Lord, truly to live!

Next to life we express gratitude for the gift of free agency. When Thou didst create man, Thou placed within him part of Thine omnipotence and bade him choose for himself. Liberty and conscience thus became a sacred part of human nature. Freedom not only to think, but to speak and to act is a God-given privilege.

Thou didst inspire Thy servant President Brigham Young to say, "Every man's independence is sacred to him—it is a portion of that same Deity that rules in the heavens. There is not a being upon the face of the earth who is made in the image of God, who stands erect and is organized as God is, that should be deprived of the free exercise of his agency so far as he does not infringe upon others' rights save by good advice and a good example." Personal liberty is the paramount essential to human dignity and human happiness.

Down through the ages men have been free to accept or to reject Thy righteous plan. History records how many have yielded to the enticements of the flesh, and how few, comparatively speaking, have followed the path of light and truth that leads to happiness and eternal life!

But Thy mercy, Thy wisdom, Thy love are infinite; and in dispensations past Thou hast pleaded, as Thou dost now plead, through chosen and authoritatively appointed servants, for Thy erring children to heed the gospel message and come to Thee. Holy temples are a means of extending Thy loving mercy to Thy children even beyond the grave.

When in the Middle Ages the Church departed from Christ's teachings Thou didst inspire honest, upright men here in Great Britain to raise their voices against corrupt practices. Mingling with the denunciatory messages of Luther and Melanchthon in Germany, and Swingli in Switzerland, were the voices of George Wishart and later John Knox of Scotland. We thank Thee that before the scorching flames silenced his tongue and reduced his body to ashes Thou didst permit George Wishart to glimpse that "this realm shall be illuminated with the light of Christ's evangel, as clearly as ever was any realm since the days of the apostles. The house of God shall be builded in it; yea, it shall not lack the very copestone."

Much clearer was the inspiration given President Wilford Woodruff, and President Joseph F. Smith, and other more recent apostles, who stated prophetically that "temples of God . . . will be erected in the divers countries of the earth," and that "Temples will appear all over the land of Joseph—North and South America—and also in Europe and elsewhere; and all the descendants of Shem, Ham, and Jaspheth, who received not the gospel in the flesh, must be officiated for in the temples of God before the Savior can present the kingdom to the Father, saying, 'It is finished.'"

We are grateful that in 1837 and 1840 authorized messengers were sent to Great Britain to announce to the people of the British Isles that

God had again spoken from the heavens and reestablished in its purity and fullness the gospel of Jesus Christ; that thousands accepted the message and subsequently emigrated to the headquarters of the Church.

We thank Thee that Thou, Great Elohim, and Jehovah, Thy Beloved Son, answered the fervent appeal of the lad Joseph Smith, and through subsequent administrations of angels, enabled and authorized him to organize the Church of Jesus Christ in its completeness with apostles, prophets, pastors, teachers, evangelists, etc., as it was established in the days of the Savior and the apostles in the meridian of time.

In keeping with the unwavering truth that Thy Church must be established by divine authority, Thou didst send heavenly messengers to confer upon the Prophet Joseph Smith and others the Aaronic and Melchizedek Priesthoods, and subsequently all the keys of the priesthood ever held by Thy prophets from Adam, the Ancient of Days, through Abraham and Moses, Malachi, and Elijah, with authority to "turn the heart of the fathers to the children, and the heart of the children to their fathers" (Mal. 4:6) down to the latest generation. For this consistency, and completeness of restoration of authority, we express gratitude on this occasion and praise Thy holy name.

We express gratitude to Thee for the leaders of Thy Church from the Prophet Joseph Smith through the years to the present General Authorities—the First Presidency, the Council of the Twelve Apostles, the Assistants to the Twelve, the Patriarch to the Church, the First Council of the Seventy, the Presiding Bishopric.

With humility and deep gratitude we acknowledge Thy nearness, Thy divine guidance and inspiration. Help us, we pray Thee, to become even more susceptible in our spiritual response to Thee.

Bless the presidencies of stakes, high councils, presidencies of missions, bishoprics of wards, presidencies of branches, presidencies of quorums, superintendencies, and presidencies of auxiliary associations throughout the world—make them keenly aware of the fact that they are trusted leaders, and that they are to hold sacred that trust as they treasure their lives.

We are grateful that the members of the Church recognize that the payment of tithes and offerings brings blessings and makes possible the proclamation of the gospel to the ends of the world, and contributes to the carrying out of Thy purposes through the building of chapels, tabernacles, and eventually temples wherever the Church is organized in all lands and climes.

It is fitting that we express appreciation of the signing of the Magna Carta in the county of Surrey, the same county in which we meet today wherein the promise is given that no freeman shall be taken or imprisoned or seized or outlawed or exiled without proper trial by his peers or by the law of the land.

This protection of the individual is in keeping with Thy divine will; and any group of men who advocate an ideology that would deprive man of this individual right and heritage and make him a vassal of the state stamp themselves at once as enemies of Thy divine purposes.

We express gratitude for the right of free peoples to resort to the ballot, and for freedom to meet in legislative halls to consider problems and settle difficulties without fear or coercion of dictators, of secret police, or of slave camps. O Father, help people everywhere more clearly to realize that government exists for the protection of the individual, not the individual for the government.

Bless, we beseech Thee, Her Majesty, Queen Elizabeth II, the Houses of Parliament, and all branches of government throughout her Majesty's realm, that the high reputation of this great government for the proper and just enforcement of law may continue to be meritoriously maintained.

May the United States government with Great Britain, her Dominions, and freedom-loving countries everywhere, including South American republics, hold so sacredly the principles of self-government, and give to their peoples such enjoyment of peace, tranquility, and opportunities for progress as will make communistic governments of dictatorship, of mock trials, of unjust imprisonment, of enforced tyranny, so universally reprehensible as to be discarded forever by liberty-loving peoples.

That peace may eventually prevail, Thou has again restored in its fullness the gospel, and established authoritatively the Church of Jesus Christ. Even so, there are millions who are being influenced by false ideologies which are disturbing the peace of mind and distorting the thinking of honest men and women. O Lord, guide and protect Thy messengers in their efforts to convince honest people in all lands and climes that Jesus Christ is "the way, the truth, and the light" (John 14:6) and that "there is none other name under heaven given among men, whereby we must be saved" (Acts 4:12).

Bless well-meaning men in all climes as they strive to hasten the day when men will renounce contention and strife and desire to use the great nuclear discoveries of the present day not for war and destruction, but for peace and spiritual advancement.

To this end, we beseech Thee to influence leaders of nations that their minds may be averse to war, their hearts cleansed from prejudice, suspicion, and hate, and filled with a desire for peace and goodwill.

While his body lay in the tomb, Christ, Thy Beloved Son, preached to the spirits in prison who once were disobedient in the days of Noah, thus evidencing that those who have passed beyond the veil must also hear the word of God and obey the eternal principles of life and salvation.

Temples are built to Thy holy name as a means of uniting Thy people, living and dead, in bonds of faith, of peace, and of love throughout eternity.

Help all, O Father, to realize more keenly and sincerely than ever before that only by obedience to eternal principles and ordinances of the gospel of Jesus Christ may loved ones who died without baptism be permitted the glorious privilege of entrance into Thy kingdom.

Increase our desire, therefore, to put forth even greater effort toward the consummation of Thy purposes.

To this end, by the authority of the holy priesthood, we dedicate this, the London Temple of the Church of Jesus Christ of Latter-day Saints, and consecrate and set it apart for the sacred purposes, for which it has been erected. We ask Thee to accept this edifice and to guard it from foundation to tower. Protect it from earthquakes, tempestuous storms, or other devastating holocausts. We dedicate the ground on which it stands and by which it is surrounded. May the baptismal font, the ordinance rooms, and especially the sealing rooms be kept holy that Thy spirit may be ever present to comfort and to inspire.

Bless the persons who are charged to look after all mechanical installations and fixtures, that they may do so skillfully, faithfully, and reverently.

Bless the president of the temple and his wife as matron. Let humility temper their feelings; wisdom, and kind consideration guide their actions. May they, and others, who will be appointed as assistants and custodians, maintain an atmosphere of cleanliness and holiness in every room. Let no unclean person or thing ever enter herein; for, "my spirit," sayeth the Lord, "will not dwell in unclean tabernacles"; neither will it remain in a house where selfish, arrogant, or unwholesome thoughts abide. Therefore, may all who enter this holy temple come with clean hands and pure hearts that Thy Holy Spirit may ever be present to comfort, to inspire, and to bless.

If any with gloomy forebodings or heavy hearts enter, may they depart with their burdens lightened and their faith increased; if any have envy or bitterness in their hearts, may such feelings be replaced by self-searching and forgiveness. May all who come within these sacred walls feel a peaceful, hallowed influence. Cause, O Lord, that even people who pass the grounds, or view the temple from afar, may lift their eyes from the groveling things of sordid life and look up to Thee and acknowledge Thy providence.

Through love for Thee, our Heavenly Father, and their fellow men, faithful members of Thy Church, and others who believe in Thee, have made possible by tithes and other generous contributions the erection and completion of this Thy holy house.

Accept of our offering, hallow it by Thy presence, protect it by Thy power.

With this prayer, we rededicate our lives to the establishment of the kingdom of God on earth for the peace of the world, and to Thy glory forever, in the name of Thy Beloved Son, Jesus Christ, amen.

Dedicatory Prayer of the Preston Temple

Plans to construct the temple were announced October 19, 1992; Church leaders broke ground June 12, 1994; and Gordon B. Hinckley, President of The Church of Jesus Christ of Latter-day Saints from 1995 to 2008, dedicated the Preston England Temple on June 7, 1998, with this prayer.

O God, our Eternal Father, we bow before Thee in solemn prayer as we dedicate this sacred house.

We worship Thee in spirit and in truth, Thou Great Elohim, the Almighty Judge of the nations, the Father of all mankind and the God of the universe.

We bow in reverence before Thy Beloved Son, the Lord Jesus Christ, who came to earth and gave His precious life in an act of Atonement that opened the gates of immortality and eternal life for each of us.

We bow in deepest gratitude for the gifts and blessings of the Holy Spirit which has borne witness of Thy divine reality and that of Thy Son.

We stand in respect and love for the Prophet Joseph Smith, the instrument in Thy hands in opening this great and final dispensation, the dispensation of the fulness of times, when Thou hast brought together in one the doctrines and practices of all previous dispensations.

Almighty God, forgive our sins on this day of dedication that we may come before Thee clean from all evil, and worthily as Thy children.

Through the centuries Thou hast smiled with favor upon England, "this sceptered isle." Great have been her ways, marvelous her destiny. She has bequeathed to the world the great principles of English law to enhance the dignity of man, and the priceless gift of the English Bible which since the year 1611 has stood as a testament of the Redeemer of the world.

This magnificent temple has been reared in this beautiful area where Thy chosen servants, in the days of their deep poverty and great sacrifice, first preached the restored gospel. Through 161 years of history this land of England, together with Scotland, Wales, and Ireland, has yielded a harvest of converts who have blessed and strengthened Thy Church. In early years thousands gave their lives when they left their homes, and with hope born of an abiding faith, sailed across the seas, and traversed a continent in search of Zion. Hallowed be their memory.

And now on this day which will long remain in our memories, acting in the authority of the eternal priesthood in us vested and in the name of Jesus Christ, we dedicate unto Thee and unto Thy Son this the Preston England Temple of The Church of Jesus Christ of Latter-day Saints. We pray that Thou wilt accept it as the sacred offering of Thy thankful people. This is Thy house and we ask that Thou wilt sanctify it with Thy presence. From this day forth may Thy Holy Spirit dwell within these walls and touch the hearts of all who enter herein.

We dedicate the grounds on which it stands, with their trees and shrubs, flowers and lawns, which add to the beauty of Thy house. We dedicate the structure from the footings of the temple to the figure of Moroni. We dedicate all of the components of the building that they may function harmoniously together to create a house that is "fitly framed."

We dedicate the Baptistry, the endowment rooms, the magnificent Celestial Room, the sealing rooms with their sacred altars, and every facility which is a part of Thy holy house.

Stay the hand of the vandal that he shall not deface or destroy. Temper the elements that they shall not damage or cause undue wear. May no unclean thing come within these hallowed walls. May Thy people come here with rejoicing in their hearts to enter into covenants with Thee, and be endowed with power from on high. May they kneel at these altars and be sealed together as families under the authority of the holy priesthood. May they return frequently to carry forward a great and selfless labor of vicarious work for the dead that the earth may not "be utterly wasted" (D&C 60:12) at the coming of Thy Son. May the multitudes of the dead, through living proxies, receive the ordinances herein offered.

Now we pray for the temple president and his counselors and the matron and her assistants. We pray for all who will serve in these hallowed precincts. May each work with an eye single to Thy glory and the building of Thy kingdom.

We pray for those who serve in temples throughout the world that all may rejoice in the glorious opportunity that is theirs to assist Thee, dear Father, in Thy work of bringing "to pass the immortality and eternal life of man" (Moses 1:39).

Bless Thy work in all the earth that it may roll forth "fair as the moon, clear as the sun, and terrible as an army with banners" (Song 6:10). We invoke Thy blessings upon Thy servants, the missionaries, wherever they labor. Watch over them, protect them from every evil, lead them to those who will accept their message, and bind their testimonies upon the hearts of all who shall hear them.

We remember before Thee those called and ordained to lead Thy Church in these days of great opportunity. Sustain them, we pray Thee, give them strength, speak through them and reveal unto them Thy divine will concerning Thy work.

Bless the Saints of the United Kingdom, these wonderful people of England, Scotland, Wales, and Northern Ireland, as well as those of the Irish Republic. As they pay their tithes and offerings, wilt Thou open the windows of heaven and shower down blessings upon them. Bless their homes and families. Bless their children that they may grow up with a love for the truth. Bless them in body and mind and spirit.

Holy Father, we love Thee. We love Thy Divine Son. We love Thy holy work. Help us to be faithful. Help us to be true. Help us to walk always with integrity. May we always look to Thee with gratitude and love and faith. May we be found always walking in Thy paths.

And now as we conclude this prayer dedicating Thy holy house, by the same authority of the holy priesthood we dedicate the other structures that comprise this complex designed and built to serve Thy purposes—the Preston England Stake Center, the Missionary Training Center, the Family History facility, the Distribution Center, the Patron Housing and Temple Missionary Accommodation facilities, and the Grounds Building—that each may fulfill its appointed purposes and be preserved and protected from evil hands and unrighteous designs.

Our dear Father, on this sacred day of dedication, we rededicate ourselves and all that we have and are to Thy holy work and that of Thy Beloved Son, and do it all in His name, even the name of the Lord Jesus Christ, Amen.

Bibliography

"50 Years of The Church of Jesus Christ of Latter-day Saints in East Kilbride." Early Day Motions. United Kingdom Parliament. Accessed April 19, 2020. https://edm.parliament.uk/early-day-motion/52402/50-years-of-the-church-of-jesus-christ-of-latter-day-saints-in-east-kilbride.

"Albert Hall." *Times* (London), August 29, 1955.

Alexander, Melvin C. Interviewed by Fred E. Woods and Martin L. Andersen, December 31, 2018. In the possession of the authors.

All-Party Parliamentary Group on Religion in the Media. "APPG On Religion in the Media Response to Call for Written Evidence: Inquiry into Religious Literacy in Print and Broadcast Media." Submission from The Church of Jesus Christ of Latter-day Saints, May 2020.

"American Chorus in Belfast." *Northern Whig*, November 6, 1936.

Amin, Mohammed. Interviewed by Malcolm Adcock and Fred E. Woods, May 8, 2019, London. Transcript in possession of the authors.

"Anglesey." *The Patch*. Aired August 10, 2020. BBC Radio 4. Accessed March 6, 2021. https://www.bbc.co.uk/programmes/m000lms0.

"Anne Gregg, Travel Journalist and Broadcaster." *Independent*, September 7, 2006.

"Anne Gregg." *Press Gazette*, September 28, 2006.

"Anti-Mormon Riot." *Derby Daily Telegraph*, June 5, 1912.

"Anti-Mormon Riot." *Manchester Courier*, June 27, 1914.

"Anti-Mormon Riot in London." *Western Daily Press*, August 27, 1885.

"The Anti-Mormon Riots at Brightside." *Sheffield Daily Telegraph*, December 9, 1884.

Armytage, W. H. G. "Liverpool, Gateway to Zion." *Pacific Northwest Quarterly* 44, no. 2 (April 1957): 39–44.

Ashton, Marvin J. "Singing Ambassadors." *Millennial Star* 100, no. 33 (August 18, 1938): 520–21.

Avant, Gerry. "Choir Begins Europe Tour in Famed London Hall." *Church News*, June 20, 1998. https://www.thechurchnews.com/archives/1998-06-20/choir-begins-europe-tour-in-famed-london-hall-127237.

———. "Temple Rededicated, Lives Renewed." *Church News*, October 31, 1992. https://www.thechurchnews.com/archives/1992-10-31/temple-rededicated-lives-renewed-143775.

Baroness Nicholson of Winterbourne. Interviewed by Malcolm Adcock, June 12, 2019. Transcript in possession of the authors.

"Basketball Makes New Speed Thrill." *Daily Mail*, April 19, 1938.

Baugh, Alexander L. "The Church in Twentieth-Century Great Britain: A Historical Overview." In *Regional Studies in Latter-day Saint Church History: The British Isles*. Edited by Cynthia Doxey, Robert C. Freedam, Richard Neitzel Holzapfel, and Dennis A. Wright. Provo, Utah: Religious Studies Center, Brigham Young University, 2007.

Bavin, Chris. *Britain in Bloom*. Series 1, episode 13, "Chorley." Aired May 2, 2018, on BBC Two.

Baxter, Lesley. "Church Members Appears on BBC TV Series." News of the Church: British Isles. *Ensign*, June 1989.

"Be Content: Talk It Over with the Family." *Romford Recorder*, May 2, 1975.

Beeny, Sarah. *Double Your House for Half the Money*. Season 3, episode 8, "Chelmsford." Aired on September 17, 2014.

Bell, Julian. Interviewed by Malcolm Adcock, July 23, 2018, Ealing. Transcript in possession of the authors.

Benson, Lee. "Jay Osmond Talks Writing Musical Play that Will Tell 'True Unvarnished Story' of Osmond Family." *Deseret News*, March 17, 2019.

Berry, William. "The Truth Will Not Set You Free." *Psychology Today*, May 6, 2012. https://www.psychologytoday.com/us/blog/the-second-noble-truth/201205/the-truth-will-not-set-you-free.

Bingham, John. "Head of Mormon Church Thomas Monson Summoned by British Magistrates' Court over Adam and Eve Teaching." *Daily Telegraph*, February 5, 2014.

Bishop, John Keith. Interviewed by Malcolm Adcock, July 29, 2017. Telephone interview. Transcript in possession of the authors.

Blake, William. "Jerusalem." Poetry Season. Accessed November 4, 2019. https://www.bbc.co.uk/poetryseason/poems/jerusalem.shtml.

Board of Deputies of British Jews. "Jews in Numbers." Accessed February 19, 2021. https://www.bod.org.uk/jewish-facts-info/jews-in-numbers/.

Boleto, Leah. "Who Are the Mormons." CBBC *Newsround*, November 1, 2012.

Bond, Peter, Peter Game, and Robert Traini. "Mounties Join Hunt for Joyce." *The Sun*, April 18, 1978.

Boone, David F. "Perpetual Emigrating Fund." In *Encyclopedia of Mormonism*. Edited by Daniel H. Ludlow. Vol 3. New York: Macmillan, 1992.

Boswell, Mary. Interviewed by Malcolm Adcock, June 16, 2018, Beverly, East Yorkshire. Telephone Interview. In the personal collection of authors.

"Bound for Bosnia." *Ensign*, September 1996.

Boyé, Alex. Interviewed by Fred E. Woods and Martin Andersen, September 11, 2019, Vineyard, Utah. Transcript in possession of the authors.

——. "Prince Charles and the Book of Mormon." Faith Section. *Deseret News*, April 23, 2012. Accessed April 17, 2020. https://www.deseret.com/2012/4/23/20501434/prince-charles-and-the-book-of-mormon.

Bradbury, Lucy Ripley. Interviewed by Richard L. Jensen, 1987. Typescript. BYU British Latter-day Saint Oral History Project.

Bradley, Ian. "Living by the Book." *The Sunday Telegraph*, July 19, 1987.

Bradley, Isabelle. "Salt Lake City Blues." Letters. *Radio Times*, October 1–7, 1977.

Brierley, Peter, ed. "Table 13.2.2 Usual Sunday Church Attendance, England, by age and denom., 1980–2030." In *UK Church Statistics No. 3: 2018 Edition*. Kent, UK: ADBC Publishers, 2018.

"British Saints Celebrate 150th Anniversary." *Ensign*, October 1987.

Brodie, Ian. "Good Samaritan Hopes for £68m in Hughes Will." *Daily Telegraph*. May 1, 1976.

——. "Mormon Ban on Black Priests Ends." *Daily Telegraph*. June 12, 1978.

Brown, Sally. Interviewed by Fred E. Woods and Malcolm Adcock, June 16, 2018, Kirkcaldy, Scotland. In the possession of the authors.

Burden, Peter and Shaun Usher. "Yard Doesn't Want Sex-in-Chains Girl." *Daily Mail*, July 20, 1979.

Burke, Lee. Interviewed by Malcolm Adcock, July 26, 2017. Telephone interview. In possession of the authors.

Burton, Richard F. "The City of the Saints, and across the Rocky Mountains to California." *The Edinburgh Review* 115, no. 233 (January 1862): 185–210.

Callister, Douglas L. and Gerald J. Day. "Region, Regional Representative." In *The Encyclopedia of Mormonism*. Vol. 3. New York: Macmillan, 1992.

Campbell, Joel J. and Kristoffer D. Boyle. "Artemus Ward: The Forgotten Influence of the Genial Showman's Mormon Lecture on Public Opinion of Mormons in the United States and Great Britain." *Journal of Popular Culture* 50, no. 5 (2017): 1107–26.

Cardon, Louis B. "The First World War and the Great Depression, 1914–1939." In *Truth Will Prevail: The Rise of the Church of Jesus Christ of Latter-day Saints in the British Isles 1837–1987*. Edited by V. Ben Bloxham, James R. Moss, and Larry C. Porter. Solihull, England: The Church of Jesus Christ of Latter-day Saints, 1987.

——. "War and Recovery." In *Truth Will Prevail: The Rise of the Church of Jesus Christ of Latter-day Saints in the British Isles 1837–1987*. Edited by V. Ben Bloxham, James R. Moss, and Larry C. Porter. Solihull, England: The Church of Jesus Christ of Latter-day Saints, 1987.

Cassidy, Sarah. "Ready to Knock on the Door of Adult Life." *Times Educational Supplement*, May 22, 1998.

"Catford Saints Win European Tournament." *Millennial Star* 100, no. 19 (May 12, 1938): 292.

"Chains' Case Boosts Mormons." *Daily Telegraph*, January 9, 1978.

Chandler, George. *Liverpool Shipping: A Short History*. London: Phoenix House, 1960.

"Changing Lives at Friendship Centres," The Church of Jesus Christ of Latter-day Saints. June 28, 2021. Accessed May 4, 2022. https://news-uk.churchofjesuschrist .org/article/changing-lives-at-friendship-centres.

Charmsen, Eargle M. "Making Friends with Fleet Street." *Improvement Era* 40, no. 7 (July 1937): 442–43, 463.

"Children and Parents: Media Use and Attitudes Report 2019." Ofcom. Last modified February 4, 2020, https://www.ofcom.org.uk/research-and-data/media-literacy -research/childrens/children-and-parents-media-use-and-attitudes-report -2019.

Christofferson, D. Todd. "Religious Freedom: The Foundation Freedom." Presented at the J. Reuben Clark Law Society, UK & Ireland Chapter, Second Annual Conference, Downing College, Cambridge University. Newsroom, The Church of Jesus Christ of Latter-day Saints, August 11, 2017. Transcript available at https://newsroom .churchofjesuschrist.org/article/transcript-elder-christofferson-cambridge-2017.

———. "Why Atheists (and Everyone Else) Should Support Freedom of Religion of Belief." Last modified May 1, 2018. https://news-gb.churchofjesuschrist.org/multimedia/file/Why-Atheists-Should-Support-Religious-Freedom.pdf.

Church of Jesus Christ of Latter-day Saints. "Book of Mormon Musical: Church's Official Statement." Newsroom. Last modified November 5, 2012. https://news-uk.churchofjesuschrist.org/article/book-of-mormon-musical.

———. "Capital Punishment." Newsroom. Accessed September 26, 2019. https://newsroom.churchofjesuschrist.org/official-statement/capital-punishment.

———. *Church History in the Fulness of Times Student Manual.* Salt Lake City: The Church of Jesus Christ of Latter-day Saints, 2003.

———. "Choir Raises Funds for 1000 Year Old Chapel." UK Newsroom. December 23, 2016. Accessed March 6, 2021. https://news-uk.churchofjesuschrist.org/article/choir-raises-funds-for-1000-year-old-chapel.

———. "Church Representative Joins Theresa May, Faith and Government Leaders in National Parliamentary Prayer Breakfast." Newsroom. Last modified June 20, 2018. https://news-uk.churchofjesuschrist.org/article/church-representative-joins-theresa-may-faith-and-government-leaders-in-national-parliamentary-prayer-breakfast.

———. "Daventry MP Receives Personal Family History." Newsroom. Last modified August 21, 2016. https://news-uk.churchofjesuschrist.org/article/daventry-mp-receives-personal-family-history.

———. "Dedicatory Prayer London England Temple, September 7, 1958." Accessed April 1, 2020. https://www.churchofjesuschrist.org/temples/details/london-england-temple/prayer/1958-09-07?lang=eng.

———. "England London Mission's Online Devotional Strengthens Christian Faith Globally." UK Newsroom. Last modified May 17, 2020. https://news-uk.churchofjesuschrist.org/article/england-london-mission-s-online-devotional-strengthens-christian-faith-globally.

———. "Exceptions to Dress Standards Announced for Young Male Missionaries." Newsroom. June 12, 2020. Accessed July 17, 2020. https://newsroom.churchofjesuschrist.org/article/dress-standards-exceptions-male-missionaries.

———. "Excerpts from Three Addresses by President Wilford Woodruff Regarding the Manifesto." In *Doctrine and Covenants.* Salt Lake City: The Church of Jesus Christ of Latter-day Saints, 2013.

———. "Gadfield Elm Chapel." United Kingdom & Ireland. Accessed April 1, 2020. https://uk.churchofjesuschrist.org/gadfield-elm-chapel.

———. "Government Minister Meets York Helping Hands." Newsroom. Last modified February 6, 2016. https://news-gb.churchofjesuschrist.org/article/government-minister-meets-york-helping-hands.

———. "History of the Church in the British Isles." Newsroom. Accessed November 4, 2019. https://www.mormonnewsroom.org.uk/article/history-of-the-mormon-church-in-the-british-isles.

———. "Kensington MP Visits Hyde Park Children." Newsroom. Last modified December 14, 2016. https://news-uk.churchofjesuschrist.org/article/kensington-mp-visits-hyde-park-children.

———. "LDS Charities Joins Humanitarian Event Hosted by Prince Charles." Newsroom. Last modified December 15, 2017. https://news-uk.churchofjesuschrist.org/article/lds-charities-joins-humanitarian-event-hosted-by-prince-charles.

———. "Local MP Attends Coventry Christmas Carol Concert." Newsroom. Last modified December 23, 2015. https://news-uk.churchofjesuschrist.org/article/local-mp-attends-coventry-christmas-carol-concert.

———. "Mormon Apostle Addresses All-Party Parliamentary Group in UK House of Lords." Newsroom. Last modified June 10, 2015. https://newsroom.churchofjesuschrist.org/article/mormon-apostle-addresses-all-party-parliamentary-group-in-uk-house-of-lords.

———. "Official Declaration 2." In *Doctrine and Covenants*. Salt Lake City: The Church of Jesus Christ of Latter-day Saints, 2013.

———. *Official Report of the First British Area General Conference of the Church of Jesus Christ of Latter-day Saints, Held in Manchester, England, August 27, 28, 29, 1971 with report of discourses*. Salt Lake City: The Church of Jesus Christ of Latter-day Saints, 1972.

———. *Official Report of the First London England Area Conference*. 1976.

———. "Oxford University and Latter-day Saints Join for King James Bible Symposium." Newsroom. Last modified May 17, 2011. https://newsroom.churchofjesuschrist.org/article/oxford-university-and-latter-day-saints-join-for-king-james-bible-symposium.

———. "Race and the Priesthood." Gospel Topics Essays. Accessed March 15, 2021. https://www.churchofjesuschrist.org/study/manual/gospel-topics-essays/race-and-the-priesthood.

———. "RootsTech Hosts International Conference in London." Newsroom. October 28, 2020. https://news-uk.churchofjesuschrist.org/article/rootstech-hosts-international-conference-in-london.

———. *The Pearl of Great Price*. Salt Lake City: The Church of Jesus Christ of Latter-day Saints, 2013.

———. "Toby Perkins, MP, Receives Community Voucher for Staveley Cemetery." Newsroom. Last modified July 15, 2017. https://news-gb.churchofjesuschrist.org/article/toby-perkins-mp-receives-community-voucher-for-staveley-cemetery.

———. "Truth Will Prevail! UK Mormons Honour British Heritage in The British Pageant." Newsroom. Last modified July 31, 2013. https://www.mormonnewsroom.org.uk/article/truth-will-prevail-uk-mormons-honour-british-heritage-in-the-british-pageant.

"Church Farms Provide Aid." *Ensign*, December 1999.

"Church Member, Elected to British Parliament." *Ensign*, February 1991.

Churchill, Rhona. "The Strangest Church I've Ever Visited." *Daily Mail*, September 9, 1958.

Clark, Ron. Interviewed by Fred E. Woods and Martin L. Andersen, July 20, 2018, Orem, Utah. Transcript in possession of authors.

Cloward, Edward. *The Steam-Ship Lines of the Mersey and Export Trade Register*. Liverpool, England: The Nautical Publishing Co., May 1880.

Cook, David. Interviewed by Malcolm Adcock, Solihull, UK. Transcript in possession of the authors.

———. "Manchester, England." In *Encyclopedia of Latter-day Saint History.* Edited by Arnold K. Garr, Donald Q. Cannon, and Richard O. Cowan. Salt Lake City: Deseret Book, 2000.

Cowan, Richard O. "Church Growth in England, 1841–1914." In *Truth Will Prevail: The Rise of the Church of Jesus Christ of Latter-day Saints in the British Isles 1837–1987.* Edited by V. Ben Bloxham, James R. Moss, and Larry C. Porter. Solihull, England: Corporation of the President of the Church of Jesus Christ of Latter-day Saints, 1987.

Croft, David. "3 Conferences Held in England, Scotland." *Church News*, June 26, 1976.

CTVC. *Meet the Mormons.* Aired June 26, 2014, on Channel 4.

Cuthbert, Derek A. "Breakthrough in Britain." *Ensign*, July 1987, https://www.lds.org/ensign/1987/07/breakthrough-in-britain?lang=eng.

———. *The Second Century: Latter-day Saints in Great Britain.* Vol. 1, 1937–1987. Cambridge: Derek Cuthbert, 1987.

D'Arc, James V. "The Mormons as Vampire: A Comparative Study of Winifred Grama's *The Love Story of a Mormon*, the Film *Trapped by the Mormons*, and Bram Stoker's *Dracula*." *BYU Studies Quarterly* 57, no. 2 (2007): 168–69.

Danvers-Walker, Michael. Interviewed by Malcolm Adcock, August 2, 2020. Telephone interview. Transcript in possession of the authors.

Dawson, Andrew. "Religious Diversity and the Shifting Sands of Political Prioritization: Reflections on the UK Context." In *The Politics and Practice of Religious Diversity: National Contexts, Global Issues.* Edited by Andrew Dawson. New York: Routledge, 2016.

Department for Transport. *Road Use Statistics Great Britain 2016.* April 7, 2016. https://www.licencebureau.co.uk/wp-content/uploads/road-use-statistics.pdf.

Dew, Sheri L. *Ezra Taft Benson, A Biography.* Salt Lake City: Deseret Book, 1987.

———. *Go Forward with Faith.* Salt Lake City: Deseret Book, 1996.

———. *Insights from a Prophet's Life: Russell M. Nelson.* Salt Lake City: Deseret Book, 2019.

Dick, Jeremy. Interviewed by Malcolm Adcock and Fred E. Woods, May 9, 2018, Oxford. Transcript in possession of the authors.

Dickens, Charles. "The Uncommercial Traveller." *All the Year Round.* July 4, 1863.

Dickens, Charles. *The Uncommercial Traveller and Reprinted Pieces etc.* Oxford: Oxford University Press, 1987.

"A Dream Come True." *Southside Magazine*, November 1987.

"Dreams Come True." *Surrey Advertiser*, October 9, 1987.

Dunn, Paul H. *The Osmonds: The Official Story of the Osmond Family.* Garden City, New York: Doubleday, 1976.

E. M. M. "Syrupy but so Fervent." *Daily Mail*, August 29, 1955.

Eade, Charles. "Salt Lake City and Utah." *Millennial Star* 94, no. 22 (June 1932): 342–43.

Eastern Daily Press. "Mormons Suggest Farm Job Instead of Dole." August 17, 1979.

Elvidge, Rowland. Interviewed by Fred E. Woods, May 22, 2017. Telephone Interview. In possession of the authors.

Embry, Jessie L. "'New Ways of Proselyting': Radio and Missionary Work in the 1930s." In *Go Ye Into all the World: The Growth and Development of Mormon Missionary Work.* Edited by Reid L. Neilson and Fred E. Woods. Salt Lake City: Deseret Book, 2012.

Entwistle, Clive and Dan Wooding. "How the Mormons Lock Out Lust." *Sunday People*, December 11, 1977.

Entwistle, Thomas. Interviewed by Fred E. Woods, June 22, 2017. FaceTime Interview. In possession of the authors.

Erasmus. "Overcoming the Mormon Legacy on Race: Building Bridges Between an Anti-Racist Movement and a Conservative Faith." *The Economist.* Last modified July 24, 2019. https://www.economist.com/erasmus/2019/07/24/overcoming-the-mormon-legacy-on-race.

Evans, Richard L. *A Century of "Mormonism" in Great Britain.* Salt Lake City: Publishers Press, 1937.

"Facts and Statistics," Newsroom, The Church of Jesus Christ of Latter-day Saints. Accessed January 14, 2021. https://newsroom.churchofjesuschrist.org/facts-and-statistics.

Fagg, Peter. Interviewed by Malcolm Adcock and Fred E. Woods, May 11, 2018, Chorley, UK. Transcript in possession of the authors.

"Family Values Award." *Ensign*, February 2019.

"Fanaticism." *Morning Advertiser*, March 10, 1831.

Farmer, Molly. "Tabernacle Organist Leaves Resonating Legacy." *Ensign*, January 2008.

"First Mormon Temple in Britain." *Times* (London), August 29, 1955.

"Flocking to Hear a 'Prophet of God.'" *Kingston and District Star*, August 13, 1987.

Foley, Charles. "Death Wish Could Start a Bloodbath." *Observer*, November 14, 1978.

Foster, Craig L. "Sacred Structure and Public Print: Mormon Public Relations and the British Response during the Building and Dedication of the London Temple." Unpublished paper.

Gadher, Dipesh. "First Black Police and Crime Commissioner: I've Been Stopped and Searched but I Back It." *Sunday Times*, May 16, 2021.

Gibbons, Francis M. *The Expanding Church: Three Decades of Remarkable Growth Among the Latter-day Saints, 1970–1999.* Springville, Utah: Cedar Fort Publishers, 1999.

Gibson, Ginger. "Mormons praise Romney's impact." *Politico*, September 2, 2012.

Gibson, Simon. Interviewed by Malcolm Adcock and Fred E. Woods, May 17, 2019, Shilton, near Burford, Oxfordshire. Transcript in possession of the authors.

Gilchrist, Roderick. "Osmonds Barred from Two London Airports." *Daily Mail*, May 22, 1975.

Givens, Terryl L. Interviewed by Fred E. Woods and Martin Andersen, July 1, 2019, Brigham Young University, Provo, Utah. Transcript in possession of the authors.

———. *The Viper on the Hearth: Mormons, Myths, and the Construction of Heresy.* New York: Oxford University Press, 2013.

Gold, Tanya. "God Will Guide Us Through." *The Sunday Times*, July 7, 2013.

"Goodwill Tour of Britain." *Gloucestershire Echo*, December 3, 1984.

Grant, Bryan J. "David Fewster: Sending a Clear Signal." *Ensign*, December 1987, 58–59.

Gray, Carol. *Miracles Among the Rubble: Bringing Convoys of Humanitarian Aid, Hugs, and Hope to a War-torn Region.* Edited by Samantha Richardson and Rebecca Johnson. Sandy, Utah: Greg Kofford Books, 2020.

"Greetings to President and Sister Clark." *Millennial Star* 99, no. 30 (July 22, 1937): 452.

Haddock, Sharon M. "Thatcher Focuses on Faith, Families." Deseret News, March 6, 1996. Last modified March 6, 1996. https://www.deseret.com/1996/3/6/19229123/thatcher-focuses-on-faith-families.

Hakarika, Ayesha and Tom Hamilton. *Punch and Judy Politics: An Insiders' Guide to Prime Minister's Questions.* London: Biteback Publishing, 2018.

Hannan, Martin. "Obituary: Brian Adam MSP, politican and biochemist." *The Scotsman.* Last modified April 27, 2013, https://www.scotsman.com/news/obituaries/obituary-brian-adam-msp-politician-and-biochemist-2469339.

Hansen, Lewis F. "The Work in Wales." *Improvement Era* 28, no. 5 (March 1925): 469–70.

Hart, John and Shauna Hart. "Sea Trek Gleans Broad Media Attention." *Deseret News*, September 8, 2001.

Hart, Shauna and John Hart. "20,000 Line Riverbanks Leading to Hull." *Church News*, August 31, 2001. Last modified August 31, 2001. https://www.thechurchnews.com/archives/2001-09-01/20-000-line-riverbanks-leading-to-hull-112726.

Hastings, Ronald. "How Lord Grade Decided to Do the Life of Jesus." *Daily Telegraph*, March 18, 1977.

Hayes, Horace. Interviewed by Chad M. Orton, 1988. Typescript. James Moyle Oral History Program, Church History Library, OH 1243.

Herbert, Shiranikha. "Mormon Temple Denied Rates Exemption." *Church Times*, May 2, 2014.

"High, You Up There." *Sunday Times*, September 27, 1987.

Hinckley, Gordon B. Remarks. Preston Temple groundbreaking June 12, 1994. Transcript in possession of the authors.

"History, 1838-1856, Volume A-1 [23 December 1805–30 August 1834]." *The Joseph Smith Papers.* Last modified September 1, 2018. https://www.josephsmithpapers.org/transcript/history-1838-1856-volume-a-1-23-december-1805-30-august-1834.

"History, 1838–1856, Volume E-1 [1 July 1843–30 April 1844]." *The Joseph Smith Papers.* Last modified September 1, 2018. https://www.josephsmithpapers.org/paper-summary/history-1838-1856-volume-e-1-1-july-1843-30-april-1844/1.

Holbrook, Kate. "Housewife in a Foreign War Zone." Pioneers in Every Land Lecture Series. Church History Library. October 8, 2015. Accessed August 23, 2020. https://history.churchofjesuschrist.org/article/pioneers-in-every-land-kate-holbrook.

Holland, Jeffrey R. "Investing in our Future with Faith." The Church of Jesus Christ of Latter-day Saints. Last modified July 2, 2018. https://news-uk.churchofjesuschrist.org/multimedia/file/Investing-in-our-Future-with-Faith-Chatham-House.pdf.

———. "The Mormon Refugee Experience; Religious Persecution: A Driver of Forced Migration Conference." Newsroom, The Church of Jesus Christ of Latter-day

Saints. Last modified September 12, 2016. https://newsroom.churchofjesuschrist
.org/article/elder-holland-transcript-mormon-refugee-experience.

———. "Transcript: Religious Conflict: Can Humanitarian Aid Help?" Newsroom, The Church of Jesus Christ of Latter-day Saints. https://newsroom.churchofjesuschrist
.org/article/transcript-religious-conflict-can-humanitarian-aid-help.

Holt, James D. *Beyond the Big Six Religions: Expanding the Boundaries in the Teaching of Religion and World Views.* Chester: University of Chester Press, 2019.

———. Interviewed by Fred E. Woods and Martin Andersen. Transcript in possession of the authors.

Hoyle, Lindsay. Interviewed by Fred E. Woods and Martin Andersen, May 11, 2019, Chorley, UK. Transcript in possession of the authors.

Hunt, Marie. Interviewed by Malcolm Adcock and Fred E. Woods, May 6, 2018, Chorley, UK. Transcript in possession of the authors.

Hyde, G. Osmond. "Movie Campaign against 'Mormons' Leads Many to Investigate Message." *Deseret News,* June 3, 1922.

"I Protest—by Lord Beaverbrook." *Sunday Express,* October 29, 1961.

"International Freedom of Religion or Belief Day." United Kingdom Parliament. Last modified October 25, 2018. Accessed March 16, 2021. https://hansard
.parliament.uk/Commons/2018-10-25/debates/B6DDA10A-5B99-494F
-81D6-395DB298CB73/InternationalFreedomOfReligionOrBeliefDay.

"Interview with Lawrence Spicer." *London News Service,* August 28, 1995.

Jeffress, Robert. Interviewed by Jeremy Paxman. Aired October 13, 2011. *Newsnight,* BBC Two.

Jensen, Richard L. "Steaming Through: Arrangements for Mormon Emigration through Europe, 1869–1887." *Journal of Mormon History* 9 (1982): 6–7.

Johnson, Pamela. "This Month We Honour Fred W. Oates." *Millennial Star* 123, no. 8 (August 1961): 395–96.

Jones, Arnold. Interviewed by Fred E. Woods, June 22, 2017. FaceTime Interview. In possession of the authors.

Jones, Leighton. Interviewed by Fred E. Woods, June 22, 2017. FaceTime Interview. In the possession of the authors.

Jones, Linda. "Missionary Memories Link Pageant Past to Pageant Present," United Kingdom & Ireland, The Church of Jesus Christ of Latter-day Saints. Accessed February 10, 2020. https://uk.churchofjesuschrist.org/missionary-memories
-link-pageant-past-to-pageant-present.

Josh Chetwynd et al. "National Champions of British Baseball." Project COBB. Accessed June 1, 2022. http://www.projectcobb.org.uk/national_champions.html.

Kear, Warrick Noel. Interviewed by David J. Whittaker, April 2, 1987. Typescript. BYU British LDS Oral History Project.

Kerr, Clifton G. M. Interviewed by Gordon Irving. Typescript. Church History Library.

———. "Now it is History." *Millennial Star* 120, no. 10 (October 1958): 293–94.

Kerr, Stephen. Interviewed by Malcolm Adcock, May 21, 2018, Portcullis House, House of Parliament. Transcript in possession of authors.

"Knocking on Heaven's Door." *Ensign,* January 1996.

Konnry, Karl. *Mormons: Fact and Fantasy.* 1978.

Kureczko, Sue. Interviewed by Fred E. Woods, June 8, 2017, Lancaster University. In possession of the authors.

Lecourt, Sebastian. "The Mormons, the Victorians, and the Idea of Greater Britain." *Victorian Studies* 56, no. 1 (Autumn): 85–111.

"Letter to James Arlington Bennet, September 8, 1842." The Joseph Smith Papers. https://www.josephsmithpapers.org/paper-summary/letter-to-james-arlington -bennet-8-september-1842/1.

"Letter to Quorum of the Twelve, December 15, 1840." The Joseph Smith Papers. https://www.josephsmithpapers.org/paper-summary/letter-to-quorum-of-the -twelve-15-december-1840/2.

Lewis, C.S. *Mere Christianity.* New York: Harper Collins, 2001.

Lipka, Michael. "U.S. Religious Groups and Their Political Leanings." Pew Research Center. Last modified February 23, 2016. http://www.pewresearch.org/fact-tank/2016/02/23/u-s-religious-groups-and-their-political-leanings/.

"The London Temple of the Church of Jesus Christ of Latter-Day Saints." *Independent,* October 6, 1992.

"London's Mormon Temple." *Time,* September 15, 1958.

Longley, Clifford and Peter Strafford. "The Mormons." *Times* (London), June 18, 1976.

Longley, Clifford. "Mormons: Second Flowering of the Church in Britain." *Times* (London), June 18, 1976.

Lord and Lady Clithroe. Interviewed by Fred E. Woods, May 11, 2019, Downham, near Clitheroe, Lancashire. Transcript in possession of the authors.

"Lord Ahmad of Wimbledon." GOV.UK. Accessed April 19, 2020. https://www.gov .uk/government/people/lord-ahmad-of-wimbledon.

Louise Manning. Interviewed by Fred E. Woods and Martin Andersen, May 5, 2019, Hill Farm, Castle Frome. Transcript in possession of authors.

Lund, Anthon H. "A Good Friend Gone." *Millennial Star* 58, no. 23 (June 4, 1896): 360–62.

Lyon, Alex, MP. "Mormon Spirit." *The Guardian,* October 26, 1977.

Mackay, Charles. *The Mormons or Latter-day Saints.* London: Henry Vizetelly, Printer and Engraver, 1852.

Maki, Elizabeth. "I Will Take It in Faith: George Rickford and the Priesthood Restriction." Pioneers in Every Land. The Church of Jesus Christ of Latter-day Saints. Accessed April 20, 2018. https://history.churchofjesuschrist.org/article/ pioneers-in-every-land-great-britain-george-rickford-priesthood-ban?lang=eng.

"Male Voice Choir." *Western Daily and Bristol Mirror,* May 10, 1938.

Mavin, Richard. "The Woodbury Years: An Insider's Look at Baseball Baptisms in Britain." *Sunstone* 19, no. 1 (March 1996): 56–60.

Mavis Airey to Elder Dennis A. Wright, April 21, 1969. From the personal collection of Dennis A. Wright.

Mawle, Myrtle. Interviewed by Malcolm Adcock and Fred E. Woods, May 6, 2018, Chorley, UK. In possession of the authors.

Maxwell, John. Interviewed by Malcolm Adcock, July 29, 2017. Transcript in possession of the authors.

McKay, David O. "A Dream Fulfilled. Remarks of President David O. McKay at the Dedication of the Hyde Park Chapel, Morning Session, February 26, 1961." *Millennial Star* 123, no. 4 (April 1961): 172–79.

———. "Text of the Dedicatory Prayer by President David O. McKay at the Hyde Park Chapel, February 26, 1961." *Millennial Star* 123, no. 4 (April 1961): 180–82.

Merriam-Webster. Accessed January 14, 2021. https://www.merriam-webster.com/.

Middleton, Anthony. "Alexander Schreiner, Organist Supreme." *Millennial Star* 123, no. 6 (June 2, 1961): 282–85.

"Missionary Experience." *Contributor* no. 4 (February 1980): 158–59.

Moore, Carrie A. "LDS Affiliate Pays Off Sea Trek Debt." *Deseret News*, March 1, 2002.

Morgan, Haydn D. Interviewed by Ronald D. Dennis, June 25, 1987. BYU Harold B. Lee Library, L. Tom Perry Special Collections. MS OH 1354.

"Mormon Drive." *Daily Telegraph*, June 19, 1976.

"Mormon Faith Is Important to Me, Says UKIP's Nathan Gill." BBC News. Last modified March 22, 2016. https://www.bbc.co.uk/news/uk-wales-politics-35870573.

"Mormon Girl Vanishes." *Observer*, April 16, 1978.

"Mormon Helping Hands Completes First Decade of Service." *Ensign*, January 2009. https://www.churchofjesuschrist.org/study/ensign/2009/01/news-of-the-church/mormon-helping-hands-completes-first-decade-of-service.

"Mormon Leader Thomas Monson Fraud Case Thrown Out." BBC News. Last modified March 20, 2014. https://www.bbc.co.uk/news/uk-26666144.

"A Mormon Maid." Mormon Literature and Creative Arts. Accessed March 11, 2021. https://mormonarts.lib.byu.edu/works/a-mormon-maid/.

"The Mormon Mission: One of the Twelve Apostles." *Sheffield Daily Telegraph*, April 9, 1928.

"Mormon Missionaries: Volume 25: Debated on Monday 8 May 1911." UK Parliament: Hansard. Accessed May 25, 2022. https://hansard.parliament.uk/Commons/1911-05-08/debates/a9605dfa-4d09-4049-bfbc-27ecb30099db/MormonMissionaries.

"A Mormon Riot." *Mormon Chronicle*, August 23, 1858.

"Mormon Riot at Sheffield." *Shields Daily Gazette and Shipping Telegraph*, December 9, 1884.

"Mormon Singers in Hull." *Daily Mail*, February 5, 1937.

"Mormon Studies Centre Founded at Nottingham University." *Ensign*, February 1991.

"The Mormonites." *Morning Advertiser*, November 8, 1831.

"Mormonism in England." *Times* (London), April 19, 1911.

"Mormons Bid for Channel on ITV." *Daily Mail*, October 2, 1965.

"Mormons Get Together." *Waltham Forest Guardian*, July 2, 1976.

"Mormons Plan Chapel in Enfield." *Southgate Gazette*, May 22, 1975.

Moss, James R. "Building the Kingdom in Europe." In *The International Church*. Edited by James R. Moss, James R. Christianson, and Richard O. Cowan. Provo, UT: Brigham Young University Press, 1982.

———. "The Great Awakening." In *Truth Will Prevail: The Rise of the Church of Jesus Christ of Latter-day Saints in the British Isles 1837–1987*. Edited by V. Ben

Bloxham, James R. Moss, and Larry C. Porter. Solihull, England: Corporation of the President of the Church of Jesus Christ of Latter-day Saints, 1987.

Nelson, Russell M. "The Correct Name of the Church." The Church of Jesus Christ of Latter-day Saints. Last modified October 2018. https://www.churchofjesuschrist .org/study/general-conference/2018/10/the-correct-name-of-the-church.

O'Flaherty, Michael. "Fear of Mormon Revenge." *Daily Express*, October 21, 1977.

Oates, Frederick W. and Gladys Q. Oates. Interviewed by Richard L. Jensen, Sunderland, England. Typescript. BYU Harold B. Lee Library, L. Tom Perry Special Collections, MSS OH 1356.

"Obituary: Clifton G. M. Kerr." *Deseret News*, June 7, 2000. https://www.deseret .com/2000/6/7/19511460/obituary-clifton-g-m-kerr.

Oldroyd, Carol. Interviewed by Fred E. Woods and Martin L. Andersen, October 15, 2018, Springville, Utah. Transcript in possession of authors.

"The Origins of Latter-day Saint Charities." Latter-day Saint Charities Blog, February 20, 2018, https://www.latterdaysaintcharities.org/blog/the-origins-of -lds-charities.

Osmond, Alan. Interviewed by Fred E. Woods and Martin L. Andersen, September 28, 2018, Orem, Utah. In possession of the authors.

Osmond, Jay. Email correspondence to Fred E. Woods, November 18, 2019.

Osmond, Jay. Interviewed by Fred E. Woods and Martin L. Andersen, April 5, 2019, Vineyard, Utah. Transcript in possession of authors.

Osmond, Marie. Interviewed by Fred E. Woods and Martin L. Andersen, February 23, 2019, Las Vegas, Nevada. In possession of authors.

Osmond, Merrill. Interviewed by Fred E. Woods and Martin L. Andersen, April 5, 2019, Eden, Utah. Transcript in possession of authors.

"An Osmond Family Tribute." Oprah. Last modified November 9, 2007. https:// www.oprah.com/oprahshow/an-osmond-family-tribute.

"The Osmonds." *Sunday Times Magazine*, January 14, 1973.

"Osmonds' Girl Fans Riot." *Daily Telegraph*, May 27, 1975.

Otterson, Michael. "In the Public Eye: How the Church is Handling Increased Global Visibility." The International Society 23rd Annual Conference, April 2, 2012.

Otterson, Michael and Cathy Otterson. Interviewed by Malcolm Adcock and Fred E. Woods, June 15, 2017, Oxford. Transcript in possession of authors.

Parrish, Alan K. "Beginnings of the *Millennial Star:* Journal of the Mission to Great Britain." *Regional Studies in Latter-day Saint Church History: British Isles*, ed. Donald Q. Cannon, 133–49. Provo, Utah: Department of Church History and Doctrine, Brigham Young University, 1990.

——. "Turning the Media Image of the Church in Great Britain, 1922–1923." In *Regional Studies in Latter-day Saint Church History: The British Isles*. Edited by Robert C. Freeman and Richard Neitzel Holzapfel. Provo, Utah: Religious Studies Center, Brigham Young University, 2007.

"People Around the World 'Meet the Mormons'—in Their Own Language." *Ensign*, April 1979.

Perry, Anne S. "The Contemporary Church." In *Truth Will Prevail: The Rise of the Church of Jesus Christ of Latter-day Saints in the British Isles 1837-1987*. Edited by V. Ben

Bloxham, James R. Moss, and Larry C. Porter. Solihull, England: Corporation of the President of the Church of Jesus Christ of Latter-day Saints, 1987.

Pickup, David M. W. "Church Leaders Attend 'Stunningly Moving' British Pageant." *Church News*, August 14, 2013.

Porch, David M. and Mary B. Porch. Interviewed by Ronald K. Esplin, July 17, 1987, Glasgow Stake Center. Transcript. BYU Harold B. Lee Library, L. Tom Perry Special Collections. MS OH 1352.

Pratt, Parley P. "Prospectus." *Millennial Star* 1, no. 1 (May 27, 1840): 1–2.

Pudding Productions. *Bare Necessities*. Aired January 11, 2001, on BBC Two.

Quinn, D. Michael. "I-Thou vs. I-It Conversions: The Mormon 'Baseball Baptism' Era." *Sunstone* 16, no. 2 (December 1993): 30–44.

Rasmussen, Matthew Lyman. *Mormonism and the Making of a British Zion*. Salt Lake City: University of Utah Press, 2016.

Redfern, John. "The 'Press-Button' Church." *Daily Express*, February 27, 1961.

Roberts, B. H. *Comprehensive History of the Church of Jesus Christ of Latter-day Saints*. Vol. 2. Salt Lake City: Deseret News, 1957.

"Rochdale Greys to Visit Craven Park." *Daily Mail*, July 21, 1937.

Roche, Ken. "When Religion Costs You 10 Per Cent of Your Pay." *TV Times*, September 22, 1977.

Rooney, Terry. Interviewed by Martin Andersen and Fred E. Woods, May 8, 2019, Bradford. Transcript in possession of the authors.

"Rose Hudson-Wilkin: First Black Female Bishop Consecrated." BBC News. Last modified November 19, 2019. https://www.bbc.com/news/uk-england-kent -50478481.

"A Royal Gift." *Ensign*, September 1997.

"Scenes of the 150th Anniversary Celebration." *Ensign*, October 1987.

Schreiner, Alexander. "Music and Fervent Faith." *Millennial Star* 123, no. 6 (June 1961): 292.

Scott, Paul. "The Book of Mormon Review: The Most Over-Hyped Show on God's Earth." Daily Mail, April 5, 2013. https://www.dailymail.co.uk/tvshowbiz/ article-2304277/The-Book-Of-Mormon-review-The-hyped-Gods-earth.html.

Searle, Don L. "The Church in the United Kingdom and Ireland." *Ensign*, June 1998, 40–51.

———. "Two-Way Window on the World." *Ensign*, July 1991, 16–20.

Sherlock, Gordon William. Interviewed by Stephen C. Young, 1987. BYU British Latter-day Saint Oral History Project.

Shute, Joe. "British Mormons Take On The Book of Mormon." *Daily Telegraph*, April 10, 2013.

Sim, Denise. Email correspondence to Fred E. Woods, May 21, 2018.

———. Interviewed by Fred E. Woods, May 21, 2018. In possession of the authors.

Smith, Joseph. "Baptisms for the Dead." *Times and Seasons* 3, no. 12 (April 15, 1842): 759–61.

Smith, Joseph, Hyrum Smith, Lyman Wight, Caleb Baldwin, and Alexander McRae. "Copy of a Letter, Written by J. Smith Jr. and Others, while in Prison." *Times and Seasons* 1 (May 7, 1840): 99–104.

Smith, Joseph Fielding Jr. and John J. Stewart. *The Life of Joseph Fielding Smith*. Salt Lake City: Deseret Book, 1972.

Smyth, Jason. Interviewed by Fred E. Woods and Martin Andersen, May 7, 2019, Dunmurry, Belfast, Northern Ireland. Transcript in possession of the authors.

Snape, Ralph. Interviewed by Malcolm Adcock and Fred E. Woods, May 7, 2018, Chorley, UK. Transcript in possession of the authors.

Snyder, Canon Sarah. Interviewed by Fred E. Woods and Martin Andersen, January 3, 2020, Cambridge. Transcript in possession of the authors.

Sonne, Conway B. *Saints on the Seas: A Maritime History of Mormon Migration 1830– 1890*. Salt Lake City: University of Utah Press, 1893.

Sorensen, Parry D. "Mormon Missionaries Under the Union Jack." *Improvement Era* 41, no. 8 (August 1938): 476, 502.

———. "A New Kind of Pioneering." *Millennial Star* 98, no. 42 (October 15, 1936): 666–69.

———. "Our Centennial Visitors." *Millennial Star* 99, no. 30 (July 29, 1937): 485.

Stevens, Robert S. "Broadcasting with the Millennial Chorus." *Improvement Era* 40, no. 2 (February 1937): 92–95.

Stevenson, Savannah. Interviewed by Fred E. Woods and Martin Andersen, May 10, 2019, London. Transcript in possession of the authors.

"Sunetra's 'So Proud of Her Past.'" *Daily Star Sunday*, February 21, 2021.

Sykes, Alan. "Mitt Romney's 'Lamentable' North of England Roots." *The Guardian*, July 24, 2012.

Talmage, John R. *The Talmage Story: Life of James E. Talmage—Educator, Scientist, Apostle*. Salt Lake City: Bookcraft, 1972.

Tate, John. Interviewed by Malcolm Adcock, July 3, 2017, Winchester, UK. Transcript in possession of the authors.

Taylor, Jerome. "Team Ireland's Sprint Star Jason Smyth: I'm Not Politically Irish or British, I Don't Really Care." *Belfast Telegraph*, September 11, 2012.

Taylor, P. A. M. "Mormons and Gentiles on the Atlantic." *Utah Historical Quarterly* 24, no. 3 (July 1956): 204.

Taylor, Scott. "The Big Picture of How London Is the Gateway for RootsTech's Global Reach." *Church News*, October 26, 2019.

Teal, Andrew, ed. *Inspiring Service: Remarks with Elder Jeffrey R. Holland at Oxford*. Provo, UT: Religious Studies Center, Brigham Young University, 2019.

———. Interviewed by Fred E. Woods, May 30, 2019. Transcript in possession of the authors.

TfL Community Team. "Tube Trivia and Facts." Made by TfL. Accessed February 19, 2021. https://madeby.tfl.gov.uk/2019/07/29/tube-trivia-and-facts.

Thatcher, Margaret. "The Moral Challenges for the Next Century." *Brigham Young University Speeches*, March 5, 1996.

Thomas, Madison H. "The Influence of Traditional British Social Patterns on LDS Church Growth in Southwest Britain." *BYU Studies* 27, no. 2 (Spring 1987): 107–17.

Thorp, Malcom R. "'The Mormon Peril': The Crusade against the Saints in Britain, 1910–1914." *Journal of Mormon History* 2 (1975): 107–21.

Tolman, Jan. "The Singing Mothers." Relief Society Women (blog). Last modified August 28, 2008. https://www.reliefsocietywomen.com/blog/2008/08/28/the -singing-mothers.

Toynbee, Polly. "Mormons Don't Smoke, Drink or Take Tea or Coffee. Statistically, They Claim, They Are the Healthiest People in The World. Their Most Prized Converts Are Young Families. The Missionaries Are at Their Most Lyrical When Extolling the Virtues of Family Life. It's So Sugary That It Sets Your Teeth on Edge." *The Guardian*, October 24, 1977.

Traini, Robert. "Mormon Kidnap: Hunt of a Girl He Jilted." *The Sun*, September 17, 1977.

Trebilcock, Peter. Interviewed by Malcolm Adcock and Fred E. Woods, Chorley, UK. Transcript in possession of the authors.

Tucker, Linda. Interviewed by Malcolm Adcock, September 25, 2018, Birmingham. In possession of the authors.

Tyson, Eric. "The Faith Merchants." *Sunday People*, April 17, 1966.

"United Kingdom Area Conference Reports." *Ensign*, August 1976.

Usborne, Simon. "Mormons: Unlikely Hi-Tech PR Wizards." *The Independent*, April 10, 2013.

Van Orden, Bruce. *Building Zion: The Latter-day Saints in Europe*. Salt Lake City: Deseret Book, 1996.

Vickers, Martin. Interviewed by Fred E. Woods and Martin Andersen, January 3, 2020, Cleethorpes, Lincolnshire. Transcript in possession of the authors.

"Vital Statistics: Jewish Population of the World (1882-Present)." Jewish Virtual Library. Accessed January 14, 2021. https://www.jewishvirtuallibrary.org/jewish-population-of-the-world#A.

Walch, Tad. "An Apostle in England: British Prime Minister Theresa May Pauses from Brexit to Meet with Elder Jeffrey R. Holland." Deseret News, November 21, 2018.

Walker, Ronald W., Richard E. Turley Jr., and Glen M. Leonard. *Massacre at Mountain Meadows*. New York: Oxford University Press, 2008.

Walsh, Bernard. Interviewed by Malcolm Adcock and Fred E. Woods, May 7, 2018, Chorley, UK. Transcript in possession of the authors.

Ward, Artemus. *Artemus Ward; His Travels*. New York: Carleton, 1865.

Watson, Daryl. Interviewed by Fred E. Woods and Martin Andersen. Transcript in possession of the authors.

Weaver, Sarah Jane. "Central America Is Evidence the Gospel Strengthens Generations Says Elder Bednar." *Church News*, December 19, 2020.

"A Welsh Anti-Mormon Meeting." *Huddersfield Daily Chronicle*, September 20, 1887.

West, Rosalie. "HULL Newspapers 1830–1950." Unpublished manuscript, received by authors January 2022.

Wheatley, Keith. "The Saints Come Marching In." *Sunday Times Magazine*, November 15, 1987.

Wheeler, Lorraine. Email correspondence to Fred E. Woods, May 21, 2019.

Woodbury, T. Bowring. Journal. Church History Library, Salt Lake City.

Woods, Fred E. "Cecil B. DeMille and David O. McKay—an Unexpected Friendship." *BYU Studies Quarterly* 57, no. 4 (2018): 78–104.

———. "George Ramsden, the Guion Line, and the Mormon Immigration Connection." *International Journal of Mormon Studies* 2, no. 1 (Spring 2009): 83–97.

——. "Osmondmania in the United Kingdom." *LDS Living*, November/December 2019.

——. "The Tide of Mormon Migration Flowing through Liverpool." *International Journal of Mormon Studies* 1, no. 1 (2008): 60–86.

Wright, Abraham. Interviewed by Ron Walker. Typescript.

Wright, Dennis A. Interviewed by Fred E. Woods and Martin L. Andersen, April 5, 2019, Springville, Utah. In the possession of the authors.

——. "Remembrances Regarding April 1969 Thames Television Appearance." May 21, 2018. In possession of the authors.

Young, Brigham, Heber C. Kimball, Orson Hyde, P. P. Pratt, Orson Pratt, Willard Richards, Wilford Woodruff, John Taylor, and G. A. Smith. "An Epistle of the Twelve." *Millennial Star* 1, no. 12 (April 1841): 311–12.

Index

Also available from
GREG KOFFORD BOOKS

Penny Tracts and Polemics:
A Critical Analysis of
Anti-Mormon Pamphleteering in
Great Britain, 1837–1860

Craig L. Foster

Hardcover, ISBN: 978-1-58958-005-3

By 1860, Mormonism had enjoyed a presence in Great Britain for over twenty years. Mormon missionaries experienced unprecedented success in conversions and many new converts had left Britain's shores for a new life and a new religion in the far western mountains of the American continent.

With the success of the Mormons came tales of duplicity, priestcraft, sexual seduction, and uninhibited depravity among the new religious adherents. Thousands of pamphlets were sold or given to the British populace as a way of discouraging people from joining the Mormon Church. Foster places the creation of these English anti-Mormon pamphlets in their historical context. He discusses the authors, the impact of the publications and the Mormon response. With illustrations and detailed bibliography.

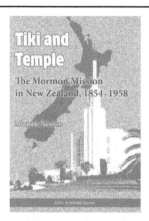

Tiki and Temple: The Mormon Mission in New Zealand, 1854–1958

Marjorie Newton

Paperback, ISBN: 978-1-58958-121-0

**2013 Best International Book Award,
Mormon History Association**

From the arrival of the first Mormon missionaries in New Zealand in 1854 until stakehood and the dedication of the Hamilton New Zealand Temple in 1958, Tiki and Temple tells the enthralling story of Mormonism's encounter with the genuinely different but surprisingly harmonious Maori culture.

Mormon interest in the Maori can be documented to 1832, soon after Joseph Smith organized the Church of Jesus Christ of Latter-day Saints in America. Under his successor Brigham Young, Mormon missionaries arrived in New Zealand in 1854, but another three decades passed before they began sustained proselytising among the Maori people—living in Maori pa, eating eels and potatoes with their fingers from communal dishes, learning to speak the language, and establishing schools. They grew to love—and were loved by—their Maori converts, whose numbers mushroomed until by 1898, when the Australasian Mission was divided, the New Zealand Mission was ten times larger than the parent Australian Mission.

The New Zealand Mission of the Mormon Church was virtually two missions—one to the English-speaking immigrants and their descendants, and one to the tangata whenua—"people of the land." The difficulties this dichotomy caused, as both leaders and converts struggled with cultural differences and their isolation from Church headquarters, make a fascinating story. Drawing on hitherto untapped sources, including missionary journals and letters and government documents, this absorbing book is the fullest narrative available of Mormonism's flourishing in New Zealand.

Although written primarily for a Latter-day Saint audience, this book fills a gap for anyone interested in an accurate and coherent account of the growth of Mormonism in New Zealand.

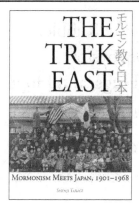

The Trek East:
Mormonism Meets Japan,
1901–1968

Shinji Takagi

Paperback, ISBN: 978-1-58958-560-7
Hardcover, ISBN: 978-1-58958-561-4

2017 Best International Book Award,
Mormon History Association

Praise for *The Trek East*:

"In *The Trek East*, Dr. Shinji Takagi has produced a masterful treatment of Mormonism's foundation in Japan. Takagi takes an approach that informs us of Mormonism in Japan in a manner that focuses on inputs and results, environmental conditions in Japan and cultural biases of a Mormonism informed by western assumptions."
— Meg Stout, *The Millennial Star*

"This is a wonderful book, full of historical knowledge on a lesser-known subject in LDS history. The author, who is Japanese, LDS and lives in Virginia, is deeply invested in the subject and carefully includes all sides of the history."
— Mike Whitmer, *Deseret News*

"A monumental work of scholarship. . . . I can't imagine that any future study of this period could hope to provide a more thorough and engrossing analytical study of the origins and growth of the Church in Japan. This remarkable contribution is unlikely ever to be supplanted."
— Van C. Gessel, *Journal of Mormon History*

Miracles Among the Rubble: Bringing Convoys of Humanitarian Aid, Hugs, and Hope to a War-torn Region

Carol R. Gray

Paperback, ISBN: 978-1-58958-578-2

"All those years ago, feeling totally overwhelmed by what I saw of fear and destruction, I turned to the Lord with a yearning I could not understand. Still to this day I do not understand why a dear and loving Heavenly Father prepared the way for me, Carol Gray, an ordinary English wife and mother, to dare to believe that in my small and humble way I could possibly make the difference to a war-wearied country."

Carol Rosemary Gray was a British mother and homemaker of seven children who became a recognized humanitarian leader in Europe and Africa. After receiving the all clear from her first battle with cancer at age 29, she made a promise to her Heavenly Father that she would live every single day to the fullest. This promise was exemplified years later when she began by organizing and transporting relief aid for victims of the Balkan War during the early 1990s, returning more than 34 times in the following nine years. She then went on to found Hugs International TLC, which, through Carol's efforts, funded the construction and operating of homes, a school, dormitories, a medical center and a sports field in Ghana for the next 10 years. Carol passed away in 2010 at age 66.

This volume comprises a selection of heart-wrenching and inspiring experiences told in Carol's poetically unique style of expression. Her stories are a testament to the extraordinary achievements of an ordinary mother, who was able to do remarkable things with nothing more than unwavering faith, the help and guidance of the Holy Ghost, and her relationship with the Savior.

Praise for *Miracles Among the Rubble*:

"A beautiful testament to courage and compassion." — Neylan McBaine, author of *Women at Church: Magnifying LDS Women's Local Impact*

"A poignant and remarkable tale of an ordinary person who responded to the calling to do extraordinary things." — Association for Mormon Letters

CPSIA information can be obtained
at www.ICGtesting.com
Printed in the USA
BVHW091351190922
647171BV00004B/4